STATES OF DEVELOPMENT

On the primacy of politics in development

Adrian Leftwich

Polity

First published in 2000 by Polity Press
in association with Blackwell Publishers Ltd

Reprinted 2005

Polity Press
65 Bridge Street
Cambridge CB2 1UR, UK

Polity Press
350 Main Street
Malden, MA 02148, USA

ISBN 0-7456-0842-6
ISBN 0-7456-0843-4 (pbk)

A catalogue record for this book is available from the British Library and has been applied for from the Library of Congress.

Typeset in 10½ on 12 pt Times
by Ace Filmsetting Ltd, Frome, Somerset
Printed and bound in Great Britain by Marston Book Services Limited, Oxford

This book is printed on acid-free paper.

For further information on Polity, visit our website: www.polity.co.uk

Contents

Acknowledgements

This book is the result of many years of research and teaching in the field of development. Although I have explored the ideas here in a number of places over the last decade, most of the work took place over the last five years, which was a time of intense complication and contestation in my life. I would never have survived that period, let alone written the book, had it not been for the purpose which my children, Maddy and Ben Leftwich, provided and for the wonderful support and friendship of many people, without whom I would have been sunk. I would like to thank the following people here: Jannie Mead, Adrian du Plessis, Margaret Lamb, Chris Clark, Dorothy Nott, Rebecca Brown, David Jockelson, Karin Bromberger, David Held, Isabelle van Notten, John and Taeko Crump, Peter Larmour, Marge Clouts and Ellie Karl, who all provided emotional and practical help when it was needed most. My colleagues in the Department of Politics in the University of York understood and facilitated the flexibility I needed to deal with the burdens of the double-day syndrome. I am grateful to Jane Duckett for insightful comments on early parts of the manuscript, and to two anonymous reviewers for Polity Press who made very useful points. I would also especially like to thank Caroline Moore, Linda Lofthouse, Jenny Bradford, Valerie Cresswell and Katy Fellows in the Department of Politics for their tolerance and good humour at the worst of times, and Jan Rollings for listening so well and helping me to keep things in perspective. A fine lawyer, Nicci Mitchell, provided detachment and wisdom when it was needed most. At Polity Press, Gill Motley and David Held were always encouraging and patient, and I am grateful to them for that and for so many other forms of support. I alone am responsible for the book and happy to be so.

Adrian Leftwich

1

The Argument: The Primacy of Politics in Development

Introduction

During the last thirty years of the twentieth century, at least, many countries in the developing world had a bad press, and with good reason. Generally, economic growth has been very sluggish. Indeed, for much of the period between 1965 and 1995 many countries (notably, but not exclusively, in sub-Saharan Africa) registered negative rates of growth (see table 1.1). This means that, by almost every conventional measure, most people in those countries were poorer at the end of the century than they were twenty years earlier. In many of these societies, despite voluble developmental rhetoric, large numbers of people remain sunk in absolute poverty and many more hover close to it, while inequality, as measured by the distribution of income or (in some countries) land, has become grotesque. Moreover, such poverty and inequality are commonly expressed in tragically high levels of infant mortality, maternal mortality during pregnancy or childbirth and infant malnutrition.

Moreover, until the very recent and, as yet, far from consolidated 'third wave' of democratization in the developing world (Huntington, 1991), political systems have been profoundly unstable, democratic politics has been overturned or distorted beyond recognition and human and civil rights have regularly been abused. At the same time, pervasive and sometimes spectacular forms of corruption are commonplace. Add to this outbreaks of often vicious civil or ethnic wars (as in Angola, Mozambique, Rwanda,

Table 1.1 Low average annual rates of growth of GNP per capita for selected countries, 1970–1995

Country	Per capita GNP growth (mean)
Angola	−6.8[a]
Brazil (D after 1985)	−0.4[a]
Cameroon	1.5
Haiti	−1.3
Algeria	−0.6
Peru	−1.1
Venezuela (D)	−1.1
Tanzania	0.8[a]
Mexico (PD)	0.9

[a] For period 1985–94
D = democracy; PD = partial democracy
Source: World Bank (1992b), 1996, 1997a, 1997b)

Myanmar and Sri Lanka in the 1980s and 1990s), military coups d'état (the so-called Latin American disease, but one which has been common throughout the developing world from Paraguay to Pakistan), as well as repeated episodes of flood, famine, drought and pestilence, which have afflicted large swathes of Africa and South Asia, especially.

The sketch is a familiar one, differing only in its forms and particulars, its intensity and extent, from place to place, whether you focus on Haiti or Honduras, Zambia or Zaire, Mexico or Myanmar, Brazil or Bangladesh. Anyone who follows current events in the developing world will be more than familiar with scenarios of this kind and would be forgiven for thinking that the Four Horsemen of the Apocalypse still roam the earth and have taken up permanent residence on the plains of the developing world.

Gloomy as this picture undoubtedly is, it is important to remember that it is *not* the *only* picture. A number of societies in the developing world *have* achieved and sustained some quite remarkable rates of growth since the 1970s and some of them have used this to lift many if not most of their people clear of the misery which so many others still experience (see table 1.2). While their number is few, the achievements of these societies are sufficiently important to justify careful attention, not only because of their developmental success but also because they may provide lessons for others.

Table 1.2   High average annual rates of growth of GNP per capita,
selected countries 1970–1995

Country	Per capita GNP growth (mean)
China	7.8[a]
Indonesia	4.7
Thailand	5.2
Botswana (D)	7.3
Mauritius (D)	5.8[b]
Malaysia (D)	4.0
Korea (D from 1987)	10.0
Singapore (D)	5.7
Chile (D from 1990)	6.5[a]

[a] For 1984–95
[b] For 1985–94
D = democracy
Source: World Bank (1996, 1997a, 1997b)

Within this high-growth category one would have to include not only
the well-known examples of the East Asian and South-east Asian 'miracles'
– such as Korea, Taiwan and Singapore – but also Botswana, Mauritius,
Malaysia, Thailand, and probably Indonesia, at least, each of which have
generated average annual rates of growth in gross national product (GNP)
per capita which were in excess of 4 per cent in the twenty-five years
between 1965 and 1990 (despite the cyclone of the oil price rises in the
1970s) and in excess of 5 per cent between 1984 and 1995 (through one of
the deepest global recessions in the post-war era). Although it must be stated
unambiguously at this point that the human and civil rights records of many
of these countries have not been good, to say the very least (but in certain
instances are improving), their levels of growth have enabled those societies to promote social policies that have had highly positive results in terms
of such important human and social indicators as life expectancy, literacy
and child health. To this group one could add Chile after 1980, Cuba and
China (at least between 1950 and 1980). Some of these societies (Botswana,
Mauritius, Singapore and Malaysia) have gone through this developmental
phase under formally democratic conditions (of varying degrees). Others
(South Korea, Taiwan, Thailand, Indonesia, Chile and China) have not,
though all (excepting China) had moved, or have moved, at different speeds
and with different results, in a democratic direction.

The fact that these few societies, both democratic and non-democratic, have been so remarkably successful from a developmental point of view is the starting point for this book. For if they can succeed, then we need to know why. For just as the general failings in development require explanation, so too do these 'successes'.

In the late 1990s some of these societies – Korea, Malaysia, Thailand and Indonesia, especially – faced major financial crises as their currencies collapsed and the extent of their indebtedness was exposed. But it would be an error of major proportions to believe that somehow these crises will wipe out the achievements of the previous 30 years. They will not. The fundamental structural change which has occurred in their economic and social structures is permanent and will not be reversed. They will have some years of difficulty, in some cases intense difficulty; there will be a heavy price to pay in terms of unemployment and a decline in living standards of the poor as Oxfam (1998) has pointed out. But these economies will not only survive, they will prosper. The pace of growth may slow down, certainly for a while, and their status as 'miracle' economies will decline. But they will remain forces to be reckoned with in the Asian regional and global economies.

The major purpose of this book is to provide an account of why societies like these have succeeded and why others have not, and hence to suggest how their experiences have implications for both the theory and practice of development. Three major arguments, or themes, underpin the whole book; these are discussed in the remainder of this chapter.

The primacy of politics

The first and major argument I shall develop will emphasize the primacy of politics in development. That is to say, the central and dominant variable determining not only the conception and shape of development, but developmental success or failure in all human societies, is their politics. For if we are to understand the different performances of developing societies we need to understand their politics and, specifically, the way in which their politics condenses in and around their *states*. In short, politics is not simply important, it is crucial for both understanding and promoting development. It shapes and is in turn influenced by the character, structure and capacity of the state.

But why is development so political and why is the state so central? Since the notion of politics plays such a central role in the argument of this book, it would be as well to spell out briefly what I mean by the term at this stage.

Politics

I start from the assumption that human societies are characterized by a diversity of interests, preferences, values and ideas and that the larger and more complex the society, the larger, sharper, more complex and, often, deeper the differences. The same is true on a world scale. This universal claim can be illustrated just as well by the conflicts and disagreements found amongst a band of the hunting and gathering BaMbuti of the Ituri forests studied by Colin Turnbull (1962) as it can be by the virulence of class conflict in Europe in the 1930s or by ethnic or religious conflict in modern Indonesia, Algeria or the former Yugoslavia. Of course, the way in which the conflict presents itself may disguise deeper and other conflicts, but all of these directly or indirectly involve the use of resources, or ways of doing things with resources, which individuals or groups seek to promote or protect. In general, also, people prefer to get their own way. But they also have to live together and cooperate if they are to prosper, and so constant war and outright victory in dispute is rarely a viable long-term solution to the problem of diversity of interests, though it often happens.

With one possible exception (de Waal, 1982), the human species is the only one to have evolved a set of conscious processes for trying to sort out or resolve these differences. These processes are what I call politics, which may be defined to mean *all the activities of conflict, cooperation and negotiation involved in the use, production and distribution of resources, whether material or ideal, whether at local, national or international levels, or whether in the private or public domains* (Leftwich, 1983: ch. 1). And of course achieving cooperation and negotiation has always been much harder where the differences between the interests, ideas and preferences have been sharp and hence less compatible.

The politics of development

I shall explore various definitions of development in the following two chapters but, however defined, the processes of development in human societies always involve the organization, mobilization, combination, use and distribution of resources *in new ways*, whether these resources take the form of capital, land, human beings or their combination. And because resources are to be used and distributed in new ways, there will inevitably be disputes amongst individuals and groups about how such resources are to be used as they calculate who will win and who will lose as a result of different configurations. It will be clear from this why all 'development' is therefore inescapably political, as defined above, not managerial or administrative in the current technicist sense. For as Hugh Stretton observed in a different context: 'People can't change the way they use resources without changing their relations with one another' (Stretton, 1976: 3). That's politics.

This is just as true at grass-roots or national levels, in a school, university, small business, multinational corporation or local government bureaucracy as it is true for the broad politics of development in any society, whether developing or not. A key difference, however, as will be made clear in chapter 6 is that in developed democratic societies, change has come to be institutionalized through generally more consensual modes of democratic politics and hence tends, in practice, to be slower, more incremental and usually less politically explosive than in developing societies, *though it was not always so*. This is probably because the winners in modern stable democracies have relatively less to win and the losers have relatively less to lose. Because the extent of policy change is not so great, the stakes are not so high and the politics not so intense.

But in many developing societies, on the other hand, inequalities are normally far greater and change can therefore threaten some interests much more directly and dramatically, especially where certain changes may be seen as an essential requirement to promote the pace and direction of development. Land reform is a good example. In many parts of Latin America land ownership remains intensely unequal: the Food and Agricultural Organization (FAO) estimated that 1.3 per cent of landowners hold 71.6 per cent of the whole cultivated area (Todaro,1997: 305–8). Inequality of land ownership remains dramatic in post-apartheid South Africa, where white ownership of land is still overwhelming. Similar patterns may be found in India and Pakistan, where landlessness is a major problem – in India some 27 per cent of the rural dwellers are landless, and the numbers are growing, though this varies from state to state in a range from 12 to 37 per cent (Mitra, 1996: 678). In Bangladesh the figure is 29 per cent (Singh,1983). And in Brazil landlessness rose from 19.2 per cent of all rural workers in 1950 to 36 per cent in 1975, prompting migration of people to the cities. Even in the 1980s, some 12 million rural people (out of a total Brazilian population, then, of about 140 million) remained landless (Hewitt,1992).

Now it is widely recognized, even by the World Bank (1991a: 10), that in some circumstances land reform can be an important condition for promoting rural development and agricultural productivity because small farmers are often more productive than large ones (Todaro, 1997: 307). This in turn contributes to wider economic growth (for instance by stimulating rural markets and hence by strengthening links between urban and rural economies) and thereby promotes political stability. This is precisely what occurred after land reform in South Korea in the 1950s, which turned the bulk of poor unmotivated tenants into landowning farmers who soon began to prosper and contribute to national development (Lee, 1979).

But the governments of Brazil, India and South Africa, which are now (2000) all democratic, have not dared to tackle the land question head on. Partly because of prior pacts and agreements, which prevent them from doing so, partly so as not to antagonize the powerful landed interests, which sometimes have close links to the army, and partly not to kill the goose which, for the present at least, lays the golden egg of food production (and sometimes agricultural export earnings), it is inconceivable that the democratic governments in those countries will seriously tackle the land question, although this may harm long-term rural development and agricultural growth – and leave a lot of people disappointed and bitter.

The case of land reform illustrates two central points in the argument of this book. First, it shows how politically explosive developmental issues can be because, as in this example of land inequality and land reform, the inequalities are so sharp and the stakes so high. Second, it raises a point that is the subject of chapter 6: how can new democracies in the developing world, especially, take on and deal with these gross forms of inequality without endangering the essential consensus that must necessarily underpin any democracy? Both points, in turn, serve to underline in distinctive ways the central theme of the book – the primacy of politics in development.

The state and development

Why then is the state important? Conventionally, development and its intimate association with economic growth have been understood as economic processes. But if, as I have argued, development must also be understood as a profoundly *political process* involving new ways in which all manner of resources – both internal and external – are mobilized, directed and deployed in new ways to promote growth and welfare, then how is this intensely complex task to be undertaken, managed and coordinated? For one thing is certain: it will not happen *solely* of its own accord – certainly not with the speed and continuity that is required if a real and sustained improvement in human welfare is to be achieved, or at least seriously begun, in the course of a generation. As has recently been pointed out afresh in a brilliant treatise of comparative historical analysis, what is required is a central 'coordinating intelligence' or 'coordinating capacity' (Weiss and Hobson, 1995: 2) which can steer, push, cajole, persuade, entice, coordinate and at times instruct the wide range of economic agents and their groupings to go this way instead of that, to do this and not that, and which itself can act where or when private agents either cannot or will not. The only agency capable of this task on a national basis is the state, or rather that kind of state with the structure and capacity to do so. As Weiss and Hobson point out, this role of the state has not been confined to the successful stories of development in the third world in the twentieth century but may be found in the history of state formation and economic development in the European context from the seventeenth century onwards, but especially in the eighteenth century and beyond.

It is important to stress that the type of state being discussed here is not what Chalmers Johnson (1982) in his classic study of Japan referred to as a 'plan-ideological' state, such as that found at the heart of the Soviet-type command economies, or its later Chinese or Cuban equivalents. In their virtual complete ownership and domination of the economies, these states sought not simply to steer or manage their economies but to control every economic movement. Inevitably, the bureaucratic sclerosis and economic slow-down which ensued meant that such statist experiments were, in the long run, doomed (Lane, 1996). But unfashionable as it may be to argue this today, especially against the savage human and environmental costs of what they did, it needs to be remembered that the Soviet and Chinese regimes (and the Cuban one, too) played enormous and transformative historical roles in levelling some profoundly uneven playing fields and unleashing modernization, not to mention achievements in education and health which were reflected, for instance, in life expectancy figures that came close to those of the West. In short, these states have turned Marx on his head. Where he saw capitalism laying the foundation for socialism (Warren, 1980), the history of these regimes suggests a different apophthegm: 'socialism, pioneer of capitalism'.

So the type of state being discussed here is not of that Soviet kind. Rather, it is one that has the authority, power and capacity to work through, in and with a market economy or, in other words, one that is able to 'manage the market' in the manner described above or, better still, in Robert Wade's phrase, to 'govern the market' (Wade, 1990). States that have this capability are now widely described as *developmental states*, and I shall discuss them in detail in later chapters. But the term is used to distinguish them not only from the 'plan-ideological' states of the Soviet variety and the 'regulatory' states of the western liberal or social-democratic kind, but also – and sharply – from states at the other end of the spectrum in the third world, what we might for convenience sake called *non-developmental* states – like Haiti under the Duvaliers, Zaire under the late President Mobuto or the Philippines under the late and ex-President Marcos – which have been characterized by varying degrees and mixtures of corruption, incompetence, cronyism, clientelism and straightforward kleptocracy, all of which have produced non-development or, at best, grotesque mal-development.

But developmental states cannot be had to order. They cannot be constructed out of institution-building kits devised in western capitals or think-tanks. The post-colonial political history of so many new states of the developing world is proof of that. For many former colonies overthrew, transformed or abandoned the constitutional and institutional arrangements bequeathed to them by the departing colonial regimes within a few years of independence. This is not to suggest that constitutions and institutions do not matter. Of course they do. But institutions cannot be seen as separate or evacuated from the raw processes and practices of politics which bring them into being, organize their evolution, sustain their continuity or manage their change. On the contrary, to underscore again the central theme here, developmental states – *like all states* – are a function of the politics associated with their provenance, development and transformation into other types of state. The idea that institutional development can be promoted and sustained independently of politics may quickly be dismissed if one remembers that however well designed they may be, no institutional arrangements – whether electoral, legislative, executive or judicial – have ever withstood the disabling effects of pervasive corruption, the thrust of the bayonet, the march of the jackboot or the rip-tide of implacably or violently antagonistic political forces which can simply wash them away. In short, no set of institutions and no code of governance is stronger than the structure of politics that both institutes and sustains it, as is illustrated by the abundant evidence of countless coups over the last thirty years of the twentieth century, from Chile to Fiji.

Democratic development

A second and related theme that the book explores concerns the extent to which democratic development is a realistic prospect for many still poor societies. By that I mean to ask whether and to what extent it is possible to combine fully democratic political processes with the inevitably transformative requirements and consequences of economic and social development. I am going to argue what I find to be an uncomfortable position, and certainly an unfashionable one. I would prefer not to argue it, but I do not think it can be avoided; and it is this.

In the course of the 1990s – after the collapse of the communist bloc – it became a central piece of official western thinking that democracy is not only a desirable feature of development, but a necessary feature as well. Where it has not been too costly for them in terms of reduced political influence or economic loss, it has become commonplace for western governments and international institutions like the World Bank to attach political conditions to aid so as to 'persuade' governments in developing countries to move in a democratic direction and to improve their human rights, processes which are sometimes regarded as an integral part of what is now referred to as 'good governance', as I shall explore later (ch. 5).

Now there are two related but distinct questions to be explored here. The first concerns the prospects for democracy – or, rather, consolidated and stable democracy – in developing countries. That is, will democracies that have come into being as part of the most recent 'third wave' of democratization become secure in the developing world? Or can we expect to see many serious reversals of democracy, as happened after the two previous 'waves'; that is, in the inter-war years (especially in Europe) and in the post-colonial world, after 1960, after the first flush of democratic decolonization? The second question concerns the extent to which developmental states can be democratic or, put slightly differently, the extent to which democratic states can also act as developmental states.

Democratic prospects

I argue that the long-term democratic prospects in many developing societies are not good, though in practice these prospects will differ from society to society. I argue – against my preferences and hopes – that the conditions that are necessary to sustain democracy are not present in many societies in the developing world and that, accordingly, their current democratic features are superficial and cosmetic and hence are likely to buckle at the first major test. Of course this is not true for all the new democracies – and it will be the purpose of the argument later to indicate where the prospects appear to be more positive.

Democracy and development

The second question that is dealt with in later chapters concerns the extent to which democratic states can and will promote rapid and sustained development. In short, what are the prospects for democratic developmental states? Is there a trade-off between democracy and development? The question has been very well researched and there is an abundant literature on the subject now, offering a number of different interpretations and possibilities.

In dealing with this issue in the context of this book, I argue that democracy is not a mono-system; that is, a single and unvaried set of constitutional and institutional arrangements. I suggest that we need to disaggregate the concept of democracy and recognize the variety of institutional and political forms it can and does take and then see their implications for developmental capacity in the third world. These forms include, for instance (i) the familiar multi-party or predominantly two-party democracies where single parties regularly alternate in power; (ii) those democratic political systems where governments are conventionally made up of coalitions; and (iii) those where single dominant parties have won every election over at least twenty or thirty years.

I further suggest that the particular form of democracy is a critical factor in determining the pace and extent of developmental achievement by the state. That is to say, I explore the idea that the developmental momentum of the state in a dominant-party democracy (like Singapore or Botswana) is *likely* to be greater than that in a coalitional democracy (like Mauritius or India) and is *likely* to be much greater still than that in democracies where political parties alternate in power (as has been the case in both Jamaica and Costa Rica).

Of course, there is more to it than this. For instance, the social factors – such as class, ethnicity and religion, and their combinations – shaping the political forces are often decisive influences on the institutional and political form that democracy may take and hence the particular developmental capacity of the state. But again, in exploring these twin aspects of the current concern for democratization and democratic development, I hope to amplify the central theme outlined above – the primacy of politics in development.

Development studies and political science

A third subsidiary but important theme running through the book has less to do with the substantive politics and processes of development as such than it has to do with the way these have been analysed and studied. In this respect, these ideas may be of more interest to academics and students of politics and development than to policy-makers.

As I have already pointed out, the centrality of politics to development cannot be stressed strongly enough. Yet for too long the study of development has often been extruded from the central concerns of political science especially, and the broader field of the social sciences more generally. Development studies rose – and fell according to some (Seers, 1979b; Apter, 1980) – largely outside the mainstream social science disciplines. Often separated symbolically in different buildings and offices (occasionally in Nissen huts), people who worked in development studies have sometimes tended to lose contact with their original disciplines. Often closely associated with, or indeed immersed in, area studies (also a strong growth field in the 1960s and 1970s), they tended to undertake research or consultancies in strange, far-away and dusty places, where difficult languages were spoken, strange cultures practised and unusual, peculiar, if not unique, practices encountered. A variety of special and distinctive frameworks, methodologies and theories emerged (Sklar,1995) to explain and help overcome the particular conditions of developing countries. Journals, conferences, schools, institutes and postgraduate courses devoted to development and area studies multiplied and expanded. Some were academic in their orientation, others focused more sharply on policy research while yet others concentrated on training, or advanced training, for those who were to work in the field of development or those already in it, from both the first and third worlds. And although economists have tended to dominate these institutes, there were also sociologists, geographers, anthropologists, a few political scientists and public administrators and a variety of other specialists in fields ranging from agricultural extension and rural development to health care, demography and education.

One should not under-estimate their achievements. A flow of fascinating books, articles and reports on an immense variety of countries, themes and subjects has characterized the field. Interesting theories and analytical approaches were developed and deployed, including modernization theory, dependency theory and a variety of neo-Marxist persuasions. In the field of policy, a range of strategic frameworks for many aspects and sectors of development succeeded one another, such as redistribution with growth, basic needs, rural development, structural adjustment and, most recently, good governance. Such a succession of diverse and changing orthodoxies, first welcomed with enthusiasm and then often discarded, may be seen as a weakness of development studies, indicating immaturity and grave theoretical inadequacy. But equally, it can be seen as a strength, as scholars sought to deal with the modern equivalents of what have always been the most difficult questions of social science, ever since the great thinkers of the nineteenth century first addressed them. In a manner of speaking development studies *is* social science and social science *is* development studies. Certainly the big questions that the giants of the social sciences have always addressed are precisely those that have been addressed by theorists working in the development field. From de Tocqueville, Comte and Adam Smith, through List, Spencer, Maine, Marx, Durkheim, Tönnies, Weber, Schumpeter and Keynes, the problem of how societies develop and how these processes may be facilitated or promoted has always been central to their concerns.

But it remains true that the study of the politics of development has tended to evolve in relative isolation from the mainstreams of the discipline of politics or political science. Parallel to that, the discipline itself moved forward in relative isolation from the work done in development politics. As I have pointed out elsewhere (Leftwich, 1990: 91): 'It would not be too grotesque a caricature to say that mainstream political scientists regard the politics of development as not only an exotic specialism, but almost as a separate (and perhaps even dubious) field beyond the discipline.' To illustrate: between 1967 and 1990, fewer than 5 per cent of all articles in the major UK journal of politics, *Political Studies*, concerned anything remotely to do with the politics of development. The figure for the *British Journal of*

Political Science (founded in 1971) is even lower. Writing in the twenty-fifth anniversary issue of *Political Studies* in 1975, Norman Chester (formerly Warden of Nuffield College, Oxford) observed both dismally and dismissively that area studies (and international relations) could be 'undertaken by those without any basic training in politics and government and in any case they tend to take such people away from the core of our subject' (Chester, 1975: 42).

Even if the remark is something of a polemical exaggeration, it remains true to say that mainstream political science and the study of the politics of development have tended to go their separate ways. In consequence, the potentially fruitful two-way traffic between the main discipline and this sub-field has not materialized. Little of the rich, complex and often challenging material about the politics of development has been assimilated into the core issues of political science. Open almost any recent standard texts on the discipline and you will find only the barest of references, if any, to the politics of development or to developing countries (Tansey, 1995; Axford et al.1997; Heywood, 1997), although those working in comparative politics have been much more attentive to non-western polities (Almond and Powell, 1996).

Likewise, in our haste or passion to analyse or expose the particular and rapidly unfolding dramas of politics in developing countries, many political scientists specializing in these areas have omitted to pause and see in what ways these apparent peculiarities of the developing world may not have been unique or special cases but rather particularly unusual and analytically taxing expressions of perennial themes in politics everywhere. For it seems to me that almost every theme, issue and problem ever dealt with in the discipline and discourses of politics – and in the central questions of political philosophy – find graphic and often raw illustrative expression in the politics of development in non-western societies. Whether it is the problem of establishing the rules of the game and securing consent for them; whether it is in providing for orderly succession or managing socio-economic and political change; whether it is the appropriate balance between the powers of the state and the rights of subjects or citizens, or about what is Caesar's and what is not; whether it is about the appropriate distinction between the public and the private; whether it is about the way in which power is constituted, distributed and controlled and who should participate in it, and how public and private resources should be used and distributed; whether it is about the definition of human rights, the requirements or limits of toleration, or the tension between the sacred and the secular in politics – all these issues are universal, and always have been, in all human societies. Yet, in general, the deep and fundamental questions of politics and political philosophy have rarely been seen as relevant in the analysis of the politics of development.

Recently, this has begun to change and it is a welcome sign, though it is not clear whether there will be a fuller re-integration of politics with the study of development. However, the third wave of democratization – especially in the 1980s and 1990s – has necessarily focused attention not only on the prospects for democracy in the developing world but on the historical conditions that have given rise to and allowed the consolidation of democracies elsewhere in the world. In this way one of the central problems of political science has become truly universal in its empirical reach. The best and the richest of the literature that has been generated around the issue of democratization has thus been genuinely comparative and hence has represented political science at its very best, and I shall return to this question in later chapters (Przeworski et al., 1995, 1996; Potter et al., 1997; Diamond, 1999 all provide a flavour of these concerns).

Put simply, the integrative flow of world economic and political history – and the variety of theories that seek to account for it – has stimulated two things. First, it has helped to undermine the dichotomous view of politics I have sketched above with respect to developed countries on the one hand, and developing countries on the other. Second, with all its problems, it has strengthened the argument for a single 'mono' discipline of politics and has, hence, helped to bring the study of the politics of development back into mainstream political science, from which it has been extruded for far too long. At the same time it has signalled the relevance of the big questions in political science for the study of developing countries and their politics of development.

It should thus be clear that this final theme that runs through the following chapters is about the need to see the politics of development, and in particular the place of the state in it, as an integral part of the discipline of political science. The more we can make the connections between them and the more closely we can align their concerns, the more enriching it will be for both. I hope to be able to contribute to that in what follows.

Structure of the book

That then is the broad thrust of the argument deployed through the chapters of this book which are structured in the following manner.

Since the concept is so central to the argument of the book, chapters 2 and 3 survey some of the approaches to and meanings of 'development'. In doing so, I hope to continue to highlight the primacy of politics in development, even in the definition of development, and hence continue to link the two together from the start. Given the failures of development, chapter 4 looks at the range of theories about the state in the third world which have been developed, in part, to explain this. The discovery by international development institutions in the late 1980s that the state and its administrative bureaucracy seemed to have something to do with development success was instrumental in unleashing a flood of optimism and a new paradigm about development – if only developing countries could get their 'governance' right. In chapter 5, therefore, I set out to explore why this discovery came so late, what it meant in practice and why, in its politically bloodless administrative and institutional form, it has been so naive.

There were some, usually outside the international agencies, who went further, or whose political status as ministers in sovereign western governments allowed them to go further than the international civil servants in, say, the World Bank, were allowed to go. They now suggested that it was not 'good' governance alone that would enhance and promote development, but *democratic* good governance. Wittingly or not, they had turned much standard official development thinking on its head. Whereas democracy had commonly been seen as a set of political and institutional arrangements that would emerge on the other side of socio-economic development, now it was held to be a precondition (or, at least, an associated condition) of economic growth. Why? Why did this new policy evolve? Why was it thought that democracies in the developing world could be encouraged or pressured into being and that, even if established, they would or could survive? In chapter 6 I explore these questions and suggest that if hopes for 'good governance' as the miracle cure were naive, hopes for *democratic* good governance as the more elaborate cure were even more so. I argue that democracies – wherever they may be – require a very special combination of circumstances to emerge, and an even more special and necessary set of circumstances to become stable and consolidated, and that many societies in the developing world are not yet characterized by those conditions. And I conclude that if development, or at the very least growth, is to occur in them, then it is likely to happen under the auspices of a political system that is a lot less pleasant than democracy but may, if successful, help to establish the conditions from which democracy may subsequently emerge. This political system is the 'developmental state' and chapter 7 is devoted to analysing the circumstances under which such states emerge, their central characteristics and problems and their achievements to date. But since both democracy and development are so important for human well-being, I go on in chapter 8 to explore the extent to which developmental states can be democratic. In doing so, I focus on some of the few consolidated third-world democracies and develop a classification of their distinctive institutional and political features which, I suggest, influence their developmental capacities.

Finally, chapter 9 draws the threads together, using illustrations from the preceding chapters to underline the primacy of politics and the state in development.

2

Progress, Growth and Modernization: Antecedents of the Development Idea

Introduction

It is not only the practice of development that is political but the very idea and definition of the process itself. And although there may seem to be a 'commonsense' consensus in everyday discussion about what 'development' is, the fact of the matter is that its meaning is far from settled because it is one of those 'essentially contested concepts' (Gallie, 1956) whose precise definition is unlikely ever to be agreed upon. But, as with the idea of 'progress' (with which, at least in one of its forms, it is so often and so intimately linked), the way 'development' is defined and understood is crucial in shaping the strategic objectives and goals of development policies and practices, and in judging their results.

On the face of it, definitional debates of this kind may seem to be of an arid, academic kind. But they are not. And I deal with them here because thinking about them is the essential first step in the analysis or promotion of development, and for two main reasons. First, 'development' is not a 'technical' process in which a number of components are assembled, combined and deployed; it is a *political process*, as explained in the previous chapter, or as one scholar describes it, a 'politico-ethical orientation' (Preston, 1982: 17). Second, these issues remind us that in the politics of development (indeed any politics), arguments about means and ends, about goals and policies, are inescapably normative in character (though not entirely so) because there will always be different interests and values seeking to impose their preferences on the definition, content and direction of developmental strategies. Indeed, one of the contemporary criticisms of 'development' as both a concept and a practice, as will emerge later, is precisely that its definition and policies have been generated mainly in western minds from within the experiences of western societies, with western (and often western capitalist) interests at heart. Moreover, the critics assert, the practices of development have been almost exclusively designed and deployed by western, western-dominated or western-influenced institutions, exercising enormous power and wealth and hence imposing western notions and strategies of development on non-western societies. In short, such critics argue, 'development' as both idea and action represents a contemporary version of western economic, political, cultural and ideological imperialism (Crush, 1995; Escobar, 1995b). I shall return to this point in chapter 3.

The purpose of this present chapter is to survey some of the big themes and approaches in the understanding of 'development', as a precursor to the next chapter where I shall look at the way in which 'development' came to be defined and redefined in the second half of the twentieth century. These chapters do not seek to provide a detailed 'archaeology' of the ideas or 'doctrines of development', as offered recently in the magisterial account by Cowen and Shenton (1996). Rather, I hope that these chapters will help to extend and illustrate the earlier argument by showing that the very *idea* of development is itself profoundly political. It is also important to stress that I am concerned here primarily with the meaning and focus of 'development' and not with theories of how it happens or how it may be promoted, though there will be some overlap because it is often necessary to extract the former from the latter.

Each of the meanings of 'development' which I deal with in this and the next chapter has a variety of forms and expressions and of course there are also many points where meanings overlap, merge and influence each other. But for the present purposes my aim is to emphasize the major features of each so as to distinguish and stress their differences.

Most major understandings of development can be located within one or more of the following broad approaches:

- development as historical progress
- development as the exploitation of natural resources
- development as the planned promotion of economic and (sometimes) social and political advancement
- development as a condition
- development as a process
- development as economic growth
- development as structural change
- development as modernization
- Marxism and development as an increase in the forces of production

Development as historical progress

'Development' has often been closely bound up (and sometimes used inter-changeably) with the concept of progress. This idea refers, fundamentally, to the 'progressive' unfolding of human history – in, between and some-times across societies. This is the notion of 'immanent' development as used by Cowen and Shenton, referring to a process happening over a long period of time, like the evolution of capitalism (1996: 4 and passim). But what is progress? With a bewildering variety of more or less explicit mean-ings (Bury, 1932; Pollard, 1968; Kumar, 1978) the modern view of 'progress' (or development) is primarily a philosophical notion, having roots deep within post-Renaissance seventeenth- and eighteenth-century Europe. This idea of progress was conceptualized as a steady, confident and onward pro-cess arising from the application of human intellect and energies in the sys-tematic understanding and transformation of the world. Such a view may be contrasted with other ideas of progress, such as the less secular and more pessimistic Graeco-Roman notions from the ancient western world, which entailed elements of scientific progress, but on a less steady and optimistic basis, combined at times with cyclical conceptions of upward and down-ward movements in the fortunes and fates of human affairs (Dodds, 1973; Blundell, 1986; Cowen and Shenton, 1996: viii).[1] Another contrasting view was the medieval notion of progress which saw it as essentially providen-tial progress, a movement in history which was concerned with the 'realiza-tion of the Kingdom of God or the achievement of a state of grace' (Bock, 1979: 42) and not with secular and human-propelled progress in the ma-terial and social constitution of human society, as is the common understand-ing today.

However, the modern idea of development as the progressive unfolding of largely secular history begins to find its clear expression in economic, social and later political terms from the late eighteenth century onwards. There is no better example of this than in the classical tradition of political economy going back to Adam Smith (though it was usually referred to as 'improvement') (Pollard,1968: 60–7). It is also found more strongly in the nineteenth-century evolutionary and diffusionist traditions of the early so-ciological theorists of modernization (Harrison, 1988), as well as in the radical tradition going back to Marx (Hobsbawm, 1964: 11–14; Bottomore et al., 1983: 398–9). Developmental changes, in this sense, are essentially the *processes of progress*, brought about by human agency. These have sometimes been understood as the discovery and application of rational or

[1] I am grateful to my colleague, Peter Nicholson, for drawing my attention to some fascinat-ing literature in this field.

scientific processes; sometimes as the unleashing of the entrepreneurial energies of people from the fetters of government control; sometimes as the deployment of concrete technological processes and economic arrangements – and sometimes all of these were conceived of as being the cause or consequence of further progressive changes in the political relations and social structure of human societies. So this early and broad understanding conceived of development essentially as progress and was anchored largely in the context of European experience. It was concerned with improvement in material circumstances, scientific understanding and, increasingly, individual human freedom, quality and autonomy. It remains a very strong influence on conceptions of development today.

Development as the exploitation of natural resources

But there has been a common second meaning of 'development', as Arndt (1987) has pointed out, and this had its roots (and certainly its rationalization) in European colonial experiences, first in Latin America from the sixteenth century but more recently and especially in Asia, Africa and the Caribbean in the nineteenth and (mainly) twentieth centuries. At its heart was the notion that development was about 'opening up' and exploiting the natural resources of the colonies and, more generally, the new world – East, West and South. In the case of the great Latin American continent, the Spanish and Portuguese view of it was summed up in the famous remark of the conqueror, Cortes, when he said: 'I came to get gold, not to till the soil, like a peasant' (Prescott, 1843–7: 130). Indeed, from the sixteenth century until well into the nineteenth century, the European colonial powers 'developed' the continent for their own interests primarily by the exploitation and export of a vast range of its raw materials, from gold to guano (Stein and Stein, 1970: 29, 41; Cammack, Pool and Tordoff, 1993), producing what some critics have called pervasive 'underdevelopment' in the continent (Frank, 1971; Stavrianos, 1981).

Sometimes (and more commonly in the later stages of imperialism and colonialism), these initially crude objectives of exploiting resources were associated with claims about serving or promoting the interests of colonial peoples. Certainly, in the earlier stages, such claims were seldom little other than self-justifying rationalizations for the greed of empire – or indeed of individuals, as in the astonishing and rapacious case of King Leopold II of the Belgians who, in effect, personally owned the vast slice of central Africa that became known as the Congo Free State (later the Belgian Congo, more recently Zaire, and now the Democratic Republic of the Congo) from 1885 to 1907. And although he spoke of 'a crusade worthy of this century of progress', to 'open to civilization the only part of our globe which has not yet been penetrated', it was under his authority that the people and resources of the Congo were ruthlessly treated and exploited (Hochschild, 1998: 44).

But the point here is that whatever the changing mix of motives and rhetoric of empire, 'development' in the official thinking of the colonial powers came to mean 'primarily development of the natural resources of the colonies for their own countries' benefit or at best that of the world at large' (Arndt, 1987: 24), and thinking about welfare was absent. In the case of Britain, the idea of linking 'development' with the 'welfare' of colonial peoples was late in its official coming, notably in the Colonial Development and Welfare Act of 1940 which replaced the Colonial Development Act of 1929 (ibid.: 28–9). Whereas the first Act of 1929 had as its objective 'aiding and developing agriculture and industries in certain colonies' (The Statutes, XX, 1950: 7), the later Act sought to make provision for 'promoting the development of colonies, protectorates, protected states and mandated territories *and the welfare of their peoples*' (The Statutes, XXV, 1950: 466, emphasis added). Similar thinking was found in France, also in the inter-war and post-war years (Hailey, 1938:139–40; Suret-Canale, 1964–72). But the idea that development was about contributing to the welfare or social development of colonial peoples was a weak impulse. And even as late as 1945, when the newly formed World Bank was specifying its goals, its Articles of Agreement treated the idea of development as the 'encouragement of the development of *productive facilities and resources in less developed countries*' (IBRD, 1989). At the time, that emphasis eclipsed any wider consideration or statements about social or welfare objectives (and political objectives were explicitly ruled out), though this was to change later, as we shall see.

Three closely associated features of this idea of development as the exploitation of resources are worth noting here. First, development was understood as something that had to be brought to the 'backward' colonies or regions by the 'advanced' metropolitan powers. Second, those colonies or regions could not have done it on their own – there was not the knowledge, energy or capital. And, third, in bringing development to the 'backward' areas, it helped to unlock potential for the benefit of all, colonized and colonizer, 'advanced' and 'poor' countries alike – a view that was made explicit in the title of Lord Lugard's classic treatise of the 1920s on colonial administration in Africa – *The Dual Mandate in British Tropical Africa* (1923). Lugard argued that the imperial powers had a dual responsibility: a moral responsibility to the 'subject races' (training, extension of some responsibility, systems of justice, appropriate education, free labour and just taxation, protection of peasants from oppression and the preservation of their lands); and a 'material' responsibility for the 'development of natural resources for the mutual benefit of the people and mankind in general'. He elaborated on this by saying that the colonial powers in the tropics were, in Chamberlain's words, 'trustees of civilization for the commerce of the world' and that their 'raw materials and foodstuffs – without which civilization cannot exist – must be developed alike in the interests of the natives and of the world at large' (Lugard, 1923: 58–62; Gann and Duignan, 1968: 209–26).

Twenty years earlier, the supposedly mutual benefits of this dual-purpose development of the colonies had been savaged as hypocritical by the Liberal economist, J. A. Hobson in his classic study, *Imperialism*. In this, he castigated the selfish interests of the 'distinctly economic forces making for Imperialism'. He went on:

In the mouth of their representatives are noble phrases, expressive of their desire to extend civilisation, to establish good government, promote Christianity, extirpate slavery and elevate the lower races. Some of the businessmen who hold such language may entertain a genuine, though usually a vague, desire to accomplish those ends, but they are primarily engaged in business. (Hobson, 1902/1954: 61)

Nonetheless, in amplifying the idea of development to include welfare or social progress, and especially in the idea of dual benefits and 'mutual interest', lay the seeds of many conceptions and purposes of development which were to emerge in the post-war era. Indeed, in the early 1960s, this view again became explicit in one of the classic and semi-official books of the time on development, Eugene Staley's *The Future of Underdeveloped Countries* (1961),[2] where he argued that successful development would

. . . simultaneously serve the interests of the people of underdeveloped countries, of the United States and the other economically advanced countries, and of the world community. (ibid.: 95)

And sixty years after Lugard, the report of the highly respected Independent Commission on International Development Issues (the Brandt Commission) of 1979 – composed of a genuinely international and developmentally committed group of people who were dedicated to recommending a 'large-scale transfer of resources' to developing countries – once more deployed the argument in support of its recommendation that 'a quickened pace of development in the South also serves people in the North' (Independent Commission on International Development Issues, 1980: 20, 276).

Nonetheless, the crispness of Hobson's observation has stood the test of

[2] I refer to Staley's book as semi-authoritative in the sense that it was funded and sponsored by the US Council on Foreign Relations, which was then a non-profit institution, but one which was close to US policy-makers.

time and the essence of his critique of the alleged hypocrisy of achieving the double purpose of imperialism has remained at the core of criticisms about the negligible benefits that 'development' (or 'aid') has brought to the mass of the people (Hayter, 1971; Hayter and Watson, 1985; Tucker, 1999).

Development as the planned promotion of economic and (sometimes) social and political advancement

However, the most familiar contemporary understanding of development as a process refers explicitly to the planned public, private or combined mobilization of resources and technology in the promotion of economic growth and, in more recent later versions, social and political progress. It has recently been compellingly argued that the intellectual origins of this lie in the thinking of the Saint-Simonians and, especially, Auguste Comte, who conceived of 'the intent to develop' as opposed to 'immanent' development (Cowen and Shenton,1996: 56) as a means to compensate for the upheaval and disorder brought about by capitalism in the form of poverty, unemployment and urban migration, and to impose some order through elite control – or 'trusteeship' – over the process in the interests of pace and stability (ibid.: 25–35).

But this meaning of development, as the intent to develop, as the purposive intervention in development, came to prominence largely in the twentieth century, and especially after the second world war. There are some (Sachs, 1990; Esteva, 1992) who even date its formal debut precisely to the inauguration address of President Truman on 20 January 1949, in which he declared that the task and responsibility of the USA was to extend the benefits of its science and industrial experience to the 'underdeveloped' world. But it is important to note that this idea of development as the conscious and planned promotion of economic growth had a number of important antecedents. One, for instance, may be found in the nineteenth-century writings of List (1844/1966) in Germany (Cowen and Shenton, 1996: 158–65); another in the theory and practice of the extraordinary economic transformation of Japan after the Meiji 'restoration' of 1868 (Gerschenkron, 1962; Moore, 1966; Akamatsu, 1972; Allen, 1981).

For List, the 'less advanced nations' (he was thinking primarily of his own Germany) needed to catch up with the advanced nations in order to compete with them and 'a perfectly developed manufacturing industry, an important mercantile marine, and foreign trade on a really large scale can only be attained by means of the interposition of the power of the State' (List, 1885/1966: 178). In the case of Japan after 1868, the Meiji regime saw that if Japan was to survive as an independent state in the face of foreign threat, it would need to build a 'modern centralized state' and a 'modern industrial economy' (Moore, 1966: 246). Speaking in the Japanese House of Representatives in 1897, the then Foreign Minister, Shigenobu, also made clear that the central purpose of the

> ... so-called opening and development of the country, or, in other words, this principle of attaining an equal footing with the Powers, was, I firmly believe the motive that has enabled Japan to become a nation advanced in civilisation and respected by the world. (Shigenobu in 1897, in Pittau, 1967: 39)

There were other twentieth-century European antecedents, too, some more and some less successful. This idea of planned (and usually state-guided) capitalist development lay at the heart of the economic policy of Italian fascism in the 1920s and 1930s, where a 'developmental regime' saw its major task as 'the rapid modernization and industrialization of a retarded socio-economic system', which would require a central role for 'the state as a centralizing, integrative and managerial agency' (Gregor, 1979: 304–11). A similar developmental objective – with its associated battery of nationalist political and economic instruments – may be seen in Spanish developmental efforts under General Primo de Rivera in the 1920s and (far less successfully) under General Franco after 1936 (Ben-Ami, 1983; Harrison, 1987, 1993).[3] Under Primo, 'the enhancement of production, the development both of the nation's economic resources and of its infrastructure, were essential if Spain was to be incorporated into modern times' (Ben-Ami, 1983: 240). Since the Spanish bourgeoisie and the liberal state had failed to bring Spain into the twentieth century, 'it was, then, up to a centralizing, coercive state to respond to the challenge, indeed to assume the tasks of the bourgeoisie' (ibid.: 240). Outlining his philosophy to the National Assembly, Primo declared:

> I am insisting, each time more strongly, upon the theory of State intervention, because I believe that, under all circumstances, States, and especially modern States where interests are so complex and contradictory, need to live under strict management ... A government, besides its essential function to govern the country ... is more than anything else a big board of directors. In the economic sphere, the government, with all its organs and advisory bodies, is the *consejo de administración* of the nation, and it should never allow either ravings or ambitions and egoism to impose themselves. Rather, it should see to it that everybody marches according to the rules ... (Cited in Ben-Ami, 1983: 241)

And although this idea of development – as planned strategies for growth –

---

[3] I owe this insight to Michelie Marin-Dogan.

may seem to have been identified only with capitalist development, and late capitalist development at that, it clearly was not, as will emerge shortly.

Development as a condition

Sometimes, development has been thought of, or described as, a *condition*, like maturity or old age. This implies that it is a stage or level of (at least) socio-economic and (possibly) political achievement, which certain societies have attained and others have not. As such, it is a notion which refers to an end-state, and this conception of development implies that societies may be ranked on a continuum, that is, along a path that leads to that end-state or condition. In his classic account of 'the stages of economic growth', W. W. Rostow advanced such a formulation in which 'all societies, in their economic dimensions' might be identified 'as lying within one of five categories', ranging from the 'traditional' to those that had reached the status of 'high mass consumption' (Rostow, 1960: 4). In other words, developed societies are those which have 'arrived', so to speak, at the terminus of high mass consumption, leaving the problems of development largely behind them. Such 'developed' societies are sometimes referred to as 'advanced', 'modern', 'industrial' or simply 'rich societies' (though it has to be said that some rich or high-income societies, like Kuwait, are not necessarily industrialized).

On the other hand, there are those societies which are not yet developed and which remain static and 'traditional', or which are 'undeveloped', 'underdeveloped', 'less developed', 'slowly developing' or, in an older language, 'backward' or simply poor. They have not 'arrived' and hence are still struggling to achieve development but may, with luck or good management, finally graduate into the category of 'developed' societies.

This kind of view entails thinking of 'developed' societies in terms of a set of defining economic, social and political characteristics, which may vary from theorist to theorist but normally include an industrial or post-industrial economy (capitalist or socialist) generating high (and steadily increasing) levels of income and material welfare; a social structure characterized by greater rather than lesser cultural homogeneity and social equality (or, at least, where any significant cultural differences are tolerated and largely confined to the private domain); and a largely secular political system characterized by both the opportunity for and reality of high levels of public participation in politics and policy-making.

There are obvious limitations to this stages, status or condition idea of development. One obvious implication and limitation is the presumption that once a society has arrived at the stage of being 'developed', the developmental process ceases. The history of the modern industrial societies of the West alone shows this to be a curious view, at best, for how does one know when a society has arrived? One example will illustrate the point. In 1851, at the time of the Great Exhibition, Britain was thought (at least by many of its elites) to represent the highwater mark of industrialism as the most 'developed' society in the world (Weiner, 1985). Though there are those who would say that Britain has declined since then – certainly in relation to the economic might of other now industrial societies such as the USA, Germany and Japan – the fact of the matter is that by the year 2000 it was almost unrecognizable by comparison with its condition in 1851. In terms of its economic, political and social structure – let alone its human-made physical features and the broad pattern of values, beliefs and ideology – Britain is for all intents and purposes another place.

Clearly, something has been happening since 1851. Change of immense proportions has been going on as people and governments have sought to adapt, innovate and borrow in response to changing and competitive circumstances in the world. But *change* is not the same as development. And while there have been winners and losers in the course of this change, what enables one to describe change as development is if that change conforms to some set of criteria by which one judges it to be *progressive* change. Such criteria may be strictly economic (such as growth in per capita GNP) or political (more democratic and participatory) or social (greater personal freedom, better and wider education for all, longer life expectancy and lower levels of infant mortality, protection of rights or equality) – all of which may be found in modern Britain. The criteria might even be psychological or emotional, referring to a decrease in stress or an increase in the capacity for toleration. Of course there may also have been costs – environmental ones are amongst the more obvious. But the argument about the example of Britain (or Japan, Germany or the USA) is that it underlines the point that, whatever our precise definition of development and whatever criteria we may use to measure it, we may need to think about development not as a condition or terminal status, but as a constant process in and between the politics of human societies.

Development as a process

Development conceived of as a process, therefore, does not necessarily or always imply a dichotomous view in terms of which there are 'developed' and 'undeveloped' societies and others ranged along a continuum between these two polar opposites. Rather, understood processually, development is considered to be a constant and regular feature of progressive (that is, improving) change in any society, irrespective of where it started, relative to all others. On this view, development is a more relative concept and countries are *not* classified according to a set of universal criteria in terms of which they may be judged to have 'arrived' or to have attained 'advanced' or 'developed' status or condition. Rather, 'development' is understood as a *process* involving the promotion and institutionalization of the capacity for constant adjustment, adaptation and change, which all societies must continually undertake as they seek to protect and promote their interests and achievements in an increasingly interdependent but still competitive world order. On this view, it could be argued, Britain did not achieve the final condition of 'development' in 1851, though it had certainly been transformed, if not revolutionized, over the previous century (Hobsbawm, 1969). Rather, it has been going through a continuous process of developmental change since then – and this will go on – even though it may have been overtaken on some criteria by other societies. Moreover, within Britain (indeed within all the industrialized countries of the Organization for Economic Cooperation and Development (OECD)) it could be said there have been experiences of both 'development' *and* its opposite in both absolute and relative terms (IDS, 1977) as some regions have prospered and others have declined. The condition of many inner-city areas in almost all the industrial countries is a clear example of this, as is the evidence of poverty, unemployment and homelessness in the 'developed' OECD countries where over 100 million people are defined as income-poor (UNDP, 1998: 27–8).

Of course, the notions of 'progress' and 'improvement' implicit in the processual view of development (as they are in the 'condition' approach) are no less normative than 'development' itself, and substituting them for 'development' solves no problems. The very idea of progress (Pollard, 1968) is steeped in contention and, like development, what it means is understood in very different ways by different groups and people and, especially, by different cultures. Even in the European homelands of its modern birth, the idea of progress has had a chequered history. The confident eighteenth-century belief in the ineluctable march of 'progress' through history – driven on by the engines of secular reasoning, science and industrialism – became much less optimistic as the nineteenth and twentieth centuries exposed many social, economic and political horrors which 'progress' brought with it in Europe (Kumar, 1978), as in Nazi Germany and, at the end of the twentieth century, in former Yugoslavia.

While such considerations serve to show the need for both caution and clarity when discussing either development or progress, this second *processual* conception of development will nonetheless require criteria and measurements that are similar to those used to measure development as a condition and may include narrowly economic ones (such as a steady increase in GNP or GNP per capita) as well as political criteria (such as greater protection of standard human rights, democratization and participation) and social criteria (such as life expectancy, education, opportunities and equality). But much of that remains highly normative. This is especially the case when one considers that such on-going goals of development as these may not be attainable *at the same time* (Huntington, 1987). If that is so – and there are good grounds for believing that it is – then both normative and political considerations will have a powerful place in determining the ranking of these goals; that is, which are more important to achieve first, and why.

What is central, however, is that development is understood here as a constant process, *not* concerned with the achievement of some end-point; that is, some terminal objective, status or condition called development or 'modernity'. Rather it is fundamentally concerned with on-going and sustained progress along a number of indices from where a society was previously. And of course as time goes by new criteria and new goals of development emerge for which new (often difficult) measures have to be evolved.

Development as economic growth

At least since Adam Smith, the idea (if not the precise term) of development has been closely identified with the idea of *economic growth*; indeed it is sometimes thought of as being the same thing, though few modern economists or other social scientists would now view development so narrowly. And, as we shall see, not even the major international financial and development institutions, like the World Bank or the International Monetary Fund (IMF) today think of development *simply* as growth, though they once did and still consider it to be fundamental. But what Adam Smith sought to encourage and explain was the achievement of economic growth in pursuit of the 'wealth of nations'.

He argued that the capital that had been 'silently and gradually accumulated by the private frugality and good conduct of individuals, by their universal, continual, and uninterrupted effort to better their own condition' had 'maintained the progress of England towards opulence and improvement' (Smith,1776/1977: 446). This had brought about 'improvement, in the productive powers of labour' so that more and more people could enjoy 'a greater share of the necessaries and conveniences of life' in what he called the 'civilized and thriving nations', in contrast to the 'savage nations of hunters and fishers' (ibid.: 104–5).

Smith was a child of eighteenth-century Europe and his language is therefore hardly surprising, but the strongly dichotomous flavour of his thinking (about savage and civilized nations) can still be found in contemporary ideas about traditional and modern societies (or undeveloped and developed ones), though not in such simplistic or judgemental terms. However, Smith's fundamental concern, the pursuit of economic growth as the irreducible and necessary central element of development, continues today in almost every country of the world and policy-makers everywhere seek to promote it. Normally, economic growth refers to steady annual increases (4 per cent per annum or more would be thought very good in a developing country) in the GNP or income per capita (Gillis et al., 1992; Ingham, 1995; Todaro, 1997: 13). Such growth may be brought about by the discovery of some valuable raw material that can be sold on highly profitable terms on the world market (such as diamonds and nickel in a poor country like Botswana, or oil in the Gulf states). But few countries have such luck and hence growth is normally the result of an intensification of productive effort and a transformation of methods and techniques in agriculture or industry, or both, resulting in increased productivity brought about by a steady rise in output per unit of input. However, in this narrow sense, the understanding and measurement of development as economic growth pays no attention to how the benefits of that growth are distributed, nor to its social, political or indeed environmental implications and costs. Brazil is a good case to illustrate the point.

At the height of the so-called Brazilian miracle, between 1969 and 1974, the economy grew at rates of over 10 per cent per annum (Hewitt, 1992: 76–7). More generally, the average annual growth in GNP per capita in Brazil during the twenty-year period between 1960 and 1981 was 4.8 per cent (World Bank, 1984). By any standards this was truly remarkable. But the distribution of the benefits of this miracle tells a different story. In the

Table 2.1 GNP per capital (1997) and mortality rates among the under-fives (1996)

Country	GNP per capita (US$)	Under-5 mortality (per 1000)
Brazil	4720	42
Venezuela	3450	28
Costa Rica	2640	15
Jamaica	1560	14
China	860	39
Sri Lanka	800	19

Source: World Bank (1998b)

previous chapter I gave figures for rural inequality and landlessness in Brazil, and if one further examines the figures on income distribution one finds that, in 1972, the poorest 20 per cent of households took only 2 per cent of household income, while the highest 10 per cent took 50.6 per cent (World Bank, 1984), making Brazil probably the most unequal society on earth at the time. The situation worsened in the 1980s, as did the sharp regional inequalities (Coes, 1995: 36–44). By 1995, this had changed little and the poorest 20 per cent of households still took only about 2.5 per cent of income and the richest 10 per cent took 47.9 per cent (World Bank, 1998b). Thus, even after the 'miracle' period, although the GNP per capita in Brazil had continued to grow from $2240 in 1982 to $4720 in 1997 (hence making the poor better off than in 1970), inequality remained stark and the country's performance on other social indicators compared very badly with some societies where GNP per capita remained much lower, as table 2.1 shows.

What the under-five mortality rate shows is that a relatively high growth rate for GNP per capita – a standard measurement of economic growth – does not automatically translate into better nutrition or improved health care for the majority of the young. Statistically, growth measured as the increase in GNP per capita is useful, but tells us nothing about how income is distributed, nor how governments use the benefits of growth (through taxation and spending).

All I mean to show by referring to these data at this stage is that while it is clear that economic growth is central to development, it is not the same thing *as* development and it is therefore unwise to define development simply as growth. For if all the benefits of growth consistently accrue mainly to a small group in the society, then it is simply not plausible to argue that there has been a sustained and all-round process of development, at least not in the short run. Nonetheless, however limited such a focus on growth may be, I shall argue in this book that growth (but not growth at any price) is a necessary component of development, but not a sufficient one. All societies require surpluses over consumption needs if physical and social infrastructure is to be maintained, expanded or improved, if welfare services are to be provided and if opportunity for all is to be expanded and realized. The capital required to undertake and support these tasks – from the provision of clean water, roads, schools and higher education to health centres, sports and cultural facilities – has to be generated and deployed, whether these things are organized entirely by the private sector or by the public sector, or a mixture of both. While growth without wider development has not been uncommon, as the Brazilian case illustrates, there can be little serious and sustained development *without* growth. And, as the rest of this book is concerned to show, what alone transforms growth into development is politics. Moreover, while economic growth has been intrinsic to the conception of *capitalist* development, it has certainly not been exclusive to it, as Stalin's view of the need for growth and structural change illustrates below.

Development as structural change

Closely associated with the idea of development as growth is the notion of development as *structural change*, a central feature of many other conceptions of development, notably those of Marxism and modernization, which I discuss below. Quite simply, structural change means a shift in the structure of an economy, and hence its output, from being primarily agricultural to being primarily industrial or, in short, industrialization. Thereafter, further structural change may involve a greater proportion of output coming from manufacturing (a specialist branch within the general category of industry) and, especially, from services (which normally include trade, transport, government activity and financial, professional and educational services) as heavy industry declines in relative importance. In short, though it has not been without its critics (Arndt, 1978; Kitching, 1982; Weiner, 1985), industrialization has been central to definitions of both economic growth and structural change and, like growth, has been consistently pursued by leaders on both the left and right of the political spectrum since the end of the nineteenth century. Consider two examples of this. The first is that of Stalin, addressing business executives in 1931:

No, comrades, . . . the pace [of industrialization] must not be slackened! On the contrary, we must quicken it as much as is within our powers and possibilities . . . To slacken the pace would mean to lag behind; and those who lag behind are beaten. We do not want to be beaten . . . The history of old . . . Russia . . . she was ceaselessly beaten for her backwardness. She was beaten by the Mongol Khans, she was beaten by Turkish Beys, she was beaten by Swedish feudal lords, she was beaten by Polish-Lithuanian *Pans*, she was beaten by Anglo- French capitalists, she was beaten by Japanese barons, she was beaten by all – for her backwardness. For military backwardness, for cultural backwardness, for political backwardness, for industrial backwardness, for agricultural backwardness . . . We are fifty or a hundred years behind the advanced countries. We must make good this lack in ten years. Either we do it or they crush us. (Deutscher, 1966: 327–9)

The second example comes from President Park Chung-hee, who led a military coup in South Korea in May 1961 and made clear what the central purpose of his regime was to be:

I want to emphasise and re-emphasise, that the key factor in the May 16th Military Revolution was to effect an industrial revolution in Korea. Since the primary objective of the revolution was to achieve a national renaissance, the revolution envisaged political, social and cultural reforms as well. My chief concern, however, was economic revolution. (Lim, 1985: 73)

In Stalin's case, the centrality of structural change in the form of industrialization was fundamental for the building of socialism, at least as he saw it, but it was equally important as a means of building up the strength of Russia (and Soviet socialism) to defend itself from a hostile world. Socialist development was simply inconceivable this side of industrialization. In the case of President Park, his concerns were equally defensive and developmental – but from a radically different political perspective. He sought to protect South Korea from the communist north and to build an economically strong society which could expunge the national humiliation of its twentieth-century colonial status under Japanese rule and become a major power in the Pacific region – and beyond.

On this view, change in structure as the essence of development is normally measured by such indicators as the changing share contributed to the gross domestic product (GDP) by agriculture, industry (which usually includes manufacturing) and services, and also by the number of people working in the different sectors. Sometimes urbanization is thought to be a useful indicator, but this is not always reliable since one may have quite rapid urbanization – as people drift to towns – *without* industrialization, as is so common in many parts of Latin America and Asia. For instance, in the 1960s in Chile and Venezuela some 46 and 47 per cent respectively of the

Table 2.2 Distribution of GDP between sectors of selected countries, 1965–1997 (%)

Country	Agriculture		Industry		Services	
	1965	1997	1965	1997	1965	1997
India	44	27	22	30	35	43
China	38	20	35	51	27	29
Korea	38	6	25	43	37	51
Botswana	34	5	19	46	47	48
Costa Rica	24	15	23	24	53	61
Jamaica	10	8	37	36	53	55
Thailand	32	11	23	40	45	50
Nepal	65	43	11	22	23	35
Ghana	44	47	19	17	38	36

Source: World Bank (1992, 1998b); UNDP (1998)

Table 2.3   Agricultural labour force of selected countries, 1965–1990 (%)

Country	1965	1990
India	73	64
China	81	72
Korea	55	18
Botswana	89	46
Costa Rica	47	26
Jamaica	37	25
Thailand	82	64
Nepal	94	94
Ghana	61	59

Source: UNDP (1992, 1998)

population lived in cities of over 20,000 people but only 16.5 and 9.8 per cent respectively were employed in industry (Skidmore, 1974: 214).

In short, the notion of *structural change* conceptualizes 'development' as the shift from a primarily rural and agricultural economy and society to a primarily urban society and industrial economy, as tables 2.2 and 2.3 show. Table 2.2 shows that the contribution of industry to GDP in countries like China, Korea, Botswana and Thailand rose dramatically in the thirty-odd years between 1965 and 1997. In India, Costa Rica and Nepal the change was less dramatic, while in Jamaica and Ghana it actually declined. Though other forces may push people from rural areas to towns, industrialization always increases urbanization and that represents another change in the structure of the society, with profound implications for its politics. These changes are also reflected in and measured by changes in the structure of the labour force, as table 2.3 shows.

Structural change, therefore, like growth, may be a useful way of defining, conceptualizing and measuring development in processual terms, but it still does not tell us much about the character or quality of life (whether social or political) or the distribution of benefits, which many regard as central components of development.

Turning now from the broad categories of thinking about development, it is appropriate to focus more sharply on some of the more specific meanings and distinctions of development found within one or more of these categories.

Development as modernization

At the heart of the modernization idea is the fundamental presumption that the structures and processes of all human societies develop from simple forms of *traditionalism* to complex expressions of *modernity*. Modern or modernizing societies *converge* in their main economic, social and ultimately political structural properties and processes (Huntington, 1971). For some, the defining process of modernization is industrialization and this has a 'central logic' to it that steers societies in a similar direction (though their paths may be different) (Kerr et al., 1973: 279–82). To this extent, development as modernization embodies both the condition and process approaches, with 'traditional' society being the status found at the start of the journey and 'modern' society, or modernity, being the destination. Modernization is the process moving societies through this immense transition from the one condition to the other.

The idea of modernization has roots which go back deep into the mainstream of social theory and imperial ideology in the nineteenth and twentieth centuries in Europe and North America (Apter, 1965; Harrison, 1988; Larrain, 1989). And precisely because of the diversity of its provenance and the variety of strands that constitute it, there is no single or simple meaning as all versions and emphases differ. But for the purpose of argument here it is possible to construct a composite account of this long-standing, influential and continuing way of defining and thinking about development as modernization.

At its best, modernization constitutes a total vision of development, as both process and condition. It refers to a total change in the structure of societies, embodying profound transformation in the economic, social, legal, institutional, political and ideological spheres – with important implications, too, for their cultures – especially in the modern era of escalating globalization (Held et al., 1999). It is a process whereby modern societies exercise greater control over their 'natural and social environment' through the expansion and application of scientific and technological knowledge (Huntington, 1971: 286). Concretely, modernization entails systematic structural differentiation (Smelser, 1968) producing an industrial or post-industrial economic order generating steadily increasing levels of material prosperity; a social structure based on the principles of individualism, equality and opportunity (whether of gender or ethnicity); a formally democratic political system of the representative kind (or at least one in which decision-makers are accountable through regular elections); a thoroughly secular political culture characterized by rational procedures for making decisions and one in which formal civil rights and liberties are entrenched in law; and a world view in which the role of reason and the application of scientific principles are said to predominate.

While economic growth and structural change are the defining features of development in 'modernizing' societies, many of the nineteenth-century (and present-day) theorists of modernization were also deeply concerned with important social, political and legal correlates of economic growth. Few described the process as modernization or development (though most thought of it as progress), but the central idea of this transformation can be found in the writings of many nineteenth-century theorists, as the following paragaphs indicate.

In terms of legal development, for instance, this movement from tradition to modernity was characterized in 1861 by Sir Henry Sumner Maine, in his classic study, *Ancient Law*, as a shift 'from status to contract' in the legal principles, processes and institutions of what he deemed 'progressive societies' (Maine, 1908: 151). For Herbert Spencer, in 1876, this transformation implied a change from simplicity to complexity, involving progress with respect to 'size, coherence, multiformity, and definiteness' in the structure of society (Spencer, 1969: 155). The German theorist, Ferdinand Tönnies wrote in 1887 that law emerged through a process of modernization from its origins in customs and folkways to its expression as formal and codified legislation. This occurred, he argued, as the structural basis of societies shifted progressively from community (*gemeinschaft*), in which what he calls 'natural will' predominated, to association *(gesellschaft),* in which 'rational will' predominated (Tönnies, 1887/1955). Durkheim, writing in 1893, saw the essential difference between traditional and modern societies as being characterized by their respective 'mechanical' and 'organic' forms of solidarity (Durkheim, 1893/1964), by which he meant that, traditionally, simple societies were constituted by similar or homologous groups (families, villages) which were linked together 'mechanically'. In 'modern' societies, by contrast, he argued that there had emerged differentiation and division of labour in the economic, social and political structures, and the different parts and specialisms in society were held together by organic solidarity. In the early years of the twentieth century Max Weber conceived of modernity, at least in terms of its politico-administrative arrangements, as being expressed in the rational-legal basis of the modern state, which had emerged from prior forms of political traditionalism such as gerontocracy, patriarchy and patrimonialism. In these traditional political systems, power and authority had been highly personalized and were largely unaccountable, not institutionalized or subject to forms of popular control, as in the modern state, which had evolved in the course of capitalist economic development (Weber, 1964).

But perhaps no theorist of the nineteenth century had a sharper conception of the distinction between 'traditional' and 'modern' societies than Karl Marx. Given that he was so deeply immersed in the scientific and social theory of Europe at the time, it is not surprising that he was so dedicated to modernization, though he had a particular view of it. Nor is it surprising that he regarded the traditional and primarily agrarian economic structure of mid-nineteenth-century French society as embodying the 'idiocy of rural life' (Marx and Engels, 1888/1958: 38), or that he likened the French peasantry to a 'sack of potatoes' (Marx, 1852/1958a: 334). Harsher still was his castigation of the economic structures of traditional Asian society in which the masses were steeped in an 'undignified, stagnatory and vegetative life' under regimes of 'oriental despotism', which 'restrained the human mind, making it the unresisting tool of superstition . . . depriving it of all grandeur and historical energies' (Marx, 1853/1958b: 350).

For Marx, as I shall elaborate more fully in the next section, the only way out of this was through industrialization (capitalist industrialization, at that), and his global prognosis was clear that 'the country that is more developed industrially only shows to the less developed, the image of its own future' (Marx, 1976: 91). For Marx, as for so many other nineteenth-century social scientists, industrialism provided the inescapable foundation for modernity – and socialism – though the Marxist version of it has its own special features.

Whether liberal or democratic-socialist in their approaches, theorists of the modernization school of the 1960s drew on all these traditions, both in their conceptions of modernity and in their analyses of the trajectories of change towards it. For S. N. Eisenstadt, for instance, modernization was best defined as

> . . . the process of change towards those types of social, economic and political systems that have developed in western Europe and North America from the seventeenth century to the nineteenth century and have then spread to other European countries and in the nineteenth and twentieth centuries to the South American, Asian and African continents. (Eisenstadt, 1966: 1)

And it is not hard to see why some regarded such a view of development as little other than more or less vaguely disguised 'westernization', and American westernization at that (O'Brien, 1972).

For David Apter, one of the most thoughtful analysts of development as modernization, the move towards modernity involved a shift from a society based on what he called the 'sacred-collectivity model' to one based on the 'secular-libertarian model' (Apter, 1965: 28–33) in which an 'ethic of science' predominated (ibid.: 461), as it had for Marx. In the West, this had arisen from industrialization, commercialization, urbanization and bureaucratization, and through these processes the fundamental principles of individualism had become firmly established, replacing collective definitions and conceptions of self.

Much of nineteenth-century modernization theory, with its evolutionary and diffusionist assumptions, has been criticized as arrogant, Eurocentric, imperialist or plain wrong. Likewise, many of the post-war theories of modernization have received intense criticism since the 1960s and 1970s for their inaccurate tradition–modern dichotomy, for being ethno- and Eurocentric and for their reductionist generality (Bernstein, 1971; O'Brien, 1972; Tipps, 1973; Tucker, 1999). But despite this, development understood as modernization still has influential advocates and takes new forms; perhaps the most renowned recent example has been Francis Fukuyama's controversial thesis about 'the end of history' (1989). In this he argued that the collapse of communism had revealed the exhaustion of viable alternatives to modern western liberal economies and that our ideological evolution has ended with the 'universalization of Western liberal democracy as the final form of human government' (Fukuyama, 1989: 4) to which all societies will move. There could be no more terminal or convergent view of development as a condition than this one, and it expresses in the language of social analysis what Flannery O'Connor expressed in a more literary form as 'everything that rises must converge' (O'Connor, 1956/1966). Nor could any of the conceptions of development as modernization of the 1960s and 1970s have expressed more sharply the idea that developmental modernization is best understood as westernization.

Marxism and development as an increase in the forces of production

Like Adam Smith before him, Marx was a Westerner and, again like Smith, he did not of course define or explore the term 'development' in any of its modern usages, although he used it constantly when discussing 'stages' in 'the development' of productive forces, for instance, or 'stages of development in the division of labour' (Marx and Engels, 1845/1965: 32). But it is nonetheless quite possible to identify Marx's understanding of development from his writings, and it is clear that his views clearly fit into the category of thought that conceived of development as the progressive unfolding of history (or pre-history as he described pre-socialist society) through structural change. The classical Marxist conception of development, then, is best understood as one that combines a view of development as involving economic growth, structural change and progress towards an end-point called communism. Though Marx was both a modernizer and modernist, a combination of original elements defines his particular perception of this process and its goal.

First, progress is not understood as a steady, evolutionary or unilinear process of growth – or improvement, as Adam Smith would have it. Progress, for Marx, meant progress or development in the characteristic structures and potentials of societies through a series of stages, each defined by its mode of production. These stages or forms stretched from the tribal, Asiatic and ancient modes, through feudalism and capitalism to socialism, with each stage giving way to the next through a revolutionary punctuation, and each stage representing an advance on the previous one.

In the social production of their life, men enter into definite relations . . . of production which correspond to a definite stage in the development of their material productive forces. . . . The mode of production of material life conditions the social, political and intellectual life process in general. (Marx, 1859/1958c: 363)

In other words, the way a society goes about making its living – that is, its system (or mode) of production – shapes and influences its social, political and ideological arrangements. And as the system of production changes, so too does change occur in the broad social, political and ideological features. Thus:

the hand-mill gives you the society with the feudal lord; the steam-mill, society with the industrial capitalist. (Marx, 1975: 102)

Development in human societies may therefore be understood as this process of progressive and revolutionary change as one mode gives way to the next and as one set of social and political relations gives way to the next.

We see, therefore, how the modern bourgeoisie is itself the product of a long course of development, of a series of revolutions in the modes of production and exchange. (Marx and Engels, 1888/1958: 35)

And, for Marx, the capitalist mode of production was the 'last antagonistic form of the social process of production'; it brought 'the pre-history of human society to a close' (Marx, 1859/1958c: 363–4).'

Second, at the core of each of these modes of production, or 'progressive epochs in the economic formations of society' (Marx, 1859/1958c: 363), is a distinctive level, or stage, of development in the *technological capacity* of the society – that is, the forces of production or the so-called 'social productive forces' (ibid.). This technology is in turn associated with a particular socio-political order, for 'the whole internal structure of the nation depends on the stage of development reached by its production and by its internal and external intercourse' (Marx and Engels, 1845/1965: 32).

Third, Marx attached enormous importance to scientific and technical knowledge and its value in both explaining and demystifying all aspects of the world, as well as in its application to agriculture, production and the harnessing of energy. For Marx, the capitalist or bourgeois stage represented the highest or most developed stage (thus far) in this process, for the bourgeoisie, during its rule of scarce one hundred years, has created more massive and more colossal productive forces than have all preceding generations together. (Marx and Engels, 1888/1958: 38)

Moreover, Marx celebrated this enthusiastically while recognizing its human costs.

Subjection of Nature's forces to man, machinery, application of chemistry to industry and agriculture, steam-navigation, railways, electric telegraphs, clearing of whole continents for cultivation, canalisation of rivers . . . what earlier century had even presentiment that such productive forces slumbered in the lap of social labour? (ibid.: 38–9).

These achievements of capitalism were fundamental and without them there would not be the technical and productive base for socialism, which could only arise out of the social and political contradictions and struggles within capitalist society. Socialism would thus represent the most advanced (and probably final) mode of production in the progressive development of human societies, *both* because it would be based on the most advanced application of science and technology in an industrial or post-industrial capitalist order, *and* because revolutionary political change would have abolished private ownership of the means of production, and hence class differences, thus providing the basis for 'true democracy' (Avineri, 1969: 31–40) in which the control of production was in the 'hands of a vast association of the whole nation . . . in which the free development of each is the condition for the free development of all' (Marx and Engels, 1888/1958: 54). Under these circumstances of 'true democracy', as Engels was to point out, the state would have withered and 'the government of persons [would be] replaced by the administration of things' – a view later underlined by Lenin (Engels, 1976: 363; Lenin, 1918/1970: 19).

One should never under-estimate the extent to which the classical Marxist conception of development was and is rigorously grounded in a secular, rational and materialist conception of modernization as the basis – and only basis – for socialism. Through this the human species would be liberated not only from the oppressive features of all previous modes of production (and particularly capitalism), but also from the wheel of nature by 'replacing the domination of circumstances and of chance over individuals by the domination of individuals over chance and circumstances' (Marx and Engels, 1845/ 1965: 482).

As I have argued elsewhere (Leftwich, 1992), this classical view holds that socialism is only possible on the other side of industrialization. The logical implication follows that there can therefore be no 'socialist path' to development because socialism can not be viewed as a means, only as an end-state. And this classical conception of industrial development as the irreducible precondition for socialism has been sustained to the present by a number of influential (and mainly) western Marxists such as Paul A. Baran (1957), Bill Warren (1980) and Gavin Kitching (1983), and those influenced by this tradition (Hyden, 1985), all of whom have been profoundly interested in questions bearing on the relationship of development, industrialization and socialism, finely summed by Baran's sharp observation that 'socialism in backward and underdeveloped countries has a powerful tendency to become a backward and underdeveloped socialism' (1957: viii).

Conclusion

Having set out the broad main approaches in terms of which the idea and practice of development have been promoted, I turn in the next chapter to look at some of the more focused conceptions of development and its major objectives which came to the fore in the post-war years.

3

The Meanings of Development: Post-war Developments

Introduction

Preoccupations with growth, modernization and structural change were the tributaries that fed the dominant orthodoxy about the meaning and purpose of development in the developing world in the immediate post-war years, in tandem with the concern for the reconstruction and development of western economies as a bulwark against communism in both the industrial and developing countries (Packenham, 1973). And although views varied about how development was to happen, and what its ultimate goals were, there was little explicit concern initially with issues such as human development or social development, as it is now called, or development as the progressive delivery of social justice. Though these questions were sometimes mentioned, the overall commitment was to growth.

This focus on growth was especially sharp in the constitutions, thinking, policies and pronouncements of the emerging post-war international institutions, like the World Bank (IBRD, 1989) and the International Monetary Fund (IMF, 1999). Given the dominance of the major industrial powers in these institutions (Payer, 1974, 1982), it is hardly surprising that the essential focus of their developmental definitions turned initially on economic growth and structural modernization and not social development, though there was later to be some modification of their official goals and pronouncements. Thinking in the United Nations (UN) was not much different in the immediate post-war period, as a report on *Measures for the Economic Development of*

Under-developed Countries (United Nations, 1951) clearly showed. In this report, development was conceived primarily in terms of per capita real income, and its recommendations, understandably for the time, focused on technology, capital, planning, development of resources and aid. More than a decade later, in another UN report on the economic development of Latin America in the post-war period (United Nations, 1964), there was still almost no discussion of the meaning of development, nor its purposes, and throughout the report the idea of development (and indeed the word itself) was used interchangeably with that of growth. The brief discussion of social development in the Latin America report refers only to some income distribution questions and the structure of population: there is no discussion of health, literacy, education, equality, gender or the environment, and certainly no reference to anything as explosively controversial as the role of participation, democracy or politics as part of the process or the goal of development. And when, in December 1961, the UN General Assembly had designated the 1960s as 'the United Nations Development decade' (United Nations, 1962: iii), it defined development as 'growth *plus* change' (ibid.: 2). With 'change' referring to 'social and cultural' aspects, it was clear that the idea of 'modernization' lay close to the surface of UN thinking at that time.

From development to social development

But the times were changing. From the early 1960s onwards a number of new factors began to undermine and expand these dominant conceptions of development. First, many formerly colonial states became independent and joined the UN, resulting in a shifting political balance within the organization, or at least the General Assembly and the UN bureaucracy (Dadzie, 1993: 300). The new states – some with radical agendas – soon began to influence the pronouncements and thinking of the UN General Assembly (though not the Security Council). And although these third-world members could not override the power (especially the veto power) of the major powers in the Security Council, they were able to use their influence to promote debates, thinking, research and a stream of resolutions, pronouncements, reports and publications, which began to focus on wider aspects of development and, in particular, on what came to be called 'social development'. This is essentially a shorthand term for improvement in such fields as education, health care, income distribution, socio-economic and gender equality and rural welfare. But it also came to signify a much more radical and sweeping conception of development involving the nationalization of major assets, the redistribution of wealth (as in land reform) and popular participation in political decision-making about both the means and ends of development.

Second, the impulse for these more radical conceptions of development (and their far-reaching policy implications) arose partly out of the political commitments of some third-world leaders, such as former President Nyerere of Tanzania who urged that the purpose of development 'is man' (by which we assume he meant humanity). He made it clear that while the pursuit of growth was not to be abandoned, it followed that its benefits must be translated into social benefits for all and, especially, for the vast majority of poor people in developing countries. Speaking to students in August 1967 about the recently formulated Arusha Declaration, he said:

in Tanzania which is implementing the Arusha declaration, the purpose of all social, economic and political activity must be man – the citizens, and all the citizens, of this country. The creation of wealth is a good thing and something which we shall have to increase. But it will cease to be good the moment wealth ceases to serve man and begins to be served by man. (Nyerere, 1968: 315)

Twenty years earlier, in his speech on the night of Indian independence on 14 August 1947, Jawaharlal Nehru had stated that the central aim of his new government was 'the ending of poverty and ignorance and disease and inequality of opportunity' (Moraes, 1957: 2). One can find countless examples of the expression of such sentiments in the public pronouncements of third-world leaders in the first years of independence. Subsequent developmental failure in many developing countries may suggest judgements of scepticism and naivety about such sentiments. But it would be folly to underestimate both the urgency with which they were pressed on the UN, and the impact which they had.

A third factor which was to provide the basis for much criticism of the narrow prevailing conceptions and strategies of development was the accumulating evidence that 'development' was simply not working or, where it was, it was either working very slowly or working only for the few. What was required, therefore, was a broader, 'unified' conception and strategy of development which recognized the importance of social development and social justice for all as both condition and outcome of effective development. The point was made explicit by a UN-sponsored Meeting of Experts on Social Policy and Planning in National Development in 1969 which reported that

development either leaves behind, or in some way even creates, large areas of poverty, stagnation, marginality and actual exclusion from economic and social progress. (International Social Development Review, 1971: 5)

The group of experts, whose ideas helped to shape the philosophy and priorities of the Second UN Development Decade of the 1970s, went on to emphasize the need to conceive of development 'as a complex whole, comprising economic elements *sensu stricto*, but also other social, as well as political and administrative elements' (ibid.: 4). While the notion of modernization was still central to their thinking, they emphasized employment, nutrition, education and health as being central to the concept of development and went on to talk of the need for radical social change, land reform, community development, the reduction of inequalities in income distribution and an increase in popular participation (especially of women) if development was to happen.

These ideas found their most substantial institutional expression in existing and newly established UN institutions, such as the United Nations Research Institute for Social Development (UNRISD), set up in 1963, and the work of the United Nations Development Programme (UNDP) (set up in1965), to which I return later (see p. 52). Following the work of the 'experts' above, and the UN resolutions arising from that work, UNRISD undertook research in the 1970s to define a 'unified approach to development analysis and planning', producing a report on this in 1980 (UNRISD, 1980). This emphasized the importance of national autonomy, participation (involving also the redistribution of power), distribution and redistribution of income and wealth, and the protection of the human environment and human relationships – though there was no mention, at least then, of the natural environment (ibid.: 16–24). These broader notions of social and unified development inevitably entailed far more radical and political conceptions of both the ends and means of development because they dealt not simply with the promotion of growth but with the social conditions for growth and, especially, how the benefits of growth were to be distributed.

But this merged with a fourth factor, which was to influence thinking about the meaning of development through the 1970s, against the background of the world oil crisis. This factor was the strengthening belief in the third world and in some radical circles in the West that growing inequalities within developing societies and, especially, between them and industrial societies, required direct attention. In particular, major institutions like the IMF, World Bank and UN themselves required root and branch reform if an effective redirection of resources in favour of the third world were to occur. Moreover, as growth stalled, debt mounted and aid declined in the 1970s, it was argued that such political and institutional reform was necessary in order to alter the pro-western bias of the prevailing international economic regime (Krasner, 1985: 5–31) so that appropriate policy measures could be evolved to protect and promote third-world interests, especially in the fields of commodity prices, trade and technology transfer (Williams, 1987: 143–51; and Dadzie, 1993: 302–3; Haynes, 1996: 66).

This thinking was partly expressed in the 1970s in various resolutions in international forums, especially that of the UN General Assembly in 1974 declaring the need for a New International Economic Order (NIEO) and defining a Charter of Economic Rights and Duties of States, which together would have involved a major shift in the balance of world economic and political power. These were very radical and threatening proposals, as western states saw them, and, had they been implemented the 'distribution of the world's economic resources would be radically altered with very great political consequences, both domestically and internationally' (Williams, 1987: 61).

Outside the UN, but closely associated with it and trying to influence its work in the 1970s, the Dag Hammarskjöld Foundation in Sweden called for 'another development' in its 1975 report, *Development and International Cooperation*, prepared on the occasion of the Seventh Special Session of the UN General Assembly in September 1975 (Dag Hammarskjöld Foundation, 1975). 'Another development' would require 'transformations of socio-economic and political structures' (ibid.: 15). These would involve, *inter alia*, land reform, urban reforms, the redistribution of wealth and the means of production within countries and of power in international institutions such as the UN and the World Bank, and would include direct attention to the provision of food, housing and health care. It would involve political autonomy for countries to define and plan their own 'endogenous and self-reliant' development which would be 'in harmony with the environment'. But none of this would happen without major structural change by the 'democratisation of the political and economic decision-making power, promoting self-management and curbing the grip of bureaucracies' (ibid.: 15–16), which would help to bring about 'ownership or control by the producers . . . of the means of production' (ibid.: 38).

Within five years, as neo-liberal economic and political philosophy came to dominate official thinking in the West from the 1980s, most of the more radical political proposals (such as the NIEO) faded or were defeated (Krasner, 1985). But though the efforts of the 1960s and 1970s to redefine and redirect development had largely failed, they had nonetheless placed questions of social development firmly on the development agenda (if rather low down). This has meant that although the commitment to growth (once again to be undertaken by the private sector rather than the state) returned to a position of dominance in most official and public conceptions of development in the late 1980s and 1990s, it would never again be possible for development to be presented solely as growth, even in institutions like the World Bank. And even if such a broad conception of development proved difficult to implement in practice, one UN official wrote in the late 1980s that development was now 'increasingly seen as a people-centred and equitable process whose goal must be the improvement of the human condition' (Dadzie, 1993: 307).

Parallel to these radical proposals for the fundamental reshaping of the idea and practice of development were some more modest (and academic) attempts to combine the necessity for growth with greater concern for both social development and social justice. One of these was the refocusing of development around the notion of basic needs.

Development as the satisfaction of basic human needs (BHN)

By the 1970s it had also become clear to many that growth and structural change in developing countries (at least where it was occurring) was not having the general or wider effect expected by the theory. In some cases – and Brazil was often cited as a dramatic example – the benefits of growth simply did not appear to be 'trickling down' as the theory suggested. On its own, growth occurring in already highly unequal societies (notably in Latin America) did not automatically seem to reduce inequalities, even if every-one got better off to some extent. Rather, growth often seemed, at best, to sustain those inequalities and, at worst, to deepen them, at least initially. And although there was theory to explain that this was a temporary and transitional phenomenon and that greater equality would happen – later – (Kuznets, 1955), there was growing dissatisfaction and unease about this and reluctance to accept (or believe) that the move towards equality was simply a matter of time and waiting. A major study, closely associated with the World Bank research group, argued in the early 1970s that:

It is now clear that more than a decade of rapid growth in underdeveloped countries has been of little or no benefit to perhaps a third of their population. Although the average per capita income of the Third World has increased by 50% since 1960, this growth has been very unequally distributed among countries, regions within countries and socio-economic groups. (Chenery et al., 1974: xiii)

Interestingly, the study was quite clear that in those few countries where 'the poor had shared equitably in income growth' (ibid.: xv), the govern-ments had taken an active role to ensure that they did. In short, the distin-guished and multinational participants who shaped the ideas that fed into the volume entitled *Redistribution with Growth*, recognized fully and force-fully the centrality of politics in development. As Richard Jolly, one of the key contributors to the study, argued: 'the political context is usually the most important determinant of whether Redistribution with Growth strate-gies will be effective' (Jolly, 1975: 11). And while the study emphasized the importance of redistribution as a condition for all-round development, it did not redefine or offer new meanings for development. But what it did do was to dramatize what others had been arguing, namely that conceptions and strategies of development which focused solely on growth were too limited with respect to both considerations of social justice and, probably, balanced growth. Indeed, later research in the 1980s showed that there was little support for the 'trickle-down' thesis and more evidence to support the 'trickle-up hypothesis', which held that initial redistribution and the meeting of needs through social development were positive conditions for economic growth (Newman and Thomson, 1989: 469).

One of the earliest academic theorists to recognize the need to expand the notion of development beyond its traditional focus on growth was the British development economist Dudley Seers (IDS, 1989). In a series of influential papers from the late 1960s he had questioned the definition of development understood as growth.

The questions to ask about a country's development are therefore: What has been happening to poverty? What has been happening to unemployment? What has been happening to inequality? If all three of these have become less severe, then beyond doubt this has been a period of development for the country concerned. If one or two of these central problems have been growing worse, especially if all three have, it would be strange to call the result 'development', even if *per capita* income has soared. (Seers, 1969: 3)

Seers was seeking to redefine the meaning and measurement of development to include the reduction of both poverty and inequality and the expansion of employment (Seers, 1969, 1972, 1979a, 1979b, 1979c). Moreover, in the early 1970s, work by the International Labour Office (ILO) and its World Employment Programme (in which Seers had an important part) began to focus attention on the importance of employment in reducing poverty and promoting development by providing for what came to be called 'basic needs' (ILO, 1976). Out of these and other influences there emerged the notion that development was a process of meeting basic (and evolving) human needs, and that development should be measured by the extent to which it met these 'primary needs of communities and individuals' (Green, 1978: 7).

What are 'basic human needs' (BHN)? It is important to note that some of the proponents of the notion of development as the provision of BHN held that these included both material and *non-material* needs. The 'basic needs approach to development is to provide opportunities for the full physical, mental and social development of the individual'. Basic needs therefore included 'the need for self-determination, self-reliance, political freedom and security, participation in decision-making, national and cultural identity, and a sense of purpose in life and work' (Streeten, 1979: 136). But, in practice, the focus was on material needs. Concern with political and human rights was to come later, in the 1990s and in a different context.

The definition of basic human needs covered five main areas (ILO, 1976:

32): basic goods for family consumption (including food, clothing, housing); basic services (including primary and adult education, water, health care and transport); participation in decision-making; the fulfilment of basic human rights; and productive employment (to generate sufficient income for a family to meet its consumption needs). In short, development as the systematic and steady provision of basic needs focussed on the 'primary redistribution . . . of income, assets and power' (Green, 1978: 8). And although one enthusiastic supporter of the approach argued that the BHN conception and strategy of development rejected the 'maximisation of the rate of growth of productive forces . . . and the primacy of accumulation' (Green, 1978: 7), the ILO was quite clear, by contrast, that 'a rapid rate of economic growth is an essential part of a basic-needs strategy' (ILO,1976: 33). And those who had been concerned with the idea of redistribution with growth were at pains to stress that aspects of redistribution of assets and income could contribute strongly and in diverse ways to the promotion of growth (Jolly, 1975; Streeten, 1979).

Just as concerns with social development and social justice had done in the 1960s and 1970s, so too the introduction and specification of basic human needs was to expand considerably the political, normative and (some would say) culturally universal implications of the idea of development. But this, too, has of course radical political implications and those who advanced the idea of basic human needs – and the idea of redistribution with growth which preceded it – were not unaware of this. It was apparent that any definition or strategy of development that turned on redistribution or on meeting basic human needs also required appropriate political action through the state (Bell, 1974). And it had been the evidence of the apparent inability of the market, on its own, to distribute the benefits of growth or to meet basic human needs, at least in the short run, that had served to reinforce the argument about the importance of state action.

But as the 1970s gave way to the 1980s, the role of the state in development came under heavy fire as the new liberalism in economic and political affairs gained ascendancy in western capitals and hence in the international institutions. It was time to roll back the state and let the free play of market forces generate the energies which would get development moving again – and that meant development was once more understood as growth, growth, growth. And it is therefore hardly surprising that just as quickly as concerns with redistribution and basic human needs arose in the first half of the 1970s, so they quickly faded out of the active languages, litany and live policies of the big development agencies. This is not to say that many of the concerns that inspired the BHN conception of development were removed from the banners of the agencies; as we shall see, in many instances they remained. But the central focus of policy and strategy moved sharply away from reliance on the state to reliance on the market in the 1980s, though by the early

1990s the role of the state was once again being more positively redefined. And no institution has better reflected these shifting fashions and priorities in the idea and practice of development than the World Bank.

The World Bank and development

No account of the evolution of the meaning and objectives of 'development' in the post-war era would be complete without reference to the World Bank (the International Bank for Reconstruction and Development, the IBRD). As perhaps the major player in the public process of 'development' since the 1950s, the influence of the World Bank on official and public conceptions and strategies of development has been immense, for it 'enjoys a unique position as a generator of ideas about economic development' (Wade, 1996: 5).The Bank has never sought to define its formal or official conception of 'development', but its shifting understanding and emphasis of the goals and processes of development has been reflected in its countless publications and statements which provide a clear indication of the evolution of its thought.

Its origins (in 1944 at the Bretton Woods meeting in the USA) as a bank designed to promote the reconstruction and development of Europe after the war were (and remain) reflected in its Articles of Agreement (revised in 1989). These state the Bank's purposes to be, *inter alia,* the reconstruction and development of productive facilities and resources, the promotion of foreign private investment and the raising of productivity, standard of living and conditions of labour of its member countries (IBRD, 1989: 1). In short, from the very beginning, the Bank's conception of development expressed the prevailing concerns with growth, structural change and modernization which dominated post-war thinking. It is true that the Bank lent to some formally (and now formerly) socialist countries that were its members (such as Algeria, Poland, former Yugoslavia, Hungary and, more recently, China). And although it is equally true that it endorsed and contributed to the conventional post-war consensus about the importance of the state in promoting development – that is, 'an activist role for government' (World Bank, 1997b: 21–2), there is simply no doubt that it has understood such growth and structural modernization in terms of the encouragement and extension of market principles and the expansion of capitalist economies.

The Bank's conception of development and its purposes has expanded significantly over the years. While in no way diminishing its commitment to economic growth as the core of development, in the 1970s the Bank came increasingly to emphasize the importance of 'social development' in its pronouncements, especially under the Presidency of Robert S. McNamara from 1968 to 1982. Reflecting some of the prevailing dissatisfaction with equating growth with development, McNamara stressed that while the Bank remained committed to 'mobilizing capital and using it for growth of the productive capacity of the developing countries' (McNamara, 1970: 6), it had to recognize that development had a social objective, aimed 'squarely at an end[ing] of grinding poverty and gross injustice'. Hence, he argued, the Bank would have to turn its attention to issues such as population, urbanization, land reform, income distribution, health and the environment (ibid.: 8).

Although the Bank now began increasingly to use 'social indicators' in order 'to complement measures of economic progress' (World Bank, 1988a: 1), another current was running fast in development thinking in the 1980s; this was to eclipse concerns with the explicit promotion of social development or social justice. The decade of the 1980s has been called 'the lost decade for development' (Esteva, 1992:16; DfID, 1997: 8) because those years saw the triumph of a 'counter-revolution in development theory and policy', which affected not only the conceptions of development but, more obviously, the strategies and policies (Toye, 1987). Fuelled by 'neo-classical' or neo-liberal economic theory (Friedman, 1980; Bauer, 1981; Lal, 1983), major western governments turned away from statist and redistributive concerns (both domestically and in their development thinking), as did governments in the developing world (notably in Latin America), in favour of ideas and policies that emphasized the role of free markets, a reduced role for the state in development and the promotion of liberal trade and foreign investment policies. As one study suggested, the core of the neo-liberal approach could be summed up in the view that, from a developmental point of view: 'imperfect markets are better than imperfect states' (Colclough, 1993: 7).

These views were absorbed, elaborated and reproduced within the World Bank and were, in turn, translated into the policy of structural adjustment lending which gripped the Bank in the 1980s. Development, as both process and goal, came to be much more sharply framed in terms of the prevailing enthusiasm for neo-liberal ideas. Specifically, these entailed the bundle of ideas that economic freedom, free markets, private-sector initiatives and the cutting away of regulations would provide the conditions and incentives for unleashing entrepreneurial energies. For some (Friedman, 1980: 21), there was a further objective: reducing and removing the economic power and control of the state would reduce the overall power of the state and hence encourage 'political freedom'. This thinking about development re-asserted 'the primacy of economic growth', rather than social development or the elimination of poverty, arguing that in the long run growth would take care of poverty (Colclough, 1993: 6), and hence explicitly rejected the ideas of the 1960s and 1970s, which saw a key role for the state in planning, redistribution and the provision of basic human needs. Structural adjustment lending, which reached almost a quarter of Bank lending by the end of the 1980s, sought to provide the incentives and the means (or loans) for re-structuring developing economies around these principles (Mosley and Toye, 1988). Reviewing the respective roles of states and markets in development in the *World Development Report, 1991*, and summing up the new emphasis in its thinking, the Bank argued that while the state did have a role in a 'market-friendly' approach to development (World Bank, 1991a: 1), 'faith in the ability of the state to direct development has given way to a greater reliance on markets' (ibid.: 31), and that government action and involvement in development should be 'employed sparingly and only where most needed' (ibid.: 49).

But even as these broad judgements were being made, the evidence was accumulating that structural adjustment and debt in the developing countries were imposing heavy costs on the poor with respect, for instance, to increases in basic food prices as well as medical and education services (R. H. Green, 1986, 1988; Cornia, Jolly and Stewart, 1987; Demery and Addison, 1987; Glewwe and de Tray, 1988; Longhurst et al., 1988).

Whether it was because of, or despite, this evidence, the Bank now offered a comprehensive view of development in its *World Development Report 1991*, defining 'economic development' as:

a sustainable increase in living standards that encompass material consumption, education, health and environmental protection.

Moreover:

Development in a broader sense is understood to include other important and related attributes as well, notably more equality of opportunity, and political freedom and civil liberties. The overall goal of development is therefore to increase the economic, political, and civil rights of all people across gender, ethnic groups, religions, races, regions, and countries. (World Bank, 1991a: 31)

Though written at the peak of the structural adjustment programmes of the 1980s, with all their costs to social development, which was likened in one Bank publication to 'crossing the desert' (Demery and Addison, 1987: 1), this wider formal definition of development nevertheless seemed to consolidate the shift in the Bank's thinking away from the older and narrower notions of development as growth. To some extent, this has been reflected in the pattern of its lending for education, health, the environment and the 'social sector' in the 1990s (World Bank, 1998a: 8).

In its current pronouncements, therefore, the Bank has now clearly returned publicly to the conception of development that ties economic growth and social development closely together. It has specified its role as 'strengthening economies and expanding markets to improve the quality of life for people everywhere, especially the poorest' (World Bank, 1998a: viii), while making sure that such development is sustainable in environmental terms (World Bank, 1999b: 5). In concert with the Organization for Economic Cooperation and Development (OECD) and the UN, the World Bank has identified six 'social goals' for the start of the new millennium: poverty reduction, universal primary education, movement towards gender equality, reduction of infant mortality rates, improvement in reproductive health services and environmental preservation (World Bank, 1999a).

Moreover, the partial politicization of the Bank's conception of development (note the references to political freedom and civil rights in the 1991 quotation above) represents the public culmination and expression of thinking inside the Bank on this issue in the form of its emerging concern with good 'governance' as both a means and end of development (World Bank, 1989, 1992a, 1994). By 1997, when the Bank surprisingly devoted its annual *World Development Report* to a reconsideration of the role of the state in development, its position had become a lot more state friendly (IDS, 1998), arguing that 'the state is central to economic and social development, not as a direct provider of growth but as a partner, catalyst and facilitator' (World Bank, 1997b: 1). Hence the state's capability, 'defined as the ability to undertake and promote collective actions efficiently', needed to be enhanced if 'sustainable development, both economic and social' was to be achieved (ibid.: 3, iii).

I return to these important questions about the means of development in later chapters. I shall point to the Bank's inability (at least publicly) to grasp the centrality of *politics*, and not simply governance, in shaping the character and capacity of states. But it is important to stress that in this chapter I am concerned only with the shifting conceptions and meanings of development, not with how it is to be achieved nor with the respective merits of different strategies. On the latter, of course, the Bank's practices have been routinely and radically criticized since the early 1970s (Hayter, 1971), suggesting something of a gap between rhetoric and reality, leading to one critic's description of the Bank as

perhaps the most important instrument of the developed capitalist countries in prying state control of its Third World member countries out of the hands of nationalists and socialists . . . and turning that power to the service of international capital. (Payer, 1982: 20)

And, more recently, the forensic dissection by Robert Wade of the Bank's role as 'part of the external infrastructural power of the US state', has illustrated how it has served to enhance the external reach and influence of the USA (Wade, 1996: 37). These criticisms have much weight and again illustrate the highly political nature of both ideas and practices of development.

Nonetheless, while growth and market forces remain central to World Bank thinking and lending operations – as they inevitably will for any bank – it is also important to recognize the immense difference between the Bank's early post-war growth-oriented obsessions and the broader understanding of the social and political goals of development for the new millennium. In many respects they articulate sharply the current official conventional wisdom of many developed and developing countries. But if these goals are truly to be pursued and achieved, then it will only be through the transformative processes of politics that it will happen – both within and beyond the Bank.

Development as freedom and the expansion of choice

While the Bank's conception of development swayed in its fashions and focuses from growth to social development to free markets to governance, and in the end sought to incorporate them all, the culmination of the unease of the 1970s in and around the UN about the meaning, focus and practice of development came to be expressed in a major new initiative of the UNDP when, in 1990, it began to publish its annual *Human Development Report*. In many ways it reflected concerns about social development, about redistribution and about basic human needs that had been prevalent in the 1970s. But the real point I think is that the UNDP was seeking to make emphatic the idea that the fundamental meaning and explicit purpose of developmental activity was to improve conditions of life for human beings, as Nyerere had argued in the 1960s, and to carve a public niche in development discourse (and practice) that was somewhat to the left of the World Bank.

Thus although they have been contentious, the *Human Development Reports* have constituted important steps in expanding the formal definition and measurement of development. In his Foreword to the first *Human Development Report 1990*, the administrator of the UNDP wrote that the

central message of this Human Development Report is that while growth in national product (GDP) is absolutely necessary to meet all essential human objectives, what is important is to study how this growth translates – or fails to translate – into human development in various societies. (UNDP, 1990: iii)

So growth remained essential, but as an explicit means for enhancing human development. But what did this mean? What is the core of human development? The UNDP's most recently refined position asserts simply that human development is a process of expanding human choices by enabling people to enjoy long, healthy and creative lives. (UNDP, 1998: 16)

There are three major components of human development: a long and healthy life, education, and access to resources that provide a decent standard of living. These components make human choice possible, for those who are ill, ignorant and poor have little real choice and hence cannot 'enjoy long, healthy and creative lives'. Additional aspects of choice require political, social and economic freedom 'for being creative and productive, and enjoying personal self-respect and guaranteed human rights' (UNDP, 1990: 10). Going much further, politically, than the World Bank was able to do in its concerns with governance, the UNDP in its 1991 *Human Development Report* concluded that 'the lack of political commitment . . . is often the real cause of human neglect' (UNDP, 1991: 1), while the 1992 *Human Development Report* was emphatic in declaring that 'political freedom is an essential element of human development' (UNDP, 1992: 27).

In trying to measure the progress of human development, the UNDP evolved its Human Development Index (HDI), which it has published in each of its annual reports since 1990. This controversial index combines indicators of life expectancy, educational attainment and income to give a composite picture of human progress in different societies. According to the UNDP, the level and progress of human development (as defined above) has been lower and slower in many countries than it could be, or ought to be, given their GDP per capita. Of the 174 countries assessed in the 1998 *Human Development Report*, for instance, 73 (mostly in the developing world) ranked lower on their HDI than on their GDP per capita, 'suggesting that they have failed to translate economic prosperity into correspondingly better lives for their people' (UNDP, 1998: 20). Some were relatively affluent countries, like Kuwait, Hong Kong and Mauritius, while others were poor, like Angola, Laos and Guatemala, suggesting that wealth is no guarantee of human development and, conversely, that relative poverty – as in Jamaica, Cuba, Western Samoa, Vietnam, Tanzania and Madagascar – is no bar to its progress (ibid.: 21). This means that some more affluent countries (both democratic and non-democratic) have been politically unable, or their states have not had the capacity (or both) to organize a more even distribution of the benefits of growth whereas some poorer countries have been able to achieve this.

It is thus not surprising that by the end of the 1990s the UNDP had sharpened its view about the importance of politics in development. It continued to emphasize that the first priority of 'sustainable human development' was poverty eradication, the creation of employment and sustainable livelihoods, the empowerment of women, and the protection and regeneration of the environment. But in keeping with the thinking of many governments, it now urged and supported the promotion not only of good governance, but also democratization through the political empowerment of the poor (UNDP, 1998: 1–4) as a necessary means of achieving the social and economic aspects of human development.

The work of the UNDP and others has shown that, at least in its official public conceptualization (if not rhetoric), the meaning and purpose of development have moved from the original narrow identification with economic growth and development, to include first the ideas of social and then human development and, most recently, to entail political development in the form of democratization and good governance.

Amartya Sen and development as freedom

These ideas of development – as both means and ends – have been most fully encapsulated in Amartya Sen's more sophisticated formulation of development as freedom (Sen, 1999). For Sen, the

expansion of freedom is viewed as both (1) the *primary end* and (2) the *principal means* of development. They can be called respectively the 'constitutive role' and the 'instrumental role' of freedom in development. (Sen, 1999: 36)

Development requires, first, however,

the removal of major sources of unfreedom: poverty as well as tyranny, poor economic opportunities as well as systematic social deprivation, neglect of public facilities as well as intolerance or overactivity of repressive states. (ibid.: 37)

Sen resists and opposes the idea that certain freedoms – especially political freedoms – may need to be postponed until social and economic development has advanced far enough to sustain them. On the contrary, he argues, political and other freedoms, such as freedom from disease and from ignorance 'are among the *constitutive components* of development' (ibid.: 5). Moreover, certain 'instrumental freedoms' enable people to live more freely and, in linking with and supporting each other, promote development. He classifies five categories of this type of freedom:

1 *political freedoms*, which enable people to shape government and government policy and maintain accountability;

2 *economic facilities*, which constitute the opportunities for individuals to use resources for consumption, production or exchange;

3 *social opportunities*, which refer to the arrangements societies make for health care and education, for instance, which have substantive but

also instrumental value in providing for more effective participation in political and economic life;

4   *transparency guarantees*, which are essentially guarantees of social and public trust achieved through 'disclosure and lucidity' which can limit corruption and graft; and

5   *protective security*, which is an instrumental freedom for development in that it provides an institutional social safety net which prevents people being reduced to abject poverty and starvation. (Sen, 1999: 38–9)

Sen's contribution appears to be that of a modern social-democratic Adam Smith. He argues that only under a regime of certain kinds of freedom (and following the elimination of certain unfreedoms) are the conditions present under which individuals can pursue their trading or productive activities to promote their own and wider social development. For these reasons, both state and society have 'extensive roles in strengthening and safeguarding human capabilities' (ibid.: 53) for development, and to that extent Sen's notion of development as freedom not only presupposes political action but directly and continuously requires it.

The key problem, however, has been that the *practice of development* does not seem to have kept up, except in a relatively few countries. For instance, the average annual rates of growth of the GNP per capita in low-income countries (excluding India and China) was negative in the decade 1985–95, as it was in middle-income countries (World Bank, 1997a: 214). Poverty remains endemic in the developing world (notably Africa and South Asia) (World Bank, 1990: 2; UNDP, 1998: 26) and, difficult as it is to measure poverty comparatively, recent data suggest that the depth and incidence of poverty between 1987 and 1993 *increased* in Latin America, the Caribbean, Central Asia and sub-Saharan Africa, while it decreased in East and South Asia (World Bank, 1997a: 53). Inequality between rich and poor countries has increased and, within some countries, internal inequalities have deepened (UNDP, 1998: 29–30). Finally, between 1980 and 1996 third-world debt increased dramatically – in sub-Saharan Arica, alone, it rose from $84 billion to $227 billion (World Bank, 1998b: 231). Of course there have been exceptions and regional variations, but the overall pattern seems clear (Escobar, 1995b: 212–13).

It has been failure of this kind that has led some theorists to declare the whole development idea and practice to be little other than a sham of domination. But before looking at that it would be appropriate to focus on the origin and idea of 'sustainable development', which came forcefully onto the agenda in the 1980s.

Sustainable development

As will have become apparent above, the notion of 'sustainable development' began to appear in pronouncements on development during the 1980s.This reflected growing official and public awareness about an increasing range of environmental concerns (Redclift, 1987). These concerns were not new; there had been earlier discussion of the problem, especially as the 'accidental internationalization' of environmental problems became apparent (Sachs, 1992b: 27) and as an emerging public consciousness was stirred by pressure groups and books (Carson, 1962; Commoner, 1971; Lele, 1991). Reacting to Swedish concerns about acid rain and the effect of pollution and pesticides on its environment, fish stocks and other wildlife, the first UN Conference on the Human Environment was held in Stockholm in 1972. This resulted in the establishment of the United Nations Environment Programme (UNEP) and a host of conferences in the 1970s on many environmental issues, ranging from atmospheric and marine pollution, population, deserts and food through to technology and energy (Sachs, 1992a: 26–7; Birnie, 1993: UNEP, 1998). Another influential document had been the Club of Rome report, entitled *Limits To Growth* (Meadows et al., 1972).This (rather dramatically) reminded the world that its resources were finite and warned that the continued exponential growth of population, industry, pollution, food production and resource depletion would bring humanity to the limits of growth. The report predicted economic and social catastrophe unless growth rates were cut back and a pattern of global equilibrium established between population and the environment, while ensuring that the basic needs of all were met (Redclift, 1987: 53; Todaro, 1997: 137).

But did this imply an end to growth and to development? Developing countries were concerned. Was it a late 'colonialist conspiracy' to hinder third-world development and impose on them the kinds of constraints that developed countries had not faced when they went through their 'pollution-generating, resource-consuming industrial revolutions' (Birnie, 1993: 338)? This has, understandably, remained a sore point with many developing countries, right up to the Earth Summit of 1992 and beyond, since it has been recognized that 'most cumulative environmental destruction to date has been caused by the First World' (Todaro, 1997: 345). And if growth were to be reined back in the third world, would the unequal status quo between rich and poor nations not be frozen? Did this not imply therefore that the 'South's continued poverty was necessary for maintaining the North's prosperity' (ibid.: 654)? As will immediately be clear, this was not simply a technical, scientific question about the depletion and destruction of global resources, but also a highly political one which, once raised, highlighted the gross and persistent material inequalities both within and between nations, and the differentials in power which went along with them.

It was thus in the context of the political need to acknowledge growth and also to recognize environmental dangers that the term 'sustainable development' emerged as a kind of conceptual compromise for establishing and maintaining 'a balance and symbiosis between environmental protection and development' (Birnie, 1993: 338). It gained currency from 1980 when the International Union for the Conservation of Nature and Natural Resources (IUCN) unveiled its World Conservation Strategy with the idea of 'sustainable development' at its core (Lele, 1991: 611). Although it was further elaborated by the IUCN, the UNEP and the World Wildlife Fund in the mid-1980s, and through many conferences and publications, a widely acceptable definition of 'sustainable development' had to await the 1987 findings of the World Commission on Environment and Development (WCED), set up as an independent commission by the UN General Assembly in 1983 and chaired by Gro Harlem Brundtland, the former prime minister of Sweden.

Although there were other conceptions of 'sustainable development' (Pearce et al., 1990), the definition evolved by the Brundtland Commission was economical and elegant and came to be widely accepted, even within the World Bank (World Bank, 1992b: 34). It provided a conceptual basis which could enable environmental concerns to be absorbed within the goals and strategies of growth and development, something that had not seriously concerned the proponents of the NIEO of the mid-1970s. The definition was:

Sustainable development is development that meets the needs of the present without compromising the ability of future generations to meet their own needs. (World Commission on Environment and Development, 1987: 43)

The threats to the environment (and hence development) that had been identified are well known. They include population growth; desertification; deforestation; pollution of air, water and sea; global warming, the emission of greenhouse gases and ozone-depleting chemicals; the production of other hazardous wastes; loss of biodiversity and atmospheric changes. And the Brundtland report went on to set out principles for the guidance of policy, both nationally and internationally. These were: to promote and maintain economic growth, but a type and quality of growth which would need to change in order to reflect 'sustainability, equity, social justice and security'; to protect the resource base; to ensure a sustainable level of population; to adapt and re-orient technology to take account of its environmental impact; to ensure that environmental issues were integral to policy-making and to enhance international relations and cooperation (World Commission on Environment and Development, 1987: 364–6).

From the time of the Brundtland report onwards, these ideas and strategies were discussed, enhanced and amplified, and aspects of them were
implemented in a wide range of regulations and agreements within and between nations. Thus, by the time the UN Conference on Environment and
Development, the so-called Earth Summit, met in Rio in June 1992 (UNEP,
1999), it was able to take the idea of 'sustainable development' largely for
granted and outline in an immense document, *Agenda 21*, a programme of
action for the global environment for the twenty-first century.

What seems to have made the concept of 'sustainable development' so
acceptable to so many public institutions and private interests around the
world in the 1980s and 1990s is that it has not threatened the urge for growth.
Rather, argue the critics, it has legitimated development, afresh, as 'an ar-
ray of interventions for boosting the GNP' (Sachs, 1992b: 29). Indeed, Principle 12 of the 1992 Rio Declaration, arising from the Earth Summit, almost
seemed to suggest that growth itself would take care of the environmental
problems:

States should cooperate to promote a supportive and open international economic
system that would lead to economic growth and sustainable development, to better
address the problems of environmental degradation. (UNEP, 1999)

Some of those who have been critical of the very idea of 'sustainable
development', especially those in the tradition of radical political ecology,
see in it a contradiction which cannot be resolved. For it is, they argue,
precisely these growth-driven open international economic processes (of
capitalism) that have been and remain the disease, not the cure. And they
draw particular attention to the 'role of a globalizing capitalist system in
the development of the Third World's environmental crisis' (Bryant and
Bailey, 1997: 104). In seeking to interpret the origins, contours and prospects of environmental and development problems, they rightly give pride
of place to politics, regarding the current situation, nationally and globally,
as any good political scientist should do, as the 'outcome of political interests and struggles' (ibid.: 5). And it is precisely that kind of approach that
has underpinned a range of views that have been intensely critical of not
only the practices (or non-practices, as they see it) of development, but of
the conception, idea and characteristics of 'development' itself. That is the
subject of the next section.

Development as domination

Anti-industrialism

In its various manifestations, the idea and practice of development has never been without its critics. For instance, in Britain, the home of the European industrial revolution, from the late eighteenth century through the nineteenth century, romantic poets like Blake and Wordsworth, and some of the greatest novelists and commentators, in their different ways cast a very critical look at the reality of development in the form of the alleged progress the industrial revolution was bringing. Some, like Trollope and Dickens, focused with brilliance on the effects of social change on the poor. Others, often forgetting the inequities and iniquities of the dying feudal order, glorified that past, or, like Arnold and Ruskin to some extent, mourned what they saw as the passing of rural Britain and its former social order, expressing their loathing of the values of industrial capitalism, technology and growth (Williams, 1963; Weiner, 1985).

While the positive idea of development as the endless and restless effort to control and improve natural, economic and social conditions was influential and dominant in nineteenth-century Britain, it was certainly not a view shared by everyone. John Stuart Mill, for example, writing in his classic mid-nineteenth-century work, *Principles of Political Economy*, expressed the hope for continued progress in 'mental culture' and social and moral matters, and what he referred to as the 'Art of Living'. But he was not 'charmed' by the exhausting prospect of constant struggle to get ahead, or by the kind of industrial and mechanical inventions which have only 'enabled a greater population to live the same life of drudgery and imprisonment' (Mill, 1848/1970: 113–16).

This critical tradition may be traced through to modern times. It was expressed, for instance in the ideas of Russian populists, neo-populists and anarchists from the end of the nineteenth century through to the revolution (Kitching, 1982), and it can be found, too, in the village-focused ideas of Gandhi in India in the first half of the twentieth century (Rao, 1968). Consider Gandhi's 1909 comment on industrialism:

When I read Mr Dutt's *Economic History of India*, I wept; and, as I think of it again, my heart sickens. It is machinery that has impoverished India. It is difficult to measure the harm that Manchester has done to us. It is due to Manchester that Indian handicraft has all but disappeared. . . . Machinery has begun to desolate Europe. Ruination is now knocking at the English gates. Machinery is the chief symbol of modern civilisation; it represents a great sin. (Gandhi, 1909/1997: 107)

This anti-industrial tradition of developmentalism crops up again, force-fully, in the work of E. F. Schumacher, whose *Small is Beautiful* in 1974 excoriated (amongst many other things) the 'soul-destroying, meaningless, mechanical, monotonous, moronic work' (1974: 30) of advanced industrial development, an image that had been wonderfully portrayed by Charlie Chaplin in the inter-war years in his film, *Modern Times*. And it is no doubt a view shared by many of those who work today in the repetitive and la-bour-intensive industries on the US–Mexican border, in Thailand, and in the booming factory cities of southern China, where wave after wave of new recruits are inducted into the ordered and oppressive structures of that kind of industrial work. And though the pulse of that sharp anti-industrial tradition continues today, it beats weakly in public debate, although the 'greens' continue to constitute one moderate and qualified – but important – critical influence in the politics of modern industrial development.

Capitalism, underdevelopment and dependency

But anti-industrialism has been only one of the strands in the complex cri-tique of the idea and practice of conventional (and mainly western or west-ern-inspired) development. Another approach – incorporating many different schools and lines of attack – has not seriously questioned the idea or goal of progressive development, understood conventionally as industrialization. On the contrary, theorists of this approach have endorsed such goals but have also regarded as naive the assumption of the modernizers that this could or would happen in the developing world in the same way as it hap-pened in the West, if at all, and simultaneously have therefore rejected Marx's prediction that 'the country that is more developed industrially only shows to the less developed, the image of its own future' (Marx, 1976: 91).

The common denominator and essential uniting theme of this strand in the critique of development has been that (whether under imperial or post-imperial relationships) foreign aid, foreign investment and international trade, such as they were, have not served to engender the dynamics of autono-mous capitalist development, but rather only to lock third-world countries into a condition of underdeveloped, impotent, peripheral and necessarily unequal subservience, or dependency, in an increasingly global economy dominated by the developed nations and their multinational corporations (Wilber and Jameson, 1988; Todaro, 1997: 82–3).

The origins of this critique are various. One influence was in the work of Marxist writers in the first two decades of the twentieth century, such as Luxemburg and Hilferding, but especially Bukharin and Lenin (Brewer, 1980; Warren, 1980). Their work gave rise to questions as to whether capi-talist imperialism, in general, could generate development in poor countries. Moreover, contrary to the fundamental thrust of Marx's thinking, these theorists seemed to provide the basis for the new conclusion that 'capitalism was thus . . . devoid of positive functions anywhere', a view that was formalized at the sixth Congress of the Communist International in 1928 (Warren, 1980: 83 and passim).

Although the long Stalinist permafrost on ideas largely prevented fresh thinking in the Marxist tradition in the inter-war years, this post-Leninist theme was taken up again after the war by the American economist Paul A. Baran, who argued in his classic study, *The Political Economy of Growth*, that

the capitalist system, once a mighty engine of economic development, has turned into a no less formidable hurdle to human advancement. (Baran, 1957: 249)

Moreover, he went on, pre-shadowing the work of later theorists of underdevelopment and dependency:

For, as we have seen, the rule of monopoly capitalism and imperialism in the advanced countries and economic and social backwardness in the underdeveloped countries are intimately related, representing merely different aspects of what is in reality a global problem. (Baran, 1957: 249–50).

These ideas were taken up initially in the context of Latin America (Larrain, 1989) where, despite a long and intimate connection through trade and investment with the developed capitalist world, the processes and features of (capitalist) development were held to be retarded and deformed, and constituted what came to be called 'underdevelopment'. Such retardation and underdevelopment in Latin America, and elsewhere (Bagchi, 1982: 20), was not simply a passing and 'necessary stage in the process of formation of modern capitalistic economies. It is a special process due to the penetration of modern capitalist enterprises into archaic structures' (Furtado, 1964: 138). In short, as another major theorist of underdevelopment in the 1960s and 1970s, was to argue: 'Economic development and underdevelopment are the opposite sides of the same coin' (Frank, 1971: 33), by which he meant that capitalist development in the industrial world had, through imperial and post-imperial economic and political relationships, created the conditions of underdevelopment found in Latin America (and elsewhere).

Development was thus not autonomous or indigenous but 'dependent capitalist development', argued two other analysts (Cardoso and Faletto, 1979: xxiii). Such dependent development produced lopsided economies of immense wealth (for the few) and pervasive poverty (for the many), employment and unemployment. It entailed complex political dynamics involving tense and precarious relations between landed, working and bourgeois classes, armies and bureaucracies, and states and external economic interests. In this context economic dependence needed to be understood as the situation where 'the accumulation and expansion of capital cannot find its essential component inside the system' (ibid.: xx). Or, as another theorist defined dependence,

a conditioning situation in which the economies of one group of countries are conditioned by the development and expansion of others. A relationship of interdependence between two or more economies or between such economies and the world trading system becomes a dependent relationship when some countries can expand through self-impulsion while others, being in a dependent position, can only expand as a reflection of the expansion of the dominant countries, which may have positive or negative effects on their immediate development. (Dos Santos, 1973: 76)

These core ideas – of underdevelopment, dependency and dependent development – were taken up, elaborated, modified or extended by other writers working in the same tradition, and were applied to the world economy as well as to both Africa and Asia. Some of the key figures included Walter Rodney (1972), Immanuel Wallerstein (1974), Colin Leys (1975), Samir Amin (1976) and A. K. Bagchi (1982). And what united these often distinctive critiques was that, in their own way, each argued that what had passed for 'development' had been little other than the global extension of capitalist exploitation, through and after formal colonialism, reducing third-world countries to the status of dependent satellites and subjecting many of their people to poverty and degradation.

In short, what had been going on was not development, but its opposite. For some, the solution to this predicament thus lay in tough measures of protective economic nationalism which crystallized round the policy of import-substituting industrialization (ISI), a policy promoted widely by the UN Economic Commission for Latin America from the 1950s and 1960s and adopted in many other parts of the developing world (Harris, 1986: 120–30; Larrain, 1989: 102–10; Todaro, 1997: 468 and passim). For others, nothing less than a revolutionary break with world capitalism and the building of socialism on a national or, preferably, a world scale could resolve the problems of underdevelopment (Baran, 1957: 261), for capitalist development could not and would not solve the plight of the majority of the people. The problem therefore remained that of 'how to construct paths toward socialism' (Cardoso and Falleto, 1979: xxiv), for without such 'liberation' from the world capitalist structure (or its collapse), the countries of the third world would remain 'condemned to underdevelopment' (Frank, 1971: 35).

Though fashionable, influential and popular in the 1970s, the potency of the ideas about underdevelopment and dependency diminished fast in the

1980s and were subject to intense critical assessment (Lall, 1975; Larrain, 1989) and some modification (Evans, 1986). Moreover, the patent advance of some third-world economies, notably in East Asia, weakened the empirical claims of the approach that saw underdevelopment as a terminal condition (Barrett and Whyte, 1982) and little is heard about it today. In any event, neo-liberalism came into the ascendance in the 1980s. And, following the disintegration of the Soviet Union and the collapse of formally constituted socialist systems around the world at the end of the decade, structural adjustment programmes of economic liberalism began to dismantle state-run economies in the East and protectionist policies of economic nationalism in the South. In the 1990s, therefore, full-frontal capitalist development, held at bay for seventy years by official 'socialisms', was once more on the march from Chile to China, where it appeared to be embraced with enthusiasm. It seemed now as if the meaning and central purpose of development was finally settled and was becoming thoroughly universalized.

But was it? For just as theorists such as Francis Fukuyama (1989) declared confidently that liberal economic and political systems were the 'final form' of political and economic development, groups of post-modernist theorists and activists were questioning the very idea of universal meanings or truths, in general (see Kiely, 1995: 153), and that of 'development' in particular.

Development as a discourse of domination

One central idea has been fundamental to the view of development as domination. Its proponents argue that, understood as the purposive intervention in the social, economic and political affairs of a society with particular social and economic objectives in mind, the concept and content of both 'development' and development programmes have largely been external in their origin (western, that is). But although they have been imposed on the third world, in practice they have come to be internalized by the bulk of its elites and masses. Both the notion of 'development' and its opposite, 'underdevelopment', the argument goes, have thus come to be broad non-indigenous cultural and ideological standards by which people or groups (peasants, workers, soldiers, teachers, bureaucrats) have learned both to define themselves or the condition of their societies and to set goals for them. Hence two-thirds of the world's population think 'of themselves as underdeveloped, with the whole burden of connotations that this carries' (Esteva, 1992: 7). Accordingly, because of this internalization of external values and beliefs, 'underdevelopment is also a state of mind, and understanding it as a state of mind or consciousness, is the critical problem', as Illich (1969/ 1973: 136) put it. For all the goals and characteristics of development that

are implicit and explicit in all the various meanings and programmes of
action, even when initiated from within, are not authentic or indigenous but
are themselves external in provenance. They include such things as industrialization and urbanism; science and technology; secularization, individualism and equality; competition and consumerism. All these apparent
objectives and values have been inherent in the 'goals of development . . .
always and everywhere stated in terms of consumer value packages stand-
ardised around the North Atlantic' (Illich, 1969/1973: 148). What this means,
in other words, is that the ideas and practices of development conveyed
through aid, trade, projects, programmes and investment, all actually represent a 'cultural invasion', whereby

the invaders penetrate the cultural context of another group, and ignoring the potential of the latter, they impose their own view of the world upon those they invade
and inhibit the creativity of the invaded by curbing their expression. (Freire, 1972b:
121)

In this context, some people in other parts of the world have even questioned whether liberalism and democracy (at least of a particular form) are
not, at least in these terms, like 'a foreign flower', unlikely to grow in local
soil (*Fiji Times*, 3 September 1992), an issue to which I return in chapter 6.
    Moreover, western 'knowledge' about development, which defines what
it is and how it happens, and what should be done and by whom and to
whom and with what objectives in mind, has been able to achieve this cultural invasion and underdevelopment of the mind and consciousness – as
well as material economic and social underdevelopment. It has been able to
do so because this 'knowledge' is intimately associated with the immense,
accumulated and articulated structures of western economic and political
power, expressed both publicly and privately in, for instance, the operations of banks, companies, government agencies and international institutions such as the regional development banks, the IMF and the World Bank.
    One early major influence shaping this approach to development as domi-
nation came from some of the critical insights of Latin American social
thinkers, educationists and developmental activists, notably such people as
Paulo Freire (1972a, 1972b) and Ivan Illich (1969/1973). In the 1960s and
1970s they were amongst the foremost exponents of the idea of cultural
action for freedom, as Freire called it, which to some extent overlapped
with the emerging radical theology of liberation in some parts of the Catholic Church in Latin America. In his work on the cultures and ideologies of
domination, Illich emphasized both a 'basic needs' approach (which would
include the majority of the people) and also the requirement of a 'cultural
revolution', which would enable people to question 'the reality that others
take for granted' (Illich, 1969/1973: 139–49). Freire (1972a: 59) argued

that a 'dependent society is a silent society' and he therefore emphasized the right of people in the third world 'to a voice . . . the right to . . . be itself, to assume direction of its own destiny' (ibid.: 17–18), which would be the point of a 'true revolutionary project . . . in which people assume the role of subject in the precarious adventure of transforming and recreating the world' (ibid.: 72). A central part of this process would be what he called *conscientization*, or 'learning to perceive social, political and economic contradictions and to take action against the oppressive elements of reality' (Freire, 1972b: 15).

The idea of 'liberation' thus came to be used widely in the 1970s in Latin America as a counter to that of 'development', despite (or perhaps even because of) the prevalence of authoritarian dictatorships in that era. The effect of these ideas of ideological, 'psychic', cultural and political liberation was to

unmask the hidden value assumptions of the conventional wisdom and replace them with a deliberate stress on self-development as opposed to aid, foreign investment, and technical assistance. (Goulet, 1971/1988: 482)

Such ideas as these did not fare well under the intense political repression which prevailed in much of Latin America into the mid-1980s (Cammack, 1997). Moreover, they seem to have been swept aside, or simply consumed, by the great waves of democratization which got under way in the mid-1980s and, after that, by the hegemony of 'market-oriented capitalist development within liberal-democratic regimes' (ibid.: 173), which foreclosed sharply on any alternative ideas about development.

But ideas do not die that easily and the notion of 'development' as a 'discourse' of domination found expression again, this time amongst a small but radical group of (mainly) anthropologists and geographers (see, for instance, Said, 1978; Escobar, 1984, 1992, 1995a, 1995b; Esteva, 1987, 1992; Ferguson, 1990; Sachs, 1990, 1992b; Crush, 1995; Tucker, 1999). Many, but not all of these, have been influenced by post-modernist 'discourse' theory and, in particular, by one of its major exponents, the French social theorist Michel Foucault (1972, 1980), whose concept of 'discourse' has come to play a critical part in organizing their analysis and applying it to questions of 'development' in the third world (Said, 1978; Escobar, 1984; Hall, 1992).

Though discourse theory has found its way into many disciplines – such as linguistics, literature and philosophy – it has made only a small impact in the study of politics and development (Howarth, 1995). Stated simply, a 'discourse' or 'discursive formation' (Foucault, 1972) consists, first, of a set or system of linked assumptions, ideas, values, definitions, themes, opinions, images, meanings, statements, techniques and interpretations which are used by people not only in conceptualizing and discussing a particular subject, with all its implications and echoes (like 'the dark continent', 'democracy' or 'development'), but also, in practice, in dealing, with it. That is to say, secondly, a discourse is not only a means of 'representing' the subject-matter but also, through that representation, of acting upon it. Discourses shape the way we understand our own societies and our place in them, and how we act upon them. And it follows, therefore, that discourses vary from society to society, from culture to culture – perhaps even from class to class within them. Discourse theory is thus hostile to the idea of universal truths, values or meanings. More important for present purposes, the 'knowledge' inherent in a particular discourse decisively influences how power is used in relation to its subject matter; indeed, such knowledge 'constitutes a kind of power' (Hall, 1992: 295).

Moreover, each society, Foucault argues

has its regime of truth, its 'general politics' of truth: that is, the types of discourse which it accepts and makes function as true, the mechanisms and instances which enable one to distinguish true and false statements, the means by which each is sanctioned; the techniques and procedures accorded value in the acquisition of truth; the status of those who are charged with saying what counts as true. (Foucault, 1980: 131)

It may seem that considerations of this kind drift the discussion somewhat away into reflective realms which are far removed from the gritty realities of poverty and development. But a moment's thought will readily reveal the implications of this approach for the meaning and pursuit of development. First, if all societies have their 'regimes of truth' and a multitude of discourses within them, then the prospect for establishing universal truths, values, goals or even rights for people everywhere are effectively denied, for there is no way of according precedence to any one 'regime of truth' over another, and therefore not a 'western' one over all others. But, second, and more relevant for present purposes, it should be clear what is involved if the 'discourse' of one society in relation to some subject or project (like 'development') is imposed on another: it becomes a 'colonizing discourse' (Escobar, 1995: 213), like the 'cultural invasion' and 'underdevelopment of the mind' from an earlier critique, discussed above (p. 65). And one of the most oft-quoted applications of this was Edward Said's analysis of what he called 'Orientalism'; that is, the western view of the Orient. Orientalism, he argued, is best thought of as

the corporate institution for dealing with the Orient – dealing with it by making statements about it, by teaching it, settling it, ruling over it; in short, Orientalism as a Western style for dominating, restructuring and having authority over the Orient

. . . Without examining orientalism as a discourse we cannot possibly understand the enormously systematic discipline by which European culture was able to manage – and even produce – the Orient politically, sociologically, ideologically, scientifically, and imaginatively during the post-Enlightenment period. (Said, 1978: 3)

Just so with development, argue its critics (Escobar, 1984). Some even date 'the era of development' and underdevelopment to 20 January 1949, the date of President Truman's inauguration address when he announced a programme of 'development' for the 'underdeveloped' areas (Sachs, 1990; Esteva, 1992). 'On that day, two billion people became underdeveloped', for that concept defined and 'belittled' them as the opposite, the 'inverted mirror', of being developed (Esteva, 1992: 6–7).

Moreover, without understanding development as a discourse

we cannot understand the systematic ways in which Western developed countries have been able to manage and control and, in many ways, even create the Third World politically, economically, sociologically and culturally; and that, although underdevelopment is a very real historical formation, it has given rise to a series of practices (promoted by the discourses of the West) which constitute one of the most powerful mechanisms for insuring domination over the Third World today. . . . In this way, development will be seen, not as a matter of scientific knowledge, a body of theories and programmes concerned with the achievement of true progress, but rather as a series of political technologies intended to manage and give shape to the reality of the Third World. (Escobar, 1984: 384)

In short, 'Western knowledge is inseparable from the exercise of Western power' and takes precedence over the 'value of alternative experiences and ways of knowing' (Crush, 1995: 3). Accordingly:

Development discourse is thus rooted in the rise of the West, in the history of capitalism, in modernity, and the globalization of western state institutions, disciplines, cultures and mechanisms of exploitation. (ibid.: 11).

This notion, wittingly or unwittingly, brings us close to the unremittingly negative characterization of 'globalization' so well described and assessed as 'hyperglobalization' (Held et al., 1999: 3–4, 326–7). Can this be reversed? Can such an immense and all-powerful discourse be changed? Michel Foucault has said 'yes', for

a change in the order of discourse does not presuppose 'new ideas', a little invention and creativity, a different mentality, but transformations in practice, perhaps also in neighbouring practices and their common articulation. (Foucault, 1972: 209)

But if this is so, how do these theorists and activists see the way out? Clearly it can only be political in the manner in which I defined politics in chapter 1;

that is, in new ways of using, producing and distributing resources. So what is to be done? What are the alternatives? What are the new ways? The main answer given to these questions is that it is from the local initiatives, ideas and communities of grass-roots organizations and the new social movements – not states, elites and foreign agencies – that the new conceptions and practices of 'development' are emerging (Esteva, 1987; Escobar, 1992: 420–35). For 'the possibility of redefining development rests largely with the action of social movements' (Escobar, 1995b: 225). These have been particularly thick on the ground in Latin America, often in the space of liberated civil society created by democratization (Hoogvelt, 1997: 233–7; Craske, 1999: 112–36) where one might find groups of 'peasants, urban marginals and de-professionalised intellectuals' seeking to 'regenerate people's space' by evolving new conceptions and practices of development (Esteva, 1987: 129–35). These practices are hugely varied. They include improving methods of food production, preserving forests, controlling fertilizer use, rebuilding houses, promoting informal exchange markets, publishing journals or establishing libraries, reinforcing traditional medicine and healing techniques, nurturing water resources, building connecting roads, promoting cooperatives, women's rights and critical thought. Whatever their form, they have a number of common elements which define their definition of development, their 'discourse', so to speak. These elements are that they are local, that they are political but distrustful of organized and established politics, that they are attuned to local cultural values and that they are sceptical of experts and governments (Escobar, 1992: 421–2).

These indigenous and participatory forms of activity define a particular kind of development and also clearly give expression to forms of resistance to poverty, injustice and inequality, and to self-help at the local level. But it still remains hard to see how they, alone, can effect the nationwide transformation of the whole society, which even their own values would endorse, without a broad political movement that could integrate and link their goals and activities in a wider, collective and transformative enterprise. Perhaps, therefore, the final word is best left with Flora Lewis, writing a bit before their time:

The aspiration for something different, better, more truly indigenous than Western systems of development, and yet as socially and materially effective is palpable everywhere. 'Our own way' is the persistent theme: but it is far more often advanced as a creed than as a plan. (Flora Lewis, in *New York Times*, 31 December 1979, cited in Wiarda, 1988: 75)

Conclusions

Taken together, this and the previous chapter have sought to provide a survey of the ways in which meanings of development have evolved, at least since the time of Adam Smith. A few important points need to be made by way of conclusion and as a basis for subsequent chapters.

First, despite the suggestion that 'development' and 'underdevelopment' were born in the immediate post-war period, it is clear that issues and concerns about these matters have been around for considerably longer, even though the sustained, conscious and focused mobilization of resources in the pursuit of development is, generally, a more recent phenomenon. Indeed, as I suggested in the first chapter, these concerns grew up as an intimate part of social science – both non-Marxist and Marxist. And in a manner of speaking the fundamental questions that have moved much social science – growth, change, equality, power, collective choice – have been developmental ones. Crudely, social science is development studies and development studies is social science.

Second, I hope it will have become clear that almost every meaning and elaboration of the concept of development has flowed from some political context or purpose, or has been a response to political circumstances or an integral part of an attempt to transform such circumstances. More than this, each meaning of development has carried with it a clear set of political implications for policy and practice. For example, like Adam Smith two hundred years earlier, advocates of development as growth in the 1980s wanted markets to be cleared of what they alleged was the clutter of governmental interference and constraint in order to give space, impetus and incentives to entrepreneurs. On the other hand, those who have regarded social development or the provision of basic human needs as the central point of development have always urged *greater* governmental action to organize the redistribution this would require. Meanwhile, proponents of the New International Economic Order as the basis for global development lobbied for inter-governmental action to contain and reshape the international market, something regarded as impossible (if not undesirable) by those for whom development is essentially an indigenous matter, defined by the cultural specificity of local discourses and community action. Modernizers – both Marxist and non-Marxist alike – have been less charmed by the significance or virtues of cultural variety and have been far more concerned with the allegedly universal validity of science, secularism and technology as the means for true social and human development. In short, politics and development are inseparable, both in concept and in practice. And whenever and wherever development has been pursued it has always enhanced the interests of some at the cost of others, in the short run and in the long run.

Third, despite the variety of meanings and purposes of development, despite persistent efforts and despite regular changes of aid priorities and policies, few countries in the developing world have achieved a regular, acceptable and sustained increase in the standard of living for most of their citizens such that poverty has been consigned to the margins. In 1973, Robert McNamara as president of the World Bank called for the ending of world poverty by the year 2000 as the major goal of development. That was more than a quarter of a century ago. Nothing even approaching that goal has been achieved, at least not in most developing countries. Such basic goals as clean water, regular diet, clothes and habitat – development by any definition – have not been achieved for more than a billion people in the so-called developing world (World Bank, 1990), while the global economy has continued to expand and others have got considerably richer. It is somewhat ironic, then, that McNamara's 1973 objective has been re-cast in one of the current goals of the Bank (in conjunction with the OECD and the UN) as reducing by half the proportion of people in extreme poverty by the year 2015 (DfID, 1997). But if the last twenty-five years of the twentieth century are anything to go by, even that elementary target is unlikely to be achieved.

The question is why? It is the central argument of this book that the explanation is primarily political. Accordingly, and consistent with that theme, I turn in the next chapter to examine and evaluate some of the theories of the state in the developing world which have been advanced to explain aspects of their slow, or failed, developmental records, while remembering – as the first chapter made clear – that not all third-world societies fall into this category.

4

States of Underdevelopment

Introduction

In the previous chapters I argued that if we are to understand the pervasive patterns of non-development or underdevelopment in much of the third world we need to focus primarily on the character and capacity of third-world states and the forms of politics that have generated and sustained them. Yet it is surprising how little attention has been given to such *political* analysis of both development and non-development (at least until relatively recently) by the major international agencies and donor governments, by the broad field of academic development studies or in concrete development programmes and projects. In short, the detailed and explicit focus on the *politics of development* has been a relatively minor and largely recent concern in both the academic study of development and in the analytical underpinning of official development and aid policy.

To illustrate, until its recent discovery of 'governance' (which I touch on in this chapter and look at in detail in the next), the World Bank maintained a virtual silence on political questions, justifying this with reference to section 10 of its Articles of Agreement (IBRD, 1989), which prohibits it from 'interfering' in the political affairs of any member country or from using political criteria in its lending decisions. The effect of this principle (though the Bank has not always adhered to it) was effectively to evacuate any professional assessment of the politics of development or non-development from its analytical concerns; this has been an immense shortcoming of its work.

Equally, little attention has historically been paid by major donor governments to political questions, though for rather different reasons. There is today a loudly voiced concern among western governments to promote democracy and civil rights in the developing world, and to use aid as a lever of conditionality to this end. But, contrary to what was often said (Packenham, 1973), this current preoccupation stands in sharp contrast to most of the post-war era, when these very same governments aided, armed and supported a wide range of non-democratic and sometimes ruthlessly oppressive (and developmentally feckless) regimes from Latin America to East Asia, commonly in countries where human and civil rights were often brutally suppressed. Why there has been this apparent change in the global development agenda of western governments is something that I also explore in the next chapter.

But this is not to suggest that political issues have never been addressed. However, where they have been, the focus of attention has tended to be very broad and often highly general, especially when dealt with by economists. For instance, in one of the earliest radical assessments of 'the political economy of growth', in 1957, Paul Baran attacked what he called the 'comprador governments' of many developing countries (his focus was mainly the oil-rich Gulf states and Latin America). He argued that their propensity for alliances with foreign companies promoted their habits of corrupt accumulation of resources for the benefit of dominant classes and groups. Moreover the unwillingness or refusal of such governments to plan for the national interest was a central element in what he termed the 'morphology of backwardness' (Baran, 1957: 163). And Gunnar Myrdal (another economist, of whom more later, see p. 80) wrote in his *Economic Theory and Underdeveloped Regions*, also in 1957, that 'underdeveloped countries need real democracy even at this early stage to break down the existing impediments to economic development' (Myrdal, 1957: 83).

Of course, during the first thirty years after the end of the second world war it had become axiomatic in most academic and official circles that development would have to be planned and implemented by the state (Robertson, 1984: 7–61). As Migdal observed:

Statesmen and scholars expected the states in Asia, Africa, and Latin America to steer the way to unprecedented levels of prosperity and new heights of human dignity through a host of both macro-level and micro-level social and economic policies. (Migdal, 1988: 39)

More recently, Colin Leys underlined the point when he argued that:

It is not a great simplification to say that 'development theory' was originally just a theory about the best way for colonial, and then ex-colonial, states to accelerate

national economic growth. . . . The goal of development was growth; the agent of
development was the state. . . . These were the taken-for-granted presuppositions of
'development theory' as it evolved from the 1950s onwards. (Leys, 1995: 7)

However, and crucially, the way in which the character and capacity of
states affected their developmental competence was seldom explored during those first thirty years when 'unrealistically optimistic expectations con-
cerning the state as an instrument of development' prevailed (Evans, 1992:
141). The prevalence of 'unreasonable expectations' was perhaps nowhere
more true than in relation to sub-Saharan Africa (Fieldhouse, 1986: 85–90).
Detailed analyses of the politics of states, and hence the politics of their
developmental propensities, were to wait until later, much later, when it
became obvious that few states in Latin America, Africa or Asia had shown
the capability to manage developmental momentum. Then, and only then,
did analytical attention begin to focus more sharply on politics, the state
and 'governance' as variables affecting developmental capacity and performance.

The publication of *Bringing the State Back In* (Evans, Rueschemeyer
and Skocpol, 1985) represented an important and substantive but also sym-
bolic milestone in this shift in academic study, though its primary focus
was not the developing world. In the World Bank, the realization that serious resistance by key interests both within and outside the state were major
political constraints on programmes of structural adjustment – liberalizing
third world economies – contributed to its interest in questions of governance and capacity-building in the 1990s (Frischtak, 1994). It began to build
cautiously on work that was beginning to be done by political scientists at
that time (Nelson, 1989a, 1990; Haggard and Kaufman, 1992).

If economists did not explore the political dimensions of development,
might one have expected more from the mainstream discipline of political
science? Perhaps, but in practice – at least until relatively recently and with
a few important exceptions – scant attention was paid to the analysis of the
relationship between politics, the state and development in the third world
in the central preoccupations of the discipline. As I pointed out in the first
chapter, issues of this kind were generally consigned to 'area' studies and
development studies. And where and when comparativists in political science did include third-world countries in their treatment, the frameworks of
analysis remained largely bound to institutional concerns of a traditional
kind (Almond and Powell, 1996). Conversely, more specific studies of politics in the third world have maintained a largely exclusive intra-third-world
focus, rarely relating the problems and issues of such politics back to the
wider universe of politics or to the concerns of the discipline of Politics
(Manor, 1991; Cammack, Pool and Tordoff, 1993; Haynes, 1996; Smith,
1996).

Nonetheless, though mainstream development studies were largely pre-occupied with broad questions of macro-economic policy, some important contributions have sought to explain developmental failure with reference to the character of third-world states. It is the purpose of this chapter to explore some of these. But before doing so, I start by reviewing briefly the main elements of established state theory. My purpose here is not to provide comprehensive accounts of such theory – for there are plenty (Alford and Friedland, 1985; Dunleavy and O'Leary, 1987; Held, 1989). Rather, my aim here is to establish some points of reference in, and linkages with, state theory so that it will be possible, later, to situate states of development and underdevelopment in or beyond these traditions. But politics is politics, wherever it occurs, and thus my secondary purpose is to locate the debate about states of development and underdevelopment full-square in the mainstream of the discipline of politics and its major preoccupations, not in some distant and dusty domain called 'area' or 'development' studies.

Traditions in state theory

Two major traditions dominate state theory and analysis in modern political science. The first and older tradition derives from Karl Marx (and Friedrich Engels), while the second and later tradition stems from Max Weber (Heper, 1987; Held, 1989). A brief sketch of the key elements of these traditions is necessary here in order to assess the theories of the third-world state against them.

Marxism and the state

While much of what Marx had to say about the state has been described by Elster (1985: 389) as being set out in 'a half-conspiratorial, half-functional-ist language', recent interpretations of Marxist theories of the state (Jessop, 1982; Elster, 1985; Dunleavy and O'Leary, 1987; Held, 1989) have all identified two main conceptions of the state in Marx (and Engels). The provenance of the first and classic one is in *The Communist Manifesto* (Marx and Engels, 1888/1958), the 'Preface to a Contribution to the Critique of Political Economy' (1859/1958c) and elsewhere. Its central thesis is that the state and its institutions are essentially the agents ('committee') of the dominant class in capitalist society, the bourgeoisie. The state and its coercive agencies act explicitly to further bourgeois interests over and against those of other classes, especially the proletariat, in advanced (or advancing) capitalism. This conception can be traced through Lenin (1918/1970) to more recent Marxist theorists such as Miliband (1969). Whether and which states in the developing world have been dominated by classes that could even begin to pass muster as bourgeois classes, and whether such states have been even remotely effective in promoting capitalist development are, of course, empirical and – above all – political questions. The obvious if stark contrast between, say, the dominant classes in the predatory Haitian state (Lundahl, 1992: 255–89) or in the 'crony capitalism' of the Philippines under the Marcos regime, on the one hand, and those of Singapore, Thailand and Taiwan, on the other hand, suggest that any easy generalizations about dominant classes and the state in the third world should be treated with great caution.

The second and less familiar Marxist conception has its fullest expression in Marx's writings on France, notably 'The Eighteenth Brumaire of Louis Bonaparte' (1852/1958a). Here Marx presents the state and its bureaucratic apparatus as largely autonomous of narrowly bourgeois interests: 'Only under the second Bonaparte does the state seem to have attained a completely autonomous position', he wrote (1852/1958a: 333). Such a state is of course constrained by the imperatives of capitalism, whose general interests it nonetheless seeks to further. Elster (1985: 426) argues that this conception provides a more accurate and representative historical picture of the state in the development of capitalist society from the sixteenth century than does the first version. This second conception was later elaborated by the Greek Marxist Nicos Poulantzas, focusing on the idea of the 'relative autonomy' of the state in capitalist society, which in turn drew on ideas in Gramsci and Althusser. Poulantzas sought to distinguish this from what he referred to as 'a simplistic and vulgarized conception which sees in the state the tool or instrument of the dominant class' (1973: 256). The central function of the state was to promote 'cohesion' in the inevitable conflict and contradictions of each capitalist society (ibid.: 44–56) and its 'relative autonomy' was both a condition and measure of that.

Considered strictly from a developmental point of view, this second conception of the state in Marx is essentially a conception of a modernizing state, one which is active, pervasive and disciplining in the promotion of capitalist development. And it is entirely consistent with Marx's historical conception of capitalism as a revolutionary modernizing force in human history. For all its conceptual and institutional imprecision, some aspects of this notion of the relatively autonomous state find occasional empirical expression in accounts of effective 'developmental states' in the contemporary third world, as will become apparent later. For it is clear that some (few) states in the third world have been successful in establishing their autonomy (though not always for the reasons given by Marx), as in South Korea or Botswana, while others, as in India, have not, as has been brilliantly analysed recently (Corbridge and Harriss, 2000).

Weber and the state

By contrast, the essence of Max Weber's account of the modern state and its bureaucracy is altogether less 'political' and conceptually altogether more precise than that of Marx and later Marxists. This is typical of Weber's concern with 'clarity and coherence of concept-formation' in the social sciences (Albrow, 1970: 37). Weber was more concerned with *how* the state operated, rather than the character of its rule or the nature of its output.

For Weber, the modern (and essentially western) state had only reached its full development recently. The character of its authority was very different from that of prior forms of the state which Weber identified in his typology of authority. Its essential form of rule and authority was different, for instance, from 'traditional' authority and, in particular, from 'patrimonial' authority, found in some pre-capitalist societies, where a 'chief' ruled through his *personal* administrative and military staff. Here, the defining characteristic of state power and authority under patrimonial rule was their identification with *personal rulership*, which, in its most extreme form involving unconstrained arbitrariness, became what Weber described as 'Sultanism' (Weber, 1964: 346–7). At the core of this, says Weber, is that:

The person exercising authority is not a 'superior' but a personal 'chief'. His administrative staff does not consist primarily of officials but of personal retainers. . . . What determines the relations of the administrative staff to the chief is not impersonal obligation of office, but personal loyalty to the chief. (Weber, 1964: 341)

And in 'the genuinely patrimonial office'

The political administration . . . is treated purely as a personal affair of the ruler and political power is considered part of his personal property. (Weber, 1968, vol. 3: 1028–9)

In practice this means that:

Instead of bureaucratic impartiality and of the ideal . . . of administering without respect to persons, the opposite principle prevails. Practically everything depends explicitly upon the personal considerations: upon the attitude toward the concrete applicant and his concrete request and upon purely personal connections, favours, promises, and privileges. (ibid.: 1041)

It is important to note (and I shall elaborate on this shortly) how these Weberian notions have influenced interpretations of third-world states as 'neo-patrimonial' (especially in relation to Africa), as 'predatory' (for instance Haiti and Zaire) and as 'cronyist' (notably the Philippines).

In contrast to these earlier states, Weber defined the modern state as a 'compulsory association with a territorial base', claiming 'the monopoly of the legitimate use of physical force' (Weber, 1964: 156) in that territory. Such a state (at least in its ideal and ideal-typical expression) is regarded as legitimate by its members and is run by an *impersonal* bureaucratic staff, in the context of a legal-administrative order, regulated and limited by legislation and representative government (Albrow, 1970: 45–9). Central to such a modern state for Weber was his ideal-typical bureaucracy, typifying what he calls 'legal-rational authority', starkly different from the highly personal form of patrimonial or Sultanist rule. Such bureaucracy was characterized by:

1   a personally free staff with impersonal duties;

2   hierarchy;

3   a clear specification of the tasks of the offices;

4   a contractual basis for employment;

5   the selection of staff by professional qualification and tested expertise;

6   payment by fixed salaries and pensions;

7   bureaucratic work being the single or major occupation for the incumbents of office;

8   promotion by merit or seniority;

9   non-ownership of the post or its resources by officials;

10 officials subject to systematic discipline (Weber, 1964: 333–4; 1965a: 196–244).

This Weberian conception of state and bureaucracy has exercised a profound influence on non-Marxist political science in the West. It has been central to both normative and analytical debates in empirical democratic theory and public administration and policy. Indeed, if one were to use the (Foucauldian) concept of a 'state discourse' in this connection, these ideas and practices would be central to western, liberal and social-democratic thinking and practices. And it is hardly surprising, therefore, that many features of this comprehensive account of the ideal bureau – and its ideal-typical nature must be remembered – have been sharply impressed in the notions of 'good governance' which have been developed and deployed in the 1980s and 1990s by the World Bank and other development agencies and donor governments and, for that reason, have also been subject to criticism and rejection by some leaders and intellectuals in the third world.

However, what is significant for present purposes about both the Marxist and Weberian traditions of state theorizing is that both have presupposed advanced or, at least, advancing industrial capitalist societies. Both traditions arose as a result of political theorizing in and about such societies and, to a considerable extent, remain embedded in them, or at least in the *idea* of such societies. For Marx, the state (especially in his second conception mentioned above) helped to promote the progressive processes of capitalist development and, in so doing, sharpen the contradictions and conflicts, while seeking to contain them (Poulantzas, 1973; Warren, 1980; Elster, 1985). Indeed, it may be argued that the imperial state in India did indeed do precisely that, by contributing political unity (but of a rather temporary and superficial kind), internal communication through the railway and the telegraph, external communication through the steamship, a 'free press', and a national system of law and order (the army). Of course Marx was quick to point out that though the Indians would 'not reap the fruits' of all this, these innovations would contribute decisively to 'the development of the productive powers of man and the transformation of material production into a scientific domination of natural agencies' (Marx, 1969: 133–8).

For Max Weber, on the other hand, the modern state and its bureaucratic character was as much the consequence as it was the condition of capitalist development. Moreover, it represented a prominent feature of the pervasive spread of 'rationalization', which had been intrinsic to the development of capitalist industrialization in the West. 'The fate of our times is characterized by rationalization and intellectualization and, above all, by the disenchantment of the world', observed Weber rather bleakly (1965b: 155). He went on to say that this meant

that principally there are no mysterious incalculable forces that come into play, but rather that one can, in principle, master all things by calculation. This means that the world is disenchanted. One need no longer have recourse to magical means in order to master or implore the spirits, as did the savage, for whom mysterious powers existed. Technical means and calculation perform the service. (ibid.: 139)

Interestingly, this rather dismal disenchantment of the world for Weber was perceived with delight by Marx as laying the foundations for an energizing, rational, secular and scientific liberation of the human species from ignorance and superstition, from the domination of nature and (ultimately) from socio-economic and political oppression. Nonetheless, what is crucial here is that for both Marx and Weber the modern state was both a function and agency of *capitalist development* – a set of coordinating and authoritative institutions which both shaped and were shaped by the relentless logics and requirements of industrialization.

But from the 1950s, when scholars intensified their study of the third world, they found only a very few societies (mainly in South-east and East Asia and to some extent in Latin America) with anything comparable to the strong or long *state traditions* of the West. Even these had few of either the Marxist or Weberian characteristics of the modern state. It is true that some were thought to illustrate Weber's notion of 'patrimonial' authority, and this was nowhere more true than of the post-colonial states of sub-Saharan Black Africa, where it has often been described as 'neo-patrimonialism' (Bratton and van de Walle, 1997). Moreover, only a handful of third-world states could be said to have been anchored in advancing industrial capitalism, at least of the western mode. And where capitalist relations had indeed penetrated on a more widespread and systematic basis (as in much of Latin America), its forms were generally held to be uneven, dependant, partial and 'distorted' (Cardoso and Faletto, 1979). Moreover, few of these Latin American states conformed with the characteristics of either Marx's capitalist state or Weber's modern and 'rational' type, given the strong legacies and traditions of '*caudillismo* (strongman politics), personalism, clientelism and centralism' (Dominguez, 1987; Craske, 1999: 28).

Yet clearly both new post-colonial and post-revolutionary states did exist, and most were committed to the active promotion of economic development (Robertson, 1984; Leys, 1995), and were encouraged to do so (Green, 1974). But on all continents, after initial, short and positive spurts of growth (Morawetz, 1977), despite interesting regional differences and apart from a few important individual exceptions, developmental records have been grim and, in fact, worsened in many countries in the twenty years after the oil crises of the 1970s. As illustrated in the previous chapters, growth slowed or stagnated, inequalities sharpened, poverty often intensified and conflict steadily increased (World Bank, 1990, 1991a).

One kind of theoretical explanation, much of which was anchored in what came to be called 'world system' theory, sought to interpret these poor developmental records in terms of the *external* constraints and hostile influences of, first, colonialism, and then, the continuing subordination to the dominant poles of the world capitalist economy (Wallerstein, 1979) in which developing countries were little more than dependent satellites. Though it has provided important and enduring insights about the implications of global inequalities and has, therefore, generated powerful political views on world trade, it is an explanatory approach which has not stood the test of time very well (Lall, 1975; Warren, 1980; Palma, 1981; Barrett and Whyte, 1982; Fieldhouse, 1986; Haggard, 1990a; Leys, 1995).

A second explanatory approach, which I shall be concerned with here, has focused on internal factors, especially the state, and a variety of theories about the character and capacity of third-world states have emerged. What was the essence of these theories and how, if at all, did they relate to the central Marxist and Weberian traditions of state theorizing in political science?

Myrdal and the 'soft state'

At the stroke of midnight when the world sleeps, India will awake to life and freedom. . . . It is fitting that at this solemn moment we take a pledge of dedication to the service of India and her people and to the still larger cause of humanity. . . . The service of India means the service of millions who suffer. It means the ending of poverty and ignorance and disease and inequality of opportunity. (Moraes, 1957: 1–2)

With these words, Jawaharlal Nehru ushered in India's independence on the night of 14 August 1947.

Despite aspects of early progress, the fact of the matter was that twenty years later many millions of Indians remained in poverty, ignorance and disease (Corbridge and Harriss, 2000). In an attempt to account for the slow pace of Indian development in the twenty years after independence, Gunnar Myrdal advanced the theory of the 'soft state' in the 1960s (Myrdal, 1968, 1970). Although based on his wider studies of South Asia it was essentially a theory of the Indian state but could also be extended (and was) to other states in the third world.

The soft state for Myrdal was characterized by:

a general lack of social discipline in underdeveloped countries, signified by deficiencies in their legislation and, in particular, in law observance and enforcement, lack of obedience to rules and directives handed down to public officials on various levels, often collusion of these officials with powerful persons or groups of persons whose conduct they should regulate, and, at bottom, a general inclination of people in all strata to resist public controls and their implementation. Within the concept of the soft state belongs also corruption, a phenomenon which seems to be generally on the increase in underdeveloped countries. (1970: 229)

The soft state grew from local socio-economic and political conditions in South Asia. Colonialism had distorted these conditions by destroying many traditional village-level organizations, in place of which no viable substitutes had been created. The soft state was also sustained by continuing attitudes of what Myrdal called 'disobedience' to authority, which had been a natural and effective weapon in the independence struggle against the authoritarianism of colonial rule (1970: 233), a view expressed later in relation to African states and societies by Peter Ekeh (1975).

The notion of the 'lack of social discipline' at the core of Myrdal's theory is highly general. But what he seemed to mean was a pervasive inability or reluctance at all levels to abide by rules and regulations or, in other words, a situation where the law and its observance and enforcement were weak (1970). The soft state for Myrdal was thus incapable of promoting urgently needed development (1968: vol. III, 1909). It failed to impose obligations and responsibilities on the masses and was unable to act decisively against corruption at all levels. As a consequence, its softness allowed conservative and reactionary elites in the rural and urban areas to undermine and resist the ideals and implementation of modernization programmes that had been at the heart of the Nehruvian vision (1968: vol I, 277–8). For instance, the 'land to the tiller' programme of land reform in India turned out to be largely rhetoric, because the soft state allowed both avoidance and evasion of the programme (1968: vol. II, 1580–1). In short, argued Myrdal, political and social life in developing countries blocked the enactment or enforcement of effective developmental legislation and regulations (1970: 235).

The ordered discipline of the affluent Scandinavian states of Myrdal's own experience seems to have provided the implicit model against which his notion of the soft state was conceived and contrasted. And although broad in its approach, this view of the state in India (and beyond it) has much intuitive appeal. More importantly, though he did not articulate it in such terms, Myrdal was one of the first to highlight the centrality of politics in development, at least in its broadest sense.

His thesis certainly goes some way towards explaining the slow pace of Indian development, when contrasted with that of China over the same period. For instance, the average annual growth rate of GNP per capita between 1965 and 1990 in India was only 1.9 per cent, compared with China's 5.8 per cent (World Bank, 1992b: 218). The central idea – of 'indiscipline' and the absence of a 'hard' or effective developmental state – has also been reflected in more recent work on India, for instance by Pranap Bardhan (1984), Atul Kohli (1991) and Corbridge and Harriss (2000). Their explanations are historically richer, analytically tighter and politically more sophisticated than Myrdal's. But they are also concerned with the absence of a strong, coherent and effective state and, crucially, with the ways in which the grandeur of the Nehruvian vision and state was slowly unravelled by the complex processes of regional, religious, intra-elite, Congressional, class and caste *politics* in the wake of Nehru's death. These politics have acted to shape what Bardhan describes as a state that came largely to regulate and dispense patronage, hence sapping it of developmental energies which might otherwise have been directed towards the achievement of the Nehruvian ideal (Bardhan, 1984: 39).

The soft state in Africa

The explanatory use of the notion of the 'soft state' has not been confined to India. Some fifteen years after Myrdal's explanation of the Indian situation, Goran Hyden's (1985) assessment of the failure of development administration in Africa focused on a similar set of characteristics, illustrated with material from both Francophone and Anglophone Africa, including Senegal, Nigeria, Tanzania, Mali and Zaire. In these contexts, the 'erosion of fundamental organizational rules' allowed clan and clientelist pressures to enter the bureaucracy and thus 'reduced the managerial autonomy of top officials', while politicians had been able to 'pervert all the norms of recruitment, promotion, termination and discipline in the public service' (Hyden, 1985: 60). Hyden identified direct parallels with Myrdal's account of the 'soft state' in India because he saw what was happening in Africa as an 'institutionalised pattern', not isolated examples. He concluded that:

The mechanisms of the soft state are the antithesis of the type of economic efficiency that is necessary for growth and development. . . . The 'soft' state is the inevitable product of a situation where no class is really in control and dominant enough to ensure the reproduction of a given macro-economic system. (Hyden, 1985: 63)

Theoretically, what is interesting here is that *neither* Myrdal's nor Hyden's accounts of the soft state display any of the characteristics attributed to modern states in either the Marxist or Weberian traditions. In the first thirty years of independence, the Indian state did not conform with either of the classical Marxist models. There was clearly no single, dominant capitalist class of bourgeois provenance – indeed both Nehru's need and commitment to consensus politics involved placating a range of urban, professional, bureaucratic and rural interests. And though no class dominated, this did not leave the state in an autonomous position, able to push through Nehru's democratic, socialist and secular developmental objectives (Corbridge and Harriss, 2000). Moreover, despite the fact that the central Indian administrative service has generally enjoyed a high reputation and is clearly not typical of a 'patrimonial' bureaucracy, it has also clearly not conformed with many of the ideal-typical characteristics of Weber's modern state and bureaucracy. And, certainly at the lower levels, it became progressively mired in the politics of corruption. Even at the end of the 1990s, the Corruption Perceptions Index produced by Transparency International (1998) ranked India at sixty-seventh out of eighty-five countries in its survey, as one of the most corrupt countries in the world, on a par with Egypt and Bulgaria. Many African states also occupy a fairly low ranking on the corruption index.

So, although Myrdal's notion of the 'soft state' lacked precision and analytical rigour, his general contention about the character of the political economy associated with such a state not only raised important questions about the role and character of states in development but also triggered implications about the universality and applicability of the two main traditions of Occidental state theorizing.

The 'overdeveloped state'

Myrdal's account of the soft state in India is a good example of the 'society-centred' approach (Nordlinger, 1987) in state theory, in emphasizing how 'social indiscipline' can infect the character and operation of the state in the developing world. Hamza Alavi's influential thesis about the 'overdeveloped state', on the other hand, had much more of an institutional and state-centred flavour to it and a broader comparative perspective.

Alavi was concerned to emphasize 'the historical specificity of the post-colonial societies' (1972: 59) in the context of their colonial histories, and hence the specificity of their states. The post-colonial state, he argued, needed to be conceptualized and understood very differently from the states that emerged in Europe following the bourgeois revolutions. In focusing on the political and economic implications of the institutional and power structure bequeathed by colonial rule, Alavi sought to challenge the utility of classical Marxist theory of the state for the analysis of post-colonial societies (1972: 59), but he nonetheless still sought to locate his argument in a broadly Marxist tradition of class analysis. And while he dealt mainly with Pakistan and Bangladesh, his thesis (like Myrdal's before him) can be, and has been, adapted and applied – to Africa, for instance (Saul, 1974).

Alavi argued that unlike the indigenous provenance of the modern European state, the colonial state had its origins in the *metropolitan* society, *not* the colonial one. This was the essence of its specificity. This colonial state, and its immediate successor, the post-colonial state, had thus not grown organically from the social or class structure, internal politics or functional economic imperatives of the indigenous society, as both Marxist and Weberian theories held. In short, in contrast to the states of modern Europe, on which so much Weberian and Marxist theory was based, the post-colonial state was not the product of the developmental history of its own society. On the contrary, it had been imposed from the outside. Its institutions and procedures were devised and deployed by the metropolitan power in pursuit of its own purposes, which included facilitating the activities of metropolitan commercial interests. It followed, argued Alavi, that the 'superstructure' in the colony is therefore 'over-developed' in relation to the 'structure' in the colony, for its basis lies in the metropolitan structure itself, from which it is later separated at the time of independence. (Alavi, 1972: 61)

At the core of this 'overdeveloped state', in the colonial period, had been a bureaucratic–military apparatus which controlled and subordinated the indigenous social classes. And it was this military–bureaucratic apparatus that was inherited at the heart of the new post-colonial state and through which 'the operations of the indigenous social classes are regulated and controlled' (ibid.: 61).

In the case of Pakistan, at least, Alavi argued that this apparatus had been in effective control of state power from independence, though it had sometimes wielded this power behind various facades of democratic politics, such as Ayub Khan's 'Basic Democracy' (ibid.: 65). Moreover, the power and reach of this overdeveloped bureaucratic–military state had been strengthened since independence by an extension of its controls through an expanding range of public agencies and parastatal authorities concerned with promoting economic development (ibid.: 64).

Like Myrdal's notion of the 'soft state', this 'overdeveloped' post-colonial state in Pakistan conformed to neither of the classical Marxist notions of the state, either in origin or structure. It was clearly not the 'instrument of a single class' (Alavi, 1972: 62), nor was it autonomous in Marx's second sense. In so far as it did enjoy autonomy, Alavi argued (as did Bardhan later for India), this was confined largely to its role as *mediator* of the competing interests of three dominant propertied classes (the metropolitan bourgeoisies, the small but powerful indigenous bourgeoisie and the substantial landed class) and *not* as an agent of capitalist transformation and development. The landlord class, especially, has been immensely powerful in Pakistan, to the extent of paying less than nominal tax on agricultural incomes and dominating economic and political life in the rural areas. While maintaining the essential political structure and socio-economic context within which each had to work, the military–bureaucratic apparatus did not seek to override any of these dominant interests in pursuit of putative national developmental objectives. Its relationship with politicians and political parties in the intermittent democratic experience of Pakistan was ambivalent and expedient. For the military–bureaucratic state did not hesitate to intervene when necessary to undermine or evade any policy, or dislodge any party, that threatened the core interests of any one of these groups. This was later amply demonstrated in the case of the late President Bhutto's attempts at land reform in the early 1970s (Herring, 1979).

So while the conceptualization of the overdeveloped state bore little resemblance to either of the classical Marxist models, there was also little here that corresponded to any of the relevant Weberian models of state authority. First, it in no way conformed to Weber's patrimonial model in which the bureaucracy, in effect, behaves and is perceived largely as the personal staff of a dominant leader or elite. Nor does the concept or reality of the overdeveloped state illustrate any of the characteristics of Weber's modern state, especially given the veritably tidal leakages (not to put too fine a point on it) between politics and bureaucracy, and the consequentially intense politicization of that bureaucracy.

While this notion of the overdeveloped state was an interesting and early (if somewhat transient) innovation in Marxist state theorizing, perhaps its greatest contribution lay in the emphasis which it placed on the organizational, bureaucratic and military legacy established and bequeathed by colonialism in explaining the character and developmental performance of post-colonial states. In short, like Myrdal's soft state, it alluded strongly to the political forces, both local and foreign, which shaped the new states and hence were critical in determining their developmental capacities, or explaining their absence, as the case may be. Such an approach has much to commend it. Moreover, it also underlines the importance of comparative analysis of the politics of the colonial state and its legacy, as illustrated by Crawford Young's work in relation to African (and other) colonial states (Young, 1994). And nothing illustrates better the primacy of politics in shaping both colonial and post-colonial states than the role played by Japan in influencing both the structure and capacity of the Korean state during its colonial rule of that country in the first half of the twentieth century (Kohli, ʾ93). The contrast with the Indian sub-continent – and all of colonial sub-aharan Africa – could not be more sharp. Japan effectively established the foundations of the modern developmental state in Korea in a manner that was virtually unique in the annals of colonialism. Importing both the personnel and the (often ruthless) techniques of developmental governance from its own experience, the Japanese transformed a

relatively corrupt and ineffectual social institution into a highly authoritarian, penetrating organization, capable of simultaneously controlling and transforming Korean society. (Kohli, 1993: 1270)

This is hardly something that can be said of British rule in India, or of French rule in Indo-China. But what it does suggest is that *some* 'overdeveloped states', whose defining feature is that their provenance lies outside the society over which they come to rule, *can* play *and have played* a far more progressive and transformative role than did the post-colonial state in Pakistan. The differences in these respects must of course be explained politically, with regard to the motives and interests of the imperial power – classically, the differences between Japanese colonialism in Korea and Taiwan, on the one hand, and British colonialism in South Asia, on the other.

The state and development in Africa: the search for a theory

There is now almost universal agreement that the generally stagnant if not negative levels of development in the African continent from the 1970s (World Bank,1989) have been associated with pervasive and deepening poverty, immense inequalities, infrastructural decay and inadequacy, widespread unemployment, pathological corruption and chronic political instability. And although there were a few signs of aggregate continental improvement in the late 1990s, measured in conventional terms of growth in GNP per capita (World Bank, 1998b: 191), the reality remains that over the last thirty years of the twentieth century Africa's developmental performance slumped. Its share of global GNP and its rates of growth and per capita consumption have declined, as has its share of world trade and third-world investment, while its debt levels have swollen. Cuts in health and educational expenditure have produced a decline in school enrolment and an increase in both malnutrition and under-five mortality rates (World Bank, 1989: 16–23; Todaro, 1997: 655–7). Human rights records have been appalling. Politically, given the dominance of military or authoritarian one-party rule, even the recent processes of democratization have been held by many to be largely cosmetic, and far from consolidated (Wiseman, 1997: 292), representing in many cases what has been referred to as 'pseudo-democracy' (Diamond, 1999: 15–16, 269–70).

Arguably, it is nowhere more important than in Africa to establish why politics has been both so venal and often so brutal, why state formation has been so 'disordered' (Chabal and Daloz, 1999), and why, in consequence, developmental performance has been so weak. But, equally, it has nowhere been more difficult than in Africa to find a coherent and plausible theory of the relationship between politics, society, the state and its developmental function or failure (Lonsdale, 1981; Ergas, 1987; Doornbos, 1990). Following Ernest Gellner's observation in his classic study of the 'Saints of the Atlas', one analyst of the earlier studies of the African state suggested that there was 'too much theory chasing too little empirical data' (Lonsdale, 1981: 140). Another distinguished observer of the African state noted grimly that:

Peasants avoid it, urban workers despise it, military men destroy it, civil servants rape it and academics ponder the short- and long-term results. There can be no gainsaying the importance of the state in Africa as both empirical phenomenon and an analytic category; yet, by a curious twist of fate, just as the concept of the state gained unprecedented vogue among Africanists, its reality seems to have dissolved into a host of invertebrate species which for the most part defy categorization. (Lemarchand, 1988: 149)

If this widespread hostility to, and abuse of, the state was the expression of a wider rejection of post-colonial forms of domination by popular movements seeking to build developmental or socialist alternatives (and there is some of that, but not much), radicals might applaud it. But it is not. And if this rejection of the state was an expression of a vibrant civil society and market, bursting with self-organizing Smithian entrepreneurial energies, determined to throw off the suffocation of the state, neo-liberals might applaud it. But it is not.

How then to conceptualize the 'precarious balance' (Rothchild and Chazan, 1988) of state–society relations in Africa? The proliferation of terms that have been devised to describe African states amply illustrates the variety of approaches and the problem of categorization (Chazan et al., 1992: 40). These include 'patrimonial' and 'neopatrimonial' states (Zolberg, 1966; Roth, 1968; Sandbrook, 1985; Bratton and van de Walle, 1997); 'underdeveloped' states (Medard, 1982); 'prebendal' states (Joseph, 1983, 1987); 'patrimonial administrative' states (Callaghy, 1987b); 'fictitious' states (Sandbrook, 1986) and 'collapsed' states (Zolberg, 1995). Other scholars have been led to describe many African states as merely 'juridical' states (Jackson and Rosberg, 1986) or as 'quasi-states' (Jackson, 1990). By this they mean that the legal substance or juridical reality of such states, in terms of their recognition in international affairs and law, eclipses their substantive or 'empirical' reality – another version of the 'fictitious' state whose developmental capacities (even if the will were present) have been minimal. Such 'fictitious' African states have been characterized as having neither effective authority nor reliable administration, as Sandbrook (following Lemarchand) has argued. Such states have been run by strongmen or groups of armed men 'without the benefit of functioning state structures' (Sandbrook, 1986: 327), a theme explored by Zartman and others (1995) in their analysis of 'collapsed states', where local-level ethnic, clan, religious, nationalist or simple brigand groups vie for power and control against the state.

There are intrinsic dangers in generalizing for the whole of sub-Saharan Africa, for one should never forget how different are the states of Botswana and, say, Nigeria or Uganda. Notwithstanding that, it is not hard to see why a persuasive account of the state in Africa has been so elusive, for few of the preconditions from which modern states have typically emerged have been present in much of sub-Saharan Africa: yet manifestly, states do exist.

The African condition

Most modern African states are both historically new and structurally insecure. The nineteenth-century colonial states (and the few earlier ones) were seldom built on the rich variety of pre-existing authority or (more rarely) state structures (Lonsdale, 1981; Bates, 1983). State borders in Africa, which bore little relation to existing socio-cultural, economic or political realities and which commonly cut across ethno-linguistic and religious boundaries, were quickly and arbitrarily carved out by the colonial powers in the second half of the nineteenth century, following the scramble for Africa (Chamberlain, 1999). These boundaries commonly produced explosively plural societies in which sharp ethnic and cultural cleavages have sometimes been made more complex and divisive where class and ethnicity have come to overlap; that is, where different ethnic groups have been 'differentially incorporated' into hierarchical national systems of wealth and power so as to advantage some and disadvantage others (Kuper and Smith, 1969; Young, 1988; Chazan et al., 1992: 105–27).

Moreover, the formal institutional structures and bureaucratic cultures of post-colonial African states had been almost entirely created and imposed by the imperial powers. At independence, few new African states were endowed with a well-prepared bureaucracy (Chazan et al., 1992) and the pool of skills on which they could draw was often very small and shallow; only 3 per cent of pupils of high-school age received a secondary education and, extremely, Zaire achieved independence without a single national doctor, lawyer or engineer (World Bank, 1991b: 10). In few African societies, under colonial rule and well into the post-colonial era, was the authoritative reach of the state complete; and its legitimacy was often very patchy (Ekeh, 1975; Hyden, 1985). This has remained true in many areas. A succession of violent civil wars, secessionist disputes and *coups d'état* from the 1960s right through the 1990s have been illustrative of this, from Zaire to Liberia, and Angola to Somalia, Sierra Leone to Sudan. And they continue.

A further confusing characteristic of many independent African states has been their facades of constitutionalism, even when competitive democratic practices were replaced by one-party or military rule, and – even after 1990 – when this was reversed again and military rule gave way to the new democracies (Bratton and van de Walle, 1997; Mayegun, 1999). Yet within and behind the interstices of this structure of apparent constitutionalism – complete with its bureaucratic apparatus, appurtenances, offices and procedures – was a spreading pattern of clientelism and corruption, which radiated out from the rulers and their cliques and which increasingly infected all levels and arenas of society, becoming 'a habitual part of everyday life, an expected element of every social transaction' (Chabal and Daloz, 1999: 99).

Furthermore, at the time of independence and ever since, the level of indigenous capital formation in most African societies has been very low. The colonial states, after all, had no serious interest in promoting local capitalist development; indeed it can be argued that the political logic of

colonial domination by a single metropolitan power in a largely closed
colonial economy obstructed the emergence of a thriving indigenous capitalism (Berman, 1984; Boone, 1994: 109ff). In consequence, the evolution
of an independent, entrepreneurial or industrial bourgeois class in most sub-
Saharan countries has been slow, as has the emergence and consolidation of
African working classes. Historically, there have always been exceptions to
this (South Africa and Rhodesia/Zimbabwe are the notable ones) and there
has been sharper class formation in other states since independence in the
1960s; Cote d'Ivoire, Nigeria and Kenya are strong examples (Sandbrook,
1975; Swainson, 1980: 288; Lubeck, 1987; Chazan et al., 1992: 118). But
the generally unclear definition of class, the fogginess of class consciousness and the generally low velocity of class relations in much of post-
colonial Africa has led theorists from many standpoints to refer to the classes
that took power in post-colonial Africa as 'unformed' (Murray, 1967), and
class formation in Africa as generally 'incomplete' (Chazan, et al., 1992:
116) or characterized by 'plasticity' (Kasfir, 1984: 6) or 'weakness' (Cooper,
1981; Callaghy, 1988: 84). Moreover, just as ethnic cleavages and their
analysis have been complicated by class factors, so too class analysis of
African politics, society and the state has been made much more difficult by
the additional salience of often sharp ethnic cleavages (Chazan et al., 1992:
106–16; Chabal and Daloz, 1999: 56–62).

The relative absence in much of sub-Saharan Africa of powerful and independent indigenous capitalist classes, willing and able to take on the historical role of capitalist development, meant that the stake of the post-colonial
state in the economy and its role in promoting economic development quickly
became substantial. This state role was consolidated and extended after independence by often far-reaching programmes of nationalization involving
the proliferation of parastatal bodies, public enterprises, public employment and a steady escalation of public expenditure as a percentage of GDP
(Diamond, 1987: 572–4). These were legitimized by the ideology and rhetoric
of radical nationalism and (sometimes) sceptical if not hostile attitudes to
foreign capital, as was so clearly stated in the late 1960s by the late Julius
Nyerere (1968: 251–6, 262–6). This, in turn, was rationalized by a widespread consensus in development theory at the time that the role of the state
was crucial (Green, 1974; Robertson, 1984).

In short, African societies at independence were characterized by arbitrary nation-state boundaries, by profoundly weak or weakened state traditions, by limited class formations and structures, by flimsiness in their
national civil societies, by weakly prepared politico-administrative elites
and by the foreign provenance of bureaucratic forms and norms, which were
rapidly eroded by clientelism and corruption. With class formation being so
indistinct, how could these new political and bureaucratic elites be seriously said to represent any clear and explicit class interests? Were they

perhaps classes in themselves? And if so, what was the basis of their power? And with the lack of a stable indigenous bureaucratic tradition could they in any way be said to have autonomous developmental purpose or capacity? It was this absence of a clear class anchorage for the African state that led Goran Hyden to describe the state in Africa as having no 'structural roots in society' or, in his much criticized formulation, like 'a balloon suspended in mid-air' which was 'punctured by excessive demands and unable to function without an indiscriminate and wasteful consumption of scarce societal resources' (Hyden,1985: 19).

Although they overlap in certain respects, two broad and early approaches to these questions can be identified: that of the 'bureaucratic bourgeois' state (and versions of it), which sought to locate class and state power in an extended Marxist frame of reference, and that of the 'underdeveloped state', which expressed the Weberian perspective.

Marxism and state failure in Africa

To understand state power, from a Marxist perspective, is to understand the forms of class domination in any particular society, for the two are inseparable. Thus, given the unformed, unclear and fluid classes and class relationships in much of sub-Saharan Africa, and especially the relative absence of both bourgeois and landed classes, the most difficult problem in theorizing about the state in Africa from a classical Marxist point of view has been how to conceptualize the dominant class or classes, and hence the class basis of the state. This is also true for other non-Marxist but class-based approaches.

Perhaps the best general statement and attempted theoretical resolution of the problem may be found in Richard Sklar's (1979) analysis of class domination in Africa. He argued that 'class relations, at bottom, are determined by relations of power, not production' (Sklar, 1979: 537), a general thesis elaborated nearly a decade later by Larry Diamond (1987). The major (though not exclusive) source of this power has been the state, and control of the state has been the means by which political and bureaucratic elites have been able to accumulate wealth and, as it were, establish themselves as a dominant class. As Callaghy has observed (for Zaire, but it is more widely relevant), the ruling group in most African states has not been a bourgeoisie, nor has it represented one. It is 'the top class, the ruling, dominating one. In its style of life and actions, it more resembles a political aristocracy' because its 'basic values, its power and its economic base result from its relationship to the state' (Callaghy,1987b: 92). More generally:

Ruling classes in post-colonial Africa were constituted through the use of state resources to satisfy the multiple and sometimes conflicting interests and political needs
of the heterogeneous elements embraced within ruling coalitions. (Boone, 1994:
134)

In conjunction with emerging business elites in the private sector – whose
size and effectiveness has varied greatly from one African country to another – these political and bureaucratic elites have become the dominant
class, a class referred to by Sklar as a 'managerial bourgeoisie' and by others as a 'state bourgeoisie', 'political class' (following Mosca) and an 'organizational bourgeoisie' as their disposition has been to 'manage the
production and distribution of wealth rather than to create new wealth-
producing enterprises' (Sklar, 1979: 546).

In the absence of any effective democratic accountability and even with
its introduction (Abrahamsen, 1996), such dispositions have routinely de-
generated into systemic rent-seeking behaviour, at best, and pervasive corruption at worst, exemplified in Zaire (now the Democratic Republic of
Congo) by a 'monstrous patronage system' (Kabwit, 1979: 397), in which
'a rapacious class of bureaucrats, army officers, and others, who enjoy a
modicum of power . . . participate with foreign businessmen through massive corruption in the spoils of exploitation of ordinary city dwellers and
rural people' (ibid.: 399).

This general approach, which focused on control of the state rather than
of the commanding heights of the economy as the source of class power and
domination, was best exemplified in the early 1970s by Issa Shivji's work
on Tanzania (1976). Shivji sought to align himself with the Marxist tradition in developing a class analysis of state and bureaucracy. But the absence of a real bourgeoisie and the weakness of the petty bourgeoisie in the
post-colonial society meant a major developmental role for the state. Control of the post-colonial state by such a weak petty bourgeoisie meant that
the state itself became the means whereby this embryonic class transformed
itself into a *ruling class* proper (Shivji, 1976: 33). In Tanzania, this ruling
group was constituted by the politico-administrative, economic and military elites, sustained by the general intelligentsia (ibid.: 88). And it was
this which Shivji described as the 'bureaucratic bourgeoisie' (ibid.: 64, 88).
There are some limited parallels here with Fred Riggs's classic account of
the 'bureaucratic polity' in Thailand, where he talks of the 'domination of
the official class as a ruling class' (1966: 396), following the coup of 1932
against the absolute monarchy and the establishment of a constitutional monarchy and representative government, aimed at westernization and modernization. The difference, of course, has been that the Thai bureaucratic
polity has historically been both more determined and successful in the promotion of socio-economic development.

In Tanzania, however, contrary to the Thai tradition, this bureaucratic bourgeoisie surrounded itself with much ideological noise about socialism, like its counterparts in Mali (Meillassoux, 1970) and Ghana (Murray, 1967). But this, argued Shivji (1976: 79), was no more than a smokescreen behind which it systematically used the state to build its own economic base and hence advance its own interests. This process was intensified after the Arusha Declaration (1967) and the establishment of a one-party state. Nationalist policies of 'socialism and self reliance' were promoted through a far-reaching programme of nationalization, rural collectivization and the suppression of independent labour organizations. The lack of developmental effectiveness of the Tanzanian state is evident in the data. Between 1965 and 1990, the annual average rate of growth of GNP per capita in Tanzania was negative at -0.2 per cent (World Bank, 1992b) and even at the end of the 1990s it remained one of the poorest countries in the world with a GNP per capita of $210 (World Bank, 1998b).

More recently, the evolution of Zimbabwean politics illustrates this thesis in highly contemporary ways. In that country, the new post-independent political elites – even in relatively promising economic circumstances, and despite the radical language and mobilizing rhetoric (Moore, 1991) of the leadership during the liberation struggle – has undergone a rapid process of 'embourgeoisement'. Members of the 'bureaucratic and political elites (the ruling elite) within the state' have 'acquired large-scale farms and business enterprises' and have consolidated themselves, through control of the state, as the 'dominant class', despite a 'leadership code' of 1984 that aimed to prevent the greed and corruption that had become pervasive (Meldrum, 1989; Dashwood, 1996: 32 and passim; Transparency International, 1998).

Max Weber in Africa: the 'underdeveloped state' – patrimonialism, neo-patrimonialism and prebendialism

The general economic, social and political characteristics of post-colonial African societies sketched above, provided few of the conditions for the emergence of anything remotely approaching the Weberian conception of the 'modern' state with its established territorial integrity, its system of legal-rational authority, its trained officials abiding by rules and laws and its monopoly of legitimate violence.

Centralization of power is a necessary but not sufficient condition for the development of a modern (Weberian) state – the fundamental attribute of which is its institutional emancipation from society. Because the African post-colonial state has failed to become differentiated from the society over which it rules, it cannot acquire the neutral political status which alone would allow its legitimation and its proper in-stitutionalization. Such a process would require at the very least that the political system overcome the particularistic constraints which presently govern its very functioning. (Chabal and Daloz, 1999: 13)

But many of the central characteristics of these states – and especially the nature of the bureaucracies and their relationship with the political elites – suggested strong parallels with Weber's other broad category of 'traditional' authority and states and, in particular, with the *patrimonial* form within it.

The distinguished Africanist Aristide Zolberg was one of the first to note this in West Africa, as early as 1966, within a few years of independence, but countless other studies have noted the same pattern since then. Follow-ing Weber (see above) Zolberg wrote:

The ruler and his personal entourage, together with a corps of ranking officials and underlings, 'satraps' (top-ranking territorial agents) and their blood relations and clients, have begun to constitute a genuine 'Bureaucratic gentry', a class based not on their relation to property but on their relation to the state apparatus. (Zolberg, 1966: 142)

Where Shivji (1976) as well as Murray (1967), Meillassoux (1970), Saul (1974), Leys (1976) and others were concerned to develop a class analysis of the emerging African state, drawing on Marxist categories of analysis, other theorists following Zolberg drew on Weber and his taxonomy of state (or authority) types. For these theorists, many states of Africa were *not* best understood in class terms, and they certainly did not seem to fit Weber's criteria of the modern legal-rational state in any way. Rather, these states were best interpreted in terms of Weber's notion of *patrimonial authority* or domination. Under this system the state machine and bureaucracy is essentially treated as the *personal* administrative staff of the ruler (Weber, 1964: 347) and members of the bureaucracy owe a *personal* loyalty to him or her.

At one end of the patrimonial continuum is what Weber called 'Sultanism' or pure 'personal rulership' (Roth, 1968). States characterized by personal rulership may 'not really be states at all, but merely the private govern-ments of those powerful enough to rule' (Roth, 1968: 196; Sandbrook, 1985: 83–111). At the other end are neo-patrimonial states, as described above: that is, states where patrimonial politics predominate behind what is noth-ing more than a facade of constitutional forms and legal-rational practices (Medard, 1982: 181; Clapham, 1985: 44–60).

The central elements in the structure of neo-patrimonial rule in Africa have been identified precisely by Bratton and van de Walle (1997:61–8) as being *presidentialism* (the concentration of political power in one person); *clientelism* (the systematic use of personal favours to reward followers and supporters with jobs, contracts and projects, for instance); and *the system-atic use (that is, abuse) of public or state resources* for private (and espe-cially private political) purposes, and to service the network of clients.

For Medard, at least, these are not overdeveloped but *underdeveloped* states, in the sense of being incomplete and not consolidated, characterized by widespread inefficiency and instability as a way of life (1982: 162). At worst, rulers have had no serious developmental objectives or interests but seek only to gain and hold power and to use that power to accumulate more power and wealth and to service their clients and supporters. The view over-laps with some of the Marxist approaches in holding that for all intents and purposes these ruling elites have no independent economic base or class identity outside the power and wealth of the state, especially where the role and stake of the state is so substantial. Therefore, contrary to the causal assumptions of Marxist analysis, political power in Africa does not flow from wealth, but *wealth flows from control of political power* and hence control of the state. This explains why those in control of the state wish to remain so. As Medard observes: 'it is political resources which give access to economic resources'. The 'state is a pie that everyone greedily wants to eat' (ibid.: 181–2), an image developed dramatically in Bayart's account of the politics which surrounds the African state as the 'politics of the belly' (Bayart, 1993: 268).

The legitimacy of the rulers of such states has generally been very low. They have thus had to rely ultimately on their armies and the use of clientelistic pay-offs to keep themselves in power and to keep others out. As Claude Ake has argued, the struggle to win and hold power in such states is desperate, since this control means in practice the ability to control or own almost everything (Ake, cited in Joseph, 1983: 24). Thus the core of patrimonial and neo-patrimonial politics is 'the privatization of public af-fairs' (Medard, 1982: 185) in which patronage, cronyism, clientelism and corruption define the daily practices of the underdeveloped state. Access to jobs, opportunities, perks, rents, income and status increasingly depends on who your patron is and whether s/he has a share of state power or can influ-ence those who do. The state, argues Bayart, acts as

a rhizome of personal networks and assures centralisation of power through the agencies of family, alliance and friendship, in a manner of ancient kingdoms. (Bayart, 1993: 261–2)

A prime example of this, the Nigerian state, has been described as 'prebendalized' by Joseph (1983, 1987). This formulation adopts Weber's notion of the '*praebend*', which he uses in association with his concept of patrimonialism. Prebendialism for Weber occurred where incumbency or control of an office entitled the holder to rents or payments for undertaking real or fictitious duties (Weber, 1965b: 207). In practice, this is the situation in Nigeria where occupation of countless state posts guarantees access to what are in practice corrupt rents and payments. As Joseph describes the Nigerian case, offices of state have been used for the 'personal benefit of office-holders as well as their reference or support groups . . . [while the] . . . statutory purposes of such offices become a matter of secondary concern' (1983: 30–1). More generally, 'state intervention in economic development frequently serves the interest of the rich and the powerful' (Diamond, 1987: 586).

There are, however, other theorists who are influenced by this approach (Bayart, 1993; Chabal and Daloz, 1999) but who do not view this syndrome of neo-patrimonial politics as 'pathological', but rather 'as one political affirmation amongst others' (Bayart, 1993: 262). 'Africa works', claims the title of a book by Chabal and Daloz (1999), by which they mean that the 'political instrumentalization of disorder' is the process

by which political actors in Africa seek to maximize their returns on the state of confusion, uncertainty, and sometimes even chaos, which characterizes most African polities. [And] that what all African states share is a generalized system of patrimonialism and an acute degree of apparent disorder. (Chabal and Daloz, 1999: xviii–xix).

The 'political instrumentalization of disorder', in other words, is 'the profit to be found in the weak institutionalization of political practices' (ibid.: 13).

Given the very slim prospects for the formal institutionalization of politics in Africa through the evolution of typically western forms of constitutional, legal and bureaucratic order (Weber's 'modern' state), their thesis is that the alleged 'disorder' of African politics is 'in fact a different "order"' (ibid.: 155), a functional one which discloses its own political rationality. 'In the end, there is an interlocking neo-patrimonial logic between the deep ambitions of the political elites and the well-grounded expectations of their clients' (ibid.: 162). In short, given the generalized incompetence of the state and the general disregard for legal-bureaucratic rules and procedures, the use of vertical and personalized solutions for societal problems (what would be seen as corrupt by western standards) is the rational means whereby 'individuals, groups and communities seek to instrumentalize the resources which they command within this general political economy of disorder' (ibid.: xix). It represents and expresses an Afro-centric path of modernization and development. For Bayart, where states do not work on the western and Weberian model, 'corruption' needs to be understood as 'social struggle', the 'politics of the belly', the 'rush for spoils in which all actors – rich and poor – participate in a world of networks' to achieve their aims (Bayart,

1993: 235). A similar thesis has been advanced in relation to the Philippines where, it has been suggested, the pervasive patterns of corruption should not be regarded as aberrant or 'pathological' but as 'deeply integrated with the course of development and political evolution' (Moran, 1999: 569).

Politics, I suggested in the first chapter, is best understood as the processes of conflict, negotiation and compromise over the use and distribution of resources. It does not have to take place within formal institutions or codified rules. That being so, all these approaches and interpretations graphically illustrate the wider point that the kinds of anti-colonial and post-colonial politics that have swirled around and through these states – whether bureaucratic, patrimonial, underdeveloped, overdeveloped or disordered – have decisively shaped the developmental character and capacity of the states and hence the outcomes of their policies and practices in this regard. For Medard, the effect of this in Africa has been to block the building of both socialism *and* capitalism (1982: 184), and much of sub-Saharan Africa stands as a grim testament to that observation.

It is important to add that while I have used the African experience to illustrate the characteristics of patrimonial state politics, the concept has also been effectively applied to explain patterns of politics and non-development in other parts of the world, notably the Philippines (Hutchcroft, 1991). There, access to state resources and the state apparatus has remained 'the major avenue to private accumulation' (ibid.: 414), giving rise to a form of patrimonialism described as 'cronyism', where 'cronies' were the particular group favoured at any time by an incumbent president. This system achieved its most extreme expression under the late President Marcos between 1965 and 1986, when patrimonialism blurred the distinctions between 'public' and 'private' spheres and hence provided immense opportunities for the systematic plunder of the state. This particular form of the politics of 'patrimonial plunder' has many of the key elements of the 'predatory' state, which I discuss shortly; in the case of the Philippines, it has been largely responsible for a virtually stagnant pattern of annual average growth in GNP per capita between 1965 and 1997 of 0.9 per cent (World Bank, 1999c: 25).

But there have been other ways in which states in the developing world have been characterized – as 'weak' states, as 'predatory' states, as 'intermediate' states and as states lacking the capacity for 'good governance'. Each of these labels – each apt in its own terms – has been used to explain the failures or relative slowness of development. They remind us not only of the importance of bringing politics back in to the study and promotion of development, but also that while economic and social development may provide solutions to political problems (the modernization thesis), it is also the case that getting the politics right, so to speak, may also be fundamental for solving developmental problems, as Sen's contribution discussed in chapter 3 so clearly illustrates.

'Weak' states and 'predatory' states

In a series of important studies, starting in the 1980s, a number of political scientists began to look more closely at the character and capacity of states in the third world. Sometimes this was done with a view to explaining the relative failures of development strategies or programmes, sometimes in order to assess their prospects or the trajectory of their politics, sometimes simply to contribute a sharper appreciation of the essential features of these states, sometimes to explore their capacity for managing economic change. Notable amongst these were studies by Bardhan (1984), Evans, Rueschemeyer and Skocpol (1985), Migdal (1988), Kohli (1991), Haggard and Kaufman (1992), Sandbrook (1992), Migdal, Kohli and Shue (1994) and Evans (1995).

If there has been a central theme to these studies it was that the state in the third world could no longer be taken for granted, either as a set of institutions that may be thought comparable to western states or as a given agency for social and economic transformation. On the contrary, the character and capacity of states in the third world vary enormously and this has been largely a function of colonial legacies and the historical and changing relations with their societies (as is axiomatically the case with all states) and, especially, the organized and organizable 'social forces' within them (Migdal, Kohli and Shue, 1994). In short, truism as it may seem to be, it is important to remember that third-world states (indeed all states) are politically constructed, politically maintained and politically transformed. So too, I would argue, has been their development.

These were of course precisely the concerns of some of the earlier theorists I have discussed above. So, although developing different slants on the materials and bringing more sophisticated theoretical approaches to bear, the more recent studies may be read as seeking to provide more detailed empirical anchorage and conceptual (and comparative) coherence to the kinds of fairly broad concerns which had been expressed by the earlier theorists in terms of such general categories as 'soft states', 'underdeveloped states', 'bureaucratic states' or 'patrimonial states'. But whether the point is made explicit or not, the evidence from these recent studies – from Brazil to India and from Egypt to China – underscores the argument in this book: if we are to understand development or the lack of it, we have to understand the state, and if we are to understand the state, we have to understand the social forces – that is, the politics – which shape and are shaped by it.

Weak states

In both his own work (Migdal, 1987, 1988) and in his collaborative work (Migdal, Kohli and Shue, 1994) on strong states and weak states, Joel Migdal has persistently drawn attention to the relationship between state and society, emphasizing what he calls the 'state-in-society perspective' (Migdal, 1994) as a means of comprehending state capacity. Weak states have a low capability 'to penetrate society, regulate social relationships, extract resources and appropriate or use resources in determined ways' (Migdal, 1988: 4). Strong states have a far greater capability in these respects. But whether 'states end up on the strong or weak end of the scale depends on the distribution of social control in society' (ibid., 1988: 275). The struggle for social control in these societies has been a struggle between the state – that is, the centre – and a range of other social actors and organizations which challenge or resist state control. This, of course, is a political struggle, and has everywhere been fundamental in shaping the strength or weakness of states (ibid.).

Many states in the third world, argues Migdal (1987, 1988), are weak in relation to their strong societies, or rather to social forces in those societies that stand out against the state and resist its drive for social control. Such states have not achieved legitimate supremacy over the 'numerous other social organizations that exercise effective control' in the wider society and that make rules and command the allegiance of significant numbers of people, sometimes *against the state* (Migdal, 1987: 397–9). Some such organizations may be the enduring (if transformed) traditional or pre-colonial grass-roots institutions. Others may have originated in the colonial era and still exercise considerable power and authority at regional or village level. These include *caciques, effendis, caudillos*, landlords, kulak-type rich peasants, moneylenders, and others (ibid.: 401). But there are also patron–client networks, friendship groups and old-boy networks, as well as formal organizations such as business groups, labour unions, social and religious movements. Federal state structures provide opportunities for local and regional state elites and centres of power and patronage, giving traditional local oligarchies and landed elites a wide range of opportunities for political action that resists social control from the centre (Migdal, Kohli and Shue, 1994). And there may be other sources of social control beyond the central state and its reach. Some may be revolutionary or secessionist organizations of more recent provenance, such as Sendero Luminoso in Peru or the Tamil separatists in northern Sri Lanka. The key point about all such organizations and individuals, however, is that their tenacious grip on local power and politics prevents states from consolidating overall social control from the centre, and that can make for weak states.

Latin American states, for example, have traditionally been understood as strong in terms of their 'despotic' power, but weak in terms of their 'infrastructural' power; that is, in terms of their 'capacity to penetrate civil society, and to implement logistically political decisions throughout the realm' (Mann, 1986: 113). Brazil is a good case in point. Here, the traditions of *caudillismo*, personalism, patronage and clientelism have been powerful in constraining a state monopoly of social control. This is hardly surprising where the legacy of oligarchic landed power endures, where external economic interests live in an uneasy relationship with internal ones, where bureaucratic tenure is often insecure and lacks the 'corporate coherence' of some East Asian developmental states, and where the state faces a 'complex and contentious structure of elites' (Craske, 1999: 28; Cammack, Pool and Tordoff, 1993: 80; Evans, 1989: 581; Evans, 1992, 1995). Even the powerful military regime in Brazil that ruled for twenty years from the mid-1960s found it impossible in the end to transform the state and state–society relations, given the political power of traditional political elites and their traditional skills of clientelism. As Hagopian observes, this illustrates that

the degree and direction of political change possible under Latin American military dictatorships were constrained by the legacy of the way in which society was organized politically and attached to the state, and how authoritarianism was formatted onto preexisting links between society and state. (Hagopian, 1994: 39)

In short, the immense legacies of the agrarian colonial economic and social structures had generated a range of social forces whose traditional patterns of politics necessarily challenged and weakened even the toughest of military regimes, and hence the state.

Comparable patterns of state–society relations, featuring strong societies and weak states, have been evident in the Philippines, deeply embedded from its colonial past which generated immensely powerful landed 'oligarchs' (Hutchcroft, 1991). Their influence on the state has been and remains profound, such that in the political balance between the formal institutions and power of the state and the informal social power of the landed oligarchy and their allies, 'the state is far more likely to be *acted upon* rather than be an independent actor' (ibid.: 424). As state involvement in the economy increased in the post-war era, landed oligarchies were able to use their position to steer state activity in their favour and to extend their power further. The effect of this – by contrast with the strong and relatively autonomous states of Japan, Korea, Taiwan and Singapore – was that 'state autonomy from powerful social classes was absent' (Moran, 1999: 577), a key point in the comparative politics of development, to which I return in chapter 7.

In India, the strength that the Congress Party once had and expressed in its control of the state, through its patronage links with influential regional and local elites, has been eroded. This has weakened what Kohli refers to as 'systematic authority links between the centre and the social periphery' which existed under Congress in the early years of independence (Kohli, 1994: 105). This has in turn lowered the legitimacy and capacity of the central state, a process accentuated by intra-elite conflict, the challenge to Nehruvian secularism by the rise of Hindu nationalism, and the spread of democratic processes from the 1980s (Corbridge and Harriss, 2000). Here, too, the weakness and weakening of the central Indian state needs to be understood as a function of unravelling Indian politics and the erosion of bureaucratic standards of universal rule-application, as the state and state policy lost coherence, purpose and shape as it responded to the particularistic claims and demands of strong sections of the society (Herring, 1999: 321ff). This had immense implications for the capacity of the state to manage, if not direct, development, producing the slow and so-called 'Hindu rate of growth'.

Weak states of this kind have been described by Evans also as 'intermediate states' (1989, 1992, 1995), a term he uses for a category of states between the dynamic successes of the 'developmental states' (which I deal with in chapter 7) and 'predatory states' to which I turn now.

Predatory states

Predatory states are not especially well theorized, though the central features of the phenomenon have long been recognized. Pareto referred to this as 'spoliation', something that 'has always existed in human societies' (Pareto, 1966: 114–17). It is 'the appropriation of the goods of others by legal or illegal means' (ibid.: 114). This process could be brought about by force but also by 'underhand methods', whereby a 'small number of individuals is able . . . to get the majority to pay tribute to a minority' (ibid.: 115). To this extent the minority preys on the majority using the state as its engine of predation. Such predatory behaviour has inevitably pushed societies down 'the road to ruin' and was only likely to cease as a result of the losses it imposed on the whole economy, even the spoliators, 'who may end up losing more than they gained'. Pareto was sharp enough to recognize that spoliation had to be explained politically, not simply as the expression of the moral defects of the spoliators, but as a social phenomenon, 'the product of all the forces operating in society' (ibid.: 116–17).

Building on Pareto's early formulation, Evans defines 'predatory' states rather more straightforwardly as those that

extract such large amounts of otherwise investable surplus while providing so little in the way of 'collective goods' in return that they do indeed impede economic transformation. Those who control these states plunder without any more regard for the welfare of the citizenry than a predator has for the welfare of its prey. (Evans, 1995: 44)

A different tradition in theorizing about states, the rational choice school of political economy, has been provocatively used by Margaret Levi to advance a 'theory of predatory rule' that contributes to our understanding of the *political* causes and conditions of predatory states (Levi, 1981, 1989). And although her historical and empirical examples are not drawn from third-world developmental contexts, her general theory can be usefully applied to them.

Levi's fundamental thesis is that all states are predatory, but the degree of their predation varies, for all rulers seek to extract as much revenue as possible from the population and use it to 'line their own pockets or to promote their personal power' (Levi, 1989: 3). Certain elements of this view are shared by some libertarian political theorists, such as Robert Nozick, who asserts that 'taxation of earnings from labour is on a par with forced labour' (Nozick, 1974: 169). What limits the capacity of rulers to extract more revenue or taxation is a function of the political constraints imposed on them and which are constituted broadly by, first, socio-political groups that 'control resources on which rulers depend', whether economic or political; and, second, the 'forms of government', including whether it is democratic or not, the type of electoral system, the powers of the executive *vis-à-vis* the legislature, state structure (federal or unitary, for instance) and much more (ibid.: 17).

In short, variation in state predatory capacity to extract revenue is a direct function of the 'relative bargaining power' of the rulers; that is, their 'degree of control over coercive, economic, and political resources' (Nozick, 1974: 2). Given Levi's assumption that rulers will seek to maximize their extraction of revenue, the greater the state's 'relative bargaining power' and the fewer or weaker the constraints upon it, the more it will prey on the citizens and the more predatory it becomes. In short, predatory rule, in form and degree, is a direct function of the politics of a society and likewise – at least by implication – will only be transformed by political action.

It is important to see predatory states as extreme versions of the patrimonial state. As I suggested earlier, the example of the Philippines – especially in the thirty-year rule of Marcos – is a good illustration of how a patrimonial system of politics can become, or come close to, predatory plunder (Hutchcroft, 1991). But Zaire under former President Mobutu Sese Seko, between 1965 and 1998, represents a classic example of predatory rule (Kabwit, 1979; Callaghy, 1984, 1987a, 1987b, 1988; Evans, 1995). From the late 1960s onwards, Mobutu proceeded to consolidate 'coercive, administrative and financial means to increase his patriarchal patrimonial power' (Callaghy, 1987b: 96). At the same time he sought to smash any alternative sources of political or economic power, thereby greatly increasing the 'relative bargaining power' of his rule. This strategy was sustained by the systematic and pervasive granting of rewards, prizes and wealth to loyal followers and by turning a blind eye to official fraud, corruption and illegal ventures (ibid.: 97–103). In short, the Zairean state under Mobutu preyed 'on its citizenry, terrorizing them, despoiling them of their common patrimony, and providing little in the way of services in return' (Evans, 1995: 45).

Moreover, with substantial western financial and military backing, Mobutu and his coterie were able to maintain power and so systematically plunder, stunt and neglect the economy to the extent that negative growth became the norm to the point where per capita income declined by an average of 3.7 per cent annually between 1965 and 1997 (World Bank, 1999c: 24). Political participation effectively ceased and the bureaucracy was emasculated to the point where a former US assistant secretary of state for Africa declared in the early 1990s:

To say that Zaire has a government today would be a gross exaggeration. A small group of military and civilian associates of President Mobutu . . . control the city of Kinshasa by virtue of the loyalty of the 5000-man Presidential Guard known as the DSP. This same group also controls the Central Bank which provides both foreign and local currency to keep the DSP loyal . . . there is no real government authority outside the capital city. (Cohen, cited in Weiss, 1995: 157)

From deep within the nineteenth century, Haiti too emerged as a classic predatory state (Lundahl, 1992). Politics there has essentially been a struggle – and commonly a violent one involving private armies – between cliques for control of the state and hence for the spoils of office, these being the only sources of wealth or immediate wealth available. Politics does not represent conflict between competing policies or ideologies, but becomes synonymous 'with the aspirations for personal wealth of those who have entered the political arena' (ibid.: 290). The state became 'a machine for grinding out private fortunes' (ibid.: 255), a process that was amplified after Duvalier took power in 1957, when expropriation, extortion, corruption and ruthless suppression of dissent became the established pattern (World Bank, 1997a: 149). The developmental consequences in Haiti have been disastrous. Between 1965 and 1990, average annual growth of GNP per capita was 0.02 per cent (ibid.). Today Haiti has the lowest GNP per capita ($380) in the western hempishere, over 60 per cent of its population remains below the poverty line, 40 per cent of the youth of the country is illiterate and barely 40 per cent of its urban population has access to sanitation (World Bank, 1988b, 1999c).

Lest it be thought that this is a phenomenon confined to societies in the developing world, it is as well to quote Harling's account of 'Old Corruption', which prevailed in Britain in the late eighteenth century and which he defined in precisely the way one might think of as typical of extreme patrimonial predatory states today:

a parasitic system that taxed the wealth of the nation and diverted it into the pockets of a narrow political clique whose only claim to privileged status was its proximity to the sources of patronage. (Harling, 1996: 1)

One could not find a more apt description of Haiti under the Duvaliers, Zaire under Mobuto or even the Philippines under Marcos than this account of eighteenth-century Britain. Predatory states, in short, bear little relationship to either the Marxist or Weberian conceptions of the state. On the one hand they are clearly not characterized by dominant capitalist or agrarian classes seeking to use the state to protect or advance their productive interests. And they can certainly not be thought of as either bureaucratic polities or systems of impartial bureaucratic rule. Rather, predatory states in the modern world can, crudely, be thought of as rogue states, whose pathology is out of control. They usually exhibit a high degree of authoritarian personal rulership – Callaghy describes Mobutu as a 'presidential monarch' (1987a: 117). Patrimonialism is central to the rulers' attempts to dominate and control in their own interest and that of their cronies. Such rulers seldom have any serious developmental purpose worth speaking of, beyond general rhetoric, and the states are characterized by a politics in which rival factions, cliques, clans or ethnic groups compete for its control, and to stay in control, and simply use state resources to promote their own wealth. Institutions have no consistency, continuity or coherence, bureaucratic rules have little meaning, predictability is low and political instability is the norm (Huntington, 1968: 398–9).

Conclusions

This chapter has sought to show that despite the general indifference of international agencies and the major donor governments in the post-war era towards a recognition of the importance of politics, power and the state in the processes of development (and particularly non-development or failed development), there has been a small but steady and important stream of explicitly political analysis that has focused on these questions. I have only dealt with some of this here. From a variety of theoretical, regional and political perspectives, these analyses help to emphasize the centrality of social and political forces in shaping the character and developmental capacity of states. Moreover, they underline how some of the central concerns of the discipline of political science today find their most interesting but taxing expression in the forms of politics, power and the state in the developing world and, especially, in their interaction with the challenges of development. The theoretical insights of both the Marxist and Weberian traditions have helped conceptually to illuminate some of these processes. But, at the same time, few of the attempts to interpret these politics have fitted easily into the analytical or classificatory categories of either the Marxist or Weberian appoaches. That is not only to be expected but is all to the good, for difficult examples serve to expand the traditions by identifying and giving greater weight to variables – in history, culture, colonial and settler legacies, international and regional relations and contexts, for instance – which help to account for the degree of variation. Or, in trying to understand the provenance of these states and the contours and function of their politics, especially where they seem so far at variance with the classical traditions of state theory, it becomes necessary to develop more synthetic frameworks of analysis for societies whose histories and structures are themselves synthetic, bearing the hallmarks of extremely varied and contradictory influences in their social, economic and political constitution, some indigenous and some external.

Despite the accumulation of these studies and insights, it took almost a quarter of a century after Myrdal first referred to the developmental defects of 'soft states' before the World Bank or any of its major members got round to a formal and public recognition that, perhaps, states and politics were significant variables in developmental performance. But the form that this recognition took was, predictably, bloodless, for when the Bank first enunciated its view in 1989, in the context of an assessment of the African situation, it held that the root cause of Africa's development problems was the failure of 'governance'. The solution to African (and many other) developmental dilemmas lay largely in the reversal of this pattern and the evolution of 'good governance'.

But what is 'governance' and what makes it 'good'? Why did concern with it arise when it did after such a long indifference to such matters? And is it possible to conceive of governance without politics? I turn to these questions in the next chapter.

5

Governance and Development: Leaving Politics Out

For Forms of Government, let fools contest;
Whate'er is best administered, is best.

Alexander Pope, 'An Essay on Man'

Introduction

During the course of the 1990s, western aid and development policy began to include the promotion of 'good governance' as one of its principal stated aims (Moore and Robinson, 1994). The landmark statement on this came in a World Bank publication on Africa, where it was argued that:

Underlying the litany of Africa's development problems is a crisis of governance. By governance is meant the exercise of political power to manage a nation's affairs. (World Bank, 1989: 60).

It should be clear from this brief definition that the concept of governance has come to mean something considerably broader than government. But this initial and (for the Bank) controversial analysis drew on many strands in the neo-patrimonial perspective discussed in the previous chapter – the weakness of civil society and the lack of political opposition (politely termed 'countervailing power'), the personalization of politics through networks of patronage, the emergence of coercive and arbitrary states and the absence of accountability (ibid.: 61). At first sight, this might appear to have been an approach that would naturally have led the Bank to embrace a much more political understanding of development. But it was not to be, largely for the reasons given earlier, namely the formal prohibition on politics in the work of the Bank. This position went right back to the founding of the

Bank when, at Bretton Woods in 1944, it was made clear that 'in deciding on loan applications, the Bank is not to be influenced by the political character of the country requesting the credits' (Shihata, 1991: 72). Although the Bank's position on governance (not politics) and the state evolved cautiously through the 1990s in a series of publications, it never seriously shifted from its fundamental preoccupation with what was, in effect, concern for the improvement of traditional public-sector management (World Bank, 1994: 1–11; World Bank, 1997b) though behind this were loud echoes of a wider ideological position about the respective merits of states and markets in development. This preoccupation both reflected and sustained the Bank's initial and enduring conception of 'good governance' as 'sound development management' (World Bank, 1992b: 1).

Few would deny that competent, open and fair administration is both a worthy aim and a self-evident requirement of development, by almost any definition. However, the current orthodoxy clearly illustrates the technicist fallacy, which is implicit in the above quotation from Pope, that the effective administration or 'management' of development is essentially a technical or practical matter: 'Whate'er is best administered is best'. By contrast, I argue that such a view and the assumptions underpinning it are seriously flawed, for as I argued in the opening chapter of this book, development is fundamentally a political matter. In this chapter I set out to explain the origins of the contemporary concern with 'governance', to explore some of the meanings associated with the idea and to show that the promotion of good governance and 'institution-building', explicitly detached (in the case of the World Bank) from a politics that can sustain it, is bound to produce feeble and flimsy developmental results. But first, some contextual points are worth making.

Context

Three major features have come to define contemporary western aid and development policy over the last decade. The first, involving a reversal of the post-war consensus about the role of the state in development – the so-called neo-liberal 'counter revolution' (Toye, 1987) – has been the use of aid to promote open, 'market-friendly' and competitive economies (World Bank, 1991a: 1). The position was made absolutely clear in a 1991 speech by the former Minister for Overseas Development of the British government, Lynda Chalker, when she said:

Just as important is the introduction of market forces and competition to ensure a more efficient use of resources. It is also vital for governments to level the playing field for the private sector and individual enterprise so that they can act as engines of growth. (Chalker, 1991a: 2)

This objective was embodied in the new economic conditionalities of structural adjustment lending developed in the 1980s and 1990s (Mosley, Harrigan and Toye, 1991: ch. 1). But in addition to this, two further (and sometimes related) features were added to the policy in the 1990s and came to constitute what is generally understood as 'political conditionality' (Stokke, 1995); that is, the requirement of political and governmental change as a condition for development aid. The changes required were movement towards democracy and the improvement of human rights, on the one hand, and insistence on what has come to be called 'good governance', on the other (Short, 1997). Taken together, the overall thrust of this new development orthodoxy insists that societies characterized by these features of open markets, competent administrations and liberal-democratic politics – essentially, capitalist democracies – not only promote growth and development, but also ensure peace because such societies do not go to war with each other (Doyle, 1983; Hurd, 1990; Chalker, 1991a; Short, 1997). As Mrs (now Lady) Chalker put it:

we will use all levers at our disposal to encourage respect for human rights, free markets, sensible economic policies, and efficient public administration. (Chalker, 1991b)

This is not the place to assess the effects of economic liberalization on economic growth and development, although it is clear that the outcomes in terms of growth have been extremely mixed (some economies have seen real and sustained growth and some have not). However, even where growth has occurred, it is also true that there has been almost universal decline in living standards of the poor, in working conditions for women, and in general social provision (education and welfare) and increases in inequality (Cornia, Jolly and Stewart, 1987; Haynes, 1997; 51–74, 124–8; Craske, 1999: 32–5). As for the argument that democratic politics is a necessary or sufficient condition for development, I explore that in the next chapter.

But what of 'good governance'? What are its implications for development? While it can hardly be doubted that this is an essential feature of *any* successful development process, I argue that the current preoccupation with good governance is naive and simplistic. It is part of a wider technicist illusion which holds that there is always a technical, administrative or managerial 'fix' in the normally difficult affairs of human societies and organizations, and also holds that this applies to the field of development, defined essentially as a matter of economics. As one former special counsel in the World Bank put it: 'the Bank's credibility and strength has traditionally depended on its status as a *quintessential technocracy* exclusively concerned with economic efficiency' (Shihata, 1991: 54; emphasis added). This was especially noticeable in the World Bank's approach to governance, which presented it almost as if it were an autonomous administrative capacity, detached from the turbulent world of social forces, politics and the structure and purpose of the state. And where (as in the case of major western governments) good governance is presented as part of a wider conception of *democratic* governance, a number of issues are jumbled together. First, desirable as it well may be, it is far from proven that democratic politics is a necessary or sufficient condition for good governance; and, second, even if it were, the question that then needs attention is whether enough democracy-sustaining conditions are present in developing countries for democracy to be consolidated and hence to protect and promote the practices of good governance (Gills and Rocamora, 1992: 504–11; Leftwich, 1993a, 1995).

Against this approach I shall argue that an effective public capacity for promoting and managing development is not a function of good governance, as currently understood, but of the kind of politics and state that can alone generate, sustain and protect it. As I shall argue in later chapters, it has been the existence of a certain type of state, the 'developmental state' (whether democratic or not) that has accounted for the most successful records of economic development in the third world over the last thirty years of the twentieth century, commonly accompanied by relatively low levels of inequality. Unattractive as many of these states may be from a liberal or socialist point of view, they have been highly effective in raising the material welfare of the majority of their citizens within a generation and, consequently, establishing (thus far) sustained democratic politics. In short, it is the structure and character of the state, politically understood, that determines the capacity for good governance, not simply the intensification of 'institution-building'.

For the moment it is important to bear in mind that the concept of good governance may be understood as having two broad sets of meanings. The first and more limited set of meanings is associated with the World Bank (see below), which has chosen to interpret governance in primarily administrative and managerial terms. The second set of meanings, associated with western governments, the Organisation for Economic Cooperation and Development (OECD) and the United Nations Development Programme (UNDP), is more political. While it includes concern for sound administration, it has also come to entail an insistence on competitive (sometimes called democratic, but often simply referred to as participatory) politics as well, and a range of other conventionally non-economic virtues. These include the promotion of equity, gender balance, respect for the rule of law, and social, cultural and individual tolerance (UNDP, 1997: 19).

It also needs to be said that insistence on good (or free or even demo-cratic) governance as a condition of aid is not by any means new in the history of western aid policy (Stokke, 1995: 21). Such conditionality, for instance, lay at the heart of President Kennedy's doomed Alliance for Progress initiative in Latin America, which was launched in March 1961 (Robinson, 1993: 58–9). For example, when a coup occurred in Peru in July 1962, President Kennedy suspended diplomatic relations and cut off aid, urging Peru to return to democracy (Packenham, 1973: 71). In practice, however, concern to promote democracy and good governance (in Latin America and elsewhere) was regularly eclipsed by foreign-policy consid-erations or economic interests. Indeed, in sharp conflict with their own cur-rent criteria, western governments and the major international institutions, the World Bank and the IMF, regularly supported 'bad' governance and cruelly authoritarian regimes. For instance, forbidden by its Articles of Agreement from using explicitly 'political' criteria in its lending operations (IBRD, 1989: 8), the World Bank has loaned to both democratic and non-democratic member governments, whether military or civil. And western governments regularly provided systematic economic, political and mili-tary aid for authoritarian regimes such as Argentina, El Salvador, Chile under Pinochet, Kenya, Iran, the Philippines and South Korea, as well as some of the least liberal, most corrupt or straightforwardly incompetent governments, such as Iraq, Zaire, Haiti and much of sub-Saharan Africa (Barya, 1993: 18; Leftwich, 1996: 11). In short, the promotion of democ-racy and good governance was sharply compromised during the Cold War years by its clash with western national security interests.

Origins and emergence of the concern with 'governance'

Why did all this change? Why did western governments begin to take an interest in good governance and democracy in the 1990s? I suggest that there were four main influences: the experience of structural adjustment lending, the dominance of official neo-liberalism (or neo-conservatism) in the West, the collapse of official communist regimes and the rise of pro-democracy movements in the developing world and elsewhere, notably Eastern Europe.

The experience of structural adjustment in the 1980s

'Structural adjustment' is the generic term used to describe a package of economic and institutional measures which the IMF, the World Bank and individual western aid donors – singly, but more often in concert – sought to persuade many developing countries to adopt during the 1980s and 1990s in return for a new wave of policy-oriented loans (Mosley, Harrigan and Toye, 1991: ch. 1; Cammack, Pool and Tordoff, 1993: 11–13). The aim of structural adjustment lending was to shatter the dominant post-war state-led and state-planned development paradigm and overcome the problems of developmental stagnation by promoting open and free competitive market economies, supervised by minimal states. In the words of one of the most persuasive advocates of markets as engines of development: an 'imperfect market mechanism' is likely to perform better in practice than an 'imperfect planning mechanism' (Lal, 1983: 106). In other words, 'imperfect markets are better than imperfect states' (Colclough, 1993: 7).

The general pattern of structural adjustment packages usually involved two main stages, 'stabilization' and 'adjustment', often deployed by the IMF and the World Bank, working in conjunction. Stabilization normally meant immediate devaluation and often quite drastic public-expenditure cuts. Adjustment followed and sought to transform economic structures and institutions through varying doses of deregulation, privatization, dismantling or diminishing allegedly over-sized and rambling public bureaucracies, reducing subsidies and encouraging realistic prices to emerge as a stimulus to greater productivity, especially for export (Mosley and Toye, 1988: 403–41; Nelson, 1990: 2–5).

But when people change the way they use resources, they change their relations with each other (Stretton, 1976: 3). And structural adjustment in the economies of developing countries certainly involved profound changes in the use, production and distribution of resources. And that is what has made it so political because it has inevitably given rise to both winners and losers (Haggard and Kaufmann, 1989b), as in Ghana, Zambia and Nigeria (Callaghy, 1990), and in some 'new democracies' (Haggard and Kaufmann, 1989a). Those who stood to lose from structural adjustment often included bureaucrats (through slimming down of the civil service and through loss of power and perks through privatization); public-sector workers (through privatization and job loss); private-sector workers (through often savage cuts in wages and welfare services); party officials (through loss of influence); and farmers and manufacturers (through reduced subsidies). They all had something to fear from a reduction in the size of the public service, diminution of the power of the party-state, more competition, withdrawal of subsidies and freer trade. But the poor also lost, for they often experienced sharp increases in basic food prices as well as in medical and education costs (Green, R. H., 1986, 1988; Demery and Addison, 1987; Glewwe and de Tray, 1988; Longhurst et al., 1988; Ghai, 1991).

These are some of the reasons why adjustment has necessarily been so political (Nelson, 1989a), for no significant change occurs in society without destabilizing some status quo, without decoupling some coalition and building another, without challenging some interests and promoting others. Thus what became clear in the course of the 1980s was that the ability to plan and implement adjustment was largely a consequence of both *political* commitment, capacity and skill, as well as *bureaucratic* competence, independence and probity (Healey and Robinson, 1992: 91, 155); in short, 'governance'.[1]

However, those who stood to lose from adjustment were often located in, or closely associated with, the state apparatus and hence could use their influence to curtail or dilute the programmes, and often did. Paradoxically, therefore, where programmes of adjustment were effectively pushed through, in practice it required a strong, determined and relatively autonomous state, whether democratic or not (Nelson, 1989c: 9–10; Whitaker, 1991: 345). This was the case in Ghana (Callaghy, 1990), Chile (Stallings, 1990); Costa Rica (Nelson, 1989b), Turkey (Mosley, Harrigan and Toye, 1991: ch. 10) and Indonesia (Soesastro, 1989). But where state autonomy, strength and capacity were not equal to it, adjustment programmes were either not implemented or not completely implemented, as in Zambia (Gulhati, 1989), India (Kohli, 1989), the Philippines (Haggard, 1990b), Jamaica (Nelson, 1989b) or Zaire (Callaghy, 1989). The significance of a strong state seems to have been lost on the prevailing orthodoxy, which aims, in part, to reduce the scope and scale of state power through both economic and political reform.

The experience with adjustment in the 1980s confronted the international institutions and bilateral donors with the reality of incompetent and often corrupt government in many developing countries (World Bank, 1991a: 128–47; Lancaster, 1993: 9). The issue could no longer be avoided as it became clear that

the political environment was the primary source of obstacles for sustained economic change . . . echoing the old intellectual debate on the relation of politics and economics. (Frischtak, 1994: 6)

This was especially true of sub-Saharan Africa and it was this that had, in part, led the Bank to identify poor governance as a major source of the African crisis in its important report on the continent, *From Crisis to Sustainable Growth* (World Bank, 1989). There was some limited acknowledgement of the *political* causes and context of this crisis of governance, but in practice the report said little about the state or the *politics* of develop-

---

[1] John Waterbury (1989: 39, 55), amongst others, has made the crucial point that effective adjustment involves the careful management of a regime's 'basic support coalition', even in authoritarian systems. This only serves to highlight the centrality of politics in all forms of change and development, especially where radical shifts in resource use and distribution are entailed, as they necessarily are.

ment. Instead it focused single-mindedly on managerial and administrative issues, as became clear in its formal statement on *Governance and Development* (World Bank, 1992a). In this and other Bank publications (such as the influential *World Development Report, 1991*), the Bank committed itself to the seemingly more apolitical and largely technical strategy of improving governance.

But even this was something of a sleight of hand, for the apparently politically neutral and largely managerial recommendations actually presupposed profound political change and represented not simply an administrative vision but also an economic and political one, as I shall explain shortly. For what was advocated was a slim but efficient administrative state, detached from its prior pervasive involvement in economic matters. While such a state might undertake basic investment in, and management of, essential physical and social infrastructure, its central role was to encourage the free and fair play of market forces in an impartial, open and accountable manner (World Bank, 1991a: 4–11). It is true that by 1997 the Bank's position on the state seemed to have mellowed and its developmental role was more fully recognized, but 'not as a direct provider of growth but as a partner, catalyst and facilitator' (World Bank, 1997a: 1; IDS, 1998). Despite this, the fundamental primacy of the indigenous and foreign private sector in open markets and trade regimes has remained central to Bank thinking.

The political influence of the neo-classical counter-revolution

Although both the World Bank and the IMF have considerable operational autonomy and are often independent sources of important development ideas, initiatives and policy, it remains the case that, politically, they are ultimately the creatures of their members and hence influences and fashions feed through from their members – and from the dominant ones in particular. The structure of voting power in these institutions (depending on financial contributions and commitments) means that the influence of the USA, Japan, Germany, Britain and France is overwhelming (World Bank, 1998a: 237). Although thinking on these matters was clearly developing within the Bank and the IMF, the new orthodoxy came to reflect the emerging neo-liberal ascendancy in economic theory and politics from the late 1970s in these countries, notably the USA and Britain (Toye, 1987: ch. 2; Killick, 1989: 9–20).

However, neo-liberalism is not only an economic doctrine but a political one as well, involving strong normative *and* functionalist theories of politics and the state. In normative terms, neo-liberal theory celebrates individual economic and political freedom as representing the good life itself. Beyond the preservation of peace and order, it is hostile to state limitation on the rights of individuals, irrespective of race, sex or creed. Neo-liberals, especially conservative libertarians such as Nozick (1974), also argue that state intervention in the economy or official discrimination impose constraints on the inalienable rights and liberties of individuals, interfere with freedom of choice, distorts the free play of markets and thus harm economic development (Olson, 1982: ch. 6; Green, D.C., 1986: 82–90).

Outside, but parallel to, the normative claims of politicians about the virtues of individualism, enterprise and minimal states, political scientists operating within the revived tradition of political economy – or the economics of politics – also contributed to the new interest in governance and the state in the process of development (Staniland, 1985; Laver, 1997). Their attack on the obesity of states in the developing world (but not only there) was based less on normative objections and more on theoretical claims that large and interventionist states, with too much control or regulation of economic life, would necessarily suffocate the evolution of thriving market economies and provide tempting opportunities for rent-seeking and corruption.

One of the classic studies to emerge early on in this tradition was Robert Bates's *Markets and States in Tropical Africa* (1981), in which he set out to explain why agricultural policy had failed so disastrously in post-colonial Africa, with such serious developmental effects. His work should be seen alongside that of Margaret Levi (1981, 1989), discussed earlier, on the basis of predatory state rule, and the work of other rational choice theorists. For Bates, political leaders in Africa used public policy instruments to keep food prices low (thereby penalizing the farmers, the producers) in order to secure urban political support on which they depended. Moreover, illustrating Levi's thesis about the propensity of the rulers of states to extract as much revenue as they can, Bates argued that post-colonial African states used their regulatory powers and, notably, the colonially established marketing boards (Ghana was a prime case), as a means of extracting revenue from farmers by buying cheap locally and (where they could) selling dear abroad and pocketing the difference to advance bureaucratic, elite or (sometimes) industrial interests. In short, Bates's highly political explanation for agricultural decline in Africa illustrates how large state involvement in the economy – through ownership or regulation – provides precisely the opportunity for political intervention in markets by politicians, bureaucrats and entrepreneurs in order to achieve ends they would otherwise not achieve by market competition (ibid.: 4), and which, if taken to extremes, becomes classically predatory behaviour, as described in the previous chapter.

In policy terms, it followed from this that reducing the role of the state in economic life would serve to reduce this extraction of revenue and the accumulation of rents and would give rise to a slimmer state and a freer, more entrepreneurial and vibrant private sector with incentives to produce more.

In this approach, then, the improvement of governance meant in practice not only the reduction in size of government but also the expansion of market forces; this indicates that concerns about 'governance' were often coded expressions for something far wider – a change of 'regime', as I will explain shortly.

However, in functional terms, neo-liberal political theory asserts that democratic politics and a slim, efficient and accountable public bureaucracy are not simply desirable but also *necessary* for a thriving free market economy, and *vice versa*, for the two are inextricably interconnected (Friedman, 1980: 21). Neo-liberals thus regard an obese state apparatus with a large stake in economic life as not simply inefficient from an administrative point of view, but also incompatible with an independent and vibrant civil society which is held to be the basis of effective democracy. Hence neo-liberal developmentalists often argue that poor development records and adjustment failures have been a direct consequence of authoritarian rule and deficient governance, all arising from excessive concentration of both economic and political power in the hands of the state (Lal, 1983: 103–9), which is incompatible with accountable and responsive good governance in a free economy. This concentration of power also explains regime reluctance or inability to institute *political* liberalization and bureaucratic contraction.

For all these reasons, resurgent neo-liberal theory from the end of the 1970s spurred western governments and international institutions to move forward from promoting economic liberalization to making good governance (and democracy) a condition of development assistance.

The collapse of communism

The collapse of East European and other 'communist' or 'state socialist' regimes (Lane, 1996) was another important strategic factor helping to shape the emergence of western interest in promoting good governance. The new international circumstances that prevailed after 1990 meant that the West could now attach explicit political and institutional conditions to its aid without fear of losing its third-world allies or clients to communism (DfID, 1997: 9). Moreover, the fate of official twentieth-century 'communism' also served to confirm neo-liberal theory that bureaucratically sclerotic, non-democratic collectivist systems were both unable to produce sustained economic growth and unable to change. Corruption, economic mismanagement, inefficiency and stagnation all flowed directly from their grotesque bureaucracies and lack of popular democratic participation. Political liberalization, administrative decentralization, reducing bureaucratic controls and the promotion of good governance on the essentially western model were seen as necessary conditions for economic liberalization and growth (World Bank, 1991a: 20).

This triumphalism – expressed in celebratory mood in the Political and Economic Declarations at the 1990 Houston Summit of the industrialized nations (the G7) (*New York Times*, 11 and 12 July 1990) – indicated the extent of western confidence in the face of the collapse of the old enemy. And this confidence was immediately and explicitly reflected in the terms of the Articles of Agreement of the new European Bank for Reconstruction and Development (EBRD), established in 1991 to help restructure the East European and former Soviet economies (Shihata, 1991: 58). In these Articles there is a direct linking of economic and political liberalism as the essence of good governance and as the objective which the new Bank was setting out to promote. Unlike the World Bank, the objectives of the EBRD were both explicitly economic and political, namely to 'promote multi-party democracy, pluralism and market economics' (EBRD, 1991: Article 1). Whereas the World Bank has always claimed to be hamstrung by its Articles – a 'hobbled giant' (Please, 1984), the EBRD made sure that its goals – both political and economic – were fully and clearly stated.

The impact of the pro-democracy movements

Finally, the pro-democracy movements in Latin America, the Philippines and latterly Eastern Europe in the 1980s stimulated similar movements elsewhere (Huntington, 1991: ch. 1). In Africa, between 1989 and 1992, internal and external pressures prompted steps in the direction of democratization in a host of countries, from Nigeria to Zaire and Guinea to Angola, though seldom without profound resistance from incumbent regimes (Riley, 1991: 17–21; Wiseman, 1997; Bratton and van de Walle, 1997). Democratization in Asia – though stalled in China and Myanmar (formerly Burma), for example, and interrupted by a coup in Pakistan in 1999 – has advanced in the Philippines, South Korea, Taiwan, Bangladesh and even Nepal. The West drew legitimacy for its pro-democracy policies from these movements and can thus be said to be supporting popular and intellectual demands for good governance in those societies (Ake, 1991). While the West may thus be said to be demonstrating its genuine preference for liberal democracy (other things being equal), some more sceptical if not realist theorists are inclined to see the contemporary orthodoxy as the most recent manifestation of the onward march of global capitalism, which had been delayed by the bipolar world (Gills and Rocamora, 1992: 506; Barya, 1993: 16–17).

It should be clear then that the concern with 'good governance' (and democratization as well) was not the sudden technical discovery of a new cure for slow development or poverty, as a new drug might be for a particularly unpleasant and crippling illness. The circumstances that brought issues of governance onto the agenda were political in origin in every conceivable respect and political in their implications. Indeed, the meanings that came to be attached to the notion of good governance were themselves also influenced by political factors. But, first, before surveying the universe of meanings attached to the notion, it is worth indicating briefly the steps marking the emergence of this new concern for good governance.

The emergence of good governance

As mentioned earlier, the first appearance of the contemporary notion of good governance came in the 1989 World Bank report on Africa, which argued that 'Underlying the litany of Africa's development problems is a crisis of governance', (World Bank, 1989: 60). This report was followed, between 1989 and 1991, by a veritable torrent of pronouncements on governance, democracy and development from a variety of sources. These included the OECD (1989); the Nordic Ministers of Development (1990); the US, British and French governments (Hurd, 1990; House of Commons Debates, 1990); *Africa Confidential* (9 March 1990); Chalker (1991a); Cohen (1991); the Commission of the European Communities (1991); the World Bank (1991a, 1992a) and the UNDP (1991). The promotion of good governance and democracy was in turn supported by many inter-governmental and regional organizations such as the Organization for African Unity (OAU), The European Council and the Commonwealth Heads of Government (IDS, 1993: 7). But what did they mean by 'good governance'?

Meanings of 'good governance'

The views of these organizations on the relationship between governance, the state and development were not identical. While some stressed democracy or the protection of human rights, others emphasized sound administration or, in the Bank's terms, efficient management, as key causal factors in development. But all failed to explore the kind of state that might be necessary for housing good governance. Even those – as was the case with many individual western governments, the UNDP and the OECD – who identified (and promoted) democracy as the institutional and political glue that would hold good governance in place failed to consider what conditions promoted and consolidated sustainable democracy itself. Furthermore, in the headlong rush to insist on good governance, they seldom paused to explore whether any or all of these conditions were present in those societies where they were advocating good or at least improved governance. That is the subject of the next chapter.

Nonetheless, despite these differences and omissions, the underlying shape of the concept of governance (and good governance) in its developmental context soon became clear. It is also important to note that the idea, thinking and language associated with 'governance' did not have its provenance in the third world or in the context of developmental aid policy, but in the developed countries in the 1980s in the course of the conceptual and organizational shift from public administration to 'new public management' (Dunleavy and Hood, 1994; Turner and Hulme, 1997: 230). In contemporary usage in these countries, the concept of governance came to have a number of different meanings, or perhaps uses. Rhodes (1995: 2–10) suggests five major uses of the concept:

1 Governance understood as the *minimal state* is a blanket term referring to the reduction of public intervention in the economy and using markets or quasi-markets to deliver 'public' service.

2 Governance conceived of as *corporate governance* is less to do with the formal institutions and structures and more to do with overall systems by which organizations (private or public) are directed and controlled, commonly including principles of openness, integrity and accountability. Simply stated this refers to the principles and philosophy of control.

3 Governance is often conceived of as *the new public management* to distinguish it from the old public administration (Dunleavy and Hood, 1994) and is understood to include the application of private-sector management principles to the public sector and, more recently, the introduction of incentive structures (like internal markets and competition) in public provision. This is a view that in Britain was absorbed into New Labour's developmental philosophy after its 1997 election victory (Short, 1997).

4 Governance as a *socio-cybernetic system* has been used to refer to the overall pattern of interventions in a society by the combined and interacting effects of central and local governments and private-sector organizations (businesses and voluntary organizations) brought about by negotiation and cooperation.

5 Governance as *self-organizing networks* refers to the new structures of widespread social coordination and interaction between both public and private institutions and organizations in the delivery of services, involving a reduction in the role of the formal institutions and agencies of the state ('hollowing out of the state') and a greater role for private, non-state or quasi-state institutions.

There is clearly much overlap between these uses of 'governance', but the central themes involved were not simply improved efficiency but a transformation in the role, range and reach of state activities in economy and society and a considerable blurring of the public–private distinction in the provision of services formerly considered the responsibility of the state. This clearly illustrates the extent to which concerns around issues of governance arose directly from the neo-liberal preoccupations of the mainly conservative governments in the West in the 1980s, though by the end of the century these ideas were no longer confined to conservatives.

As these ideas came to be assimilated into development ideas and debates, there was no more agreement about the meaning and forms of good governance in developmental processes than there had been in the context of discussion in the industrialized countries. But, surveying the variety of meanings of the concept (Frischtak, 1994: 11–16), it is possible to distil three broad categories, or levels, of meaning that emerged. Ranging from the most inclusive down to the narrowest, these may be termed systemic (or regime) level, political, and administrative/managerial.

Systemic or regime-level governance

From a broad systemic point of view, the concept of *governance* is wider than that of *government*. The latter conventionally refers to the formal institutional structure and location of authoritative decision-making in the modern state. 'Governance', on the other hand, refers to a looser and wider distribution of both internal and external political *and* economic power (Lofchie, 1989: 121–2). In this broad sense, governance denotes the structures of political and, crucially, *economic* principles and relationships and rules by which the total productive and distributive life of a society is governed (Frischtak, 1994: 4). In short, it refers to a *system* of political and socio-economic relations governed by agreed rules or, more loosely, a regime, which has been aptly defined in the following way:

Regimes are principles, norms, rules and decision-making procedures around which actor expectations converge. (Krasner, 1985:4)

Of course, a neutral reading of this would suggest that regimes may differ greatly and hence cultures of governance may also do so. And, as will become clear in the later chapter on developmental states (chapter 7), there are those who suggest that the culture of both politics and governance in these states is very different from the typical Weberian model which informs most western thinking (Johnson, 1995). But there can be little doubt that standing behind much of the rhetoric and the apparently neutral technical language surrounding the concept of good governance in current development usage (whether in its broad or narrow sense) has been this wider, normative and systemic understanding of the term. Quite simply, it means a democratic capitalist regime presided over by a minimal state which is part of the wider governance of the new world order (House of Commons Debates, 1990: cols 1235–99; Chalker, 1991a: 2–3). This was the central and explicit message of the Houston Summit of 1990, when western leaders stated that they officially

celebrated the renaissance of democracy throughout much of the world . . . and the increased recognition of the principles of the open and competitive economy . . . and the encouragement of enterprise . . . [and] of incentives for individual initiative and innovation. (*New York Times*, 12 July 1990)

Douglas Hurd, British Foreign Secretary at the time, echoed this view when he wrote that

free markets, open trade and private property are the best way known to mankind for improving its standard of living. (Hurd, 1990: 4)

Good governance as participatory politics and (sometimes) democratic government

This second, more limited and obviously *political* sense of good governance clearly presupposes such a free-market economic regime outlined above. But it also explicitly means a state enjoying legitimacy and authority, derived from a participatory (not always called 'democratic') mandate and built on the traditional liberal notion of a clear separation of legislative, executive and judicial powers. And, whether presidential or parliamentary, this presupposes a pluralist polity with a freely and regularly elected representative legislature, with the capacity at least to influence and check executive power. This, indeed, has come to be the position of most western governments but also that of cooperative inter-governmental organizations of the major industrial powers, like the European Union or the OECD, whose Development Assistance Committee (DAC) emphasized the importance of democracy and 'participatory development' as major elements of good governance (OECD, 1997: 6). It has also come to be the position of the UNDP. In its concern to promote 'sustainable development', the UNDP has emphasized the virtues of 'public participation, accountability and transparency' for 'effective democratic forms of governance' (UNDP, 1997: 9). In listing the many attributes of 'good governance' (ranging from the promotion of equality, through toleration, mobilizing resources for social purposes, efficiency of resource usage, promotion of gender balance, regulatory rather than controlling) it emphasized that:

good governance systems are participatory, implying that all members of governance institutions have a voice in decision-making. This is the foundation of legitimacy in democratic systems. (UNDP, 1997: 19–20)

Most western governments made it clear that not only were they in favour of promoting democracy but that progress towards democratization would become a condition to be attached to aid. Successive British foreign secretaries and ministers for overseas development through the 1990s were explicit on the point (Hurd, 1990; Chalker, 1991a; Short, 1997), but perhaps Hurd's statement is the most unambiguous:

So the moral imperative is clearly understood. In practical terms, it means that we should state explicitly that we will reward democratic governments and any political reform which leads to greater accountability and democracy. The corollary is that we should penalise particularly bad cases of repression and abuse of human rights. Those principles should increasingly inform our aid programme. (Hurd, 1990: 4)

Good governance as managerial/administrative efficiency and probity

This level represents the lowest, narrowest and most universal common denominator of meaning and usage of the term 'good governance', found in both the above and broader conceptions and, in the case of the World Bank, apparently (or at least presented as) detached from political considerations. Clearly, given its Articles of Agreement (its constitution in effect), the Bank resolved that it should not be influenced by the 'political character' of its members; that it should not interfere in the domestic politics of its members; that, as a multilateral giver and coordinator of aid, it should not act as a conduit of pressure to influence the 'political orientation or behaviour' of the recipients of aid; and, more generally, it should not allow 'political factors' to influence its aid or advisory work (Shihata, 1991: 82–4). In short, the Bank needed to focus on 'good order' (in the sense of applied and functioning rules and institutions), stability and predictability, for effective good governance required stable, predictable and efficient institutions systematically applying clear rules with impartiality. It followed that the Bank would not address issues to do with political regimes, but only those matters that concerned the 'processes by which authority is exercised in the management of a country's economic and social resources for development' and 'the capacity of governments to design, formulate and implement policies and discharge functions' (World Bank, 1994: xiv).

Within this narrower administrative and managerial perspective, good governance has come to mean, universally, an efficient, independent, accountable and open public service, stripped of corruption and dedicated to the public good. This is the World Bank's position, which is fully outlined in its definitive statements on *Governance and Development*, which treats good governance as 'synonymous with sound development management' (World Bank, 1992a: 1), and *Governance: The World Bank's Experience* (World Bank, 1994). These policy documents focus on four main areas of public administration in general, and public-sector management in particular, which it considers fall legitimately within its mandate:

1   *Accountability*, which in essence means holding officials responsible for their actions.

2   A *legal framework for development*, which means a structure of rules and laws which provide clarity, predictability and stability for the private sector, which are impartially and fairly applied to all, and which provide the basis for conflict resolution through an independent judicial system.

3   *Information*, by which is meant that information about economic conditions, budgets, markets and government intentions is reliable and accessible to all, something that is crucial for private-sector calculations.

4   Finally, insistence on *transparency* is basically a call for open government, to enhance accountability, limit corruption and stimulate consultative processes between government and private interests over policy development.

It should be clear, then, that in its first and most *extensive* form (above), the idea of good governance as a *regime* is not simply a new technical answer to the difficult administrative problems of development, though it is often presented as that. On the contrary, good governance is best understood as an intimate part of the emerging politics of the new world order. And, clearly, the barely submerged structural model and ideal of politics, economics and society on which all notions of good governance rests is nothing less than that of western liberal (or social) capitalist democracy – the focal concern and teleological terminus of much modernization theory.

Even though the Bank made no public commitment to regime-level conceptions of governance and remained close to the narrowest of operational definitions, it is clear that many of the projects that it funded had profound regime-level implications and carried that overall political objective forward. For its projects included not only programmes like civil service reform, improving the legal and institutional framework for development, but also state-enterprise reform and general management of an increasingly privatized economy (World Bank, 1994). The Bank does not identify 'governance' loans, as such, in its annual reports, but includes these within its 'public sector management' category, which in 1998 accounted for only 7 per cent of Bank lending (World Bank, 1998a: 7). On its own admission it is difficult to estimate 'precisely how much governance work is being carried out in the World Bank . . . because governance is a broad term that straddles the functional classifications the Bank uses to classify its lending operations' (World Bank, 1994: xv). But amongst the kind of governance projects undertaken by the Bank in the 1990s have been measures to speed up judicial processes in Chile, surveying the attitudes of Zambian civil servants, assistance with the privatization of state enterprises in Argentina, improving public and private accounting procedures in Indonesia, legal reform to support private-sector development in the newly marketized economies of the former Soviet Republics, enhancing property rights for private-sector development and the empowerment of women in Africa, reform and privatization of the banking sector in Nicaragua, assisting decentralization in Bolivia by enhancing public-sector auditing and monitoring, privatization of urban transport and utilities in the state of Rio de Janeiro in Brazil and support for private-sector development in Côte d'Ivoire (World Bank, 1994, 1998a). While these unquestionably fit under the broad rubric of managing a country's economic and social resources ('development management'), it should be clear, too, that they have an unambiguous politico-economic theme to them, with explicit regime implications that are far from neutral or technical and are profoundly political in their effects.

Where the Bank took on these kinds of tasks, individual donor governments such as that of Britain saw the practical forms of good governance as going beyond these to include more explicitly political issues, including support for 'participatory processes' and the legitimacy of governments as well as the promotion of human rights. In the 1990s this involved 'supporting the strengthening of government as a good in itself' (Short, 1997: 5), by training and institution-building and, where necessary, by slimming down obese bureaucratic superstructures. Western governments also sought to enhance the capacity of public bodies – in the case of Britain this included prison and police services and revenue collection agencies. More politically, through their own aid programmes, and in concert with non-public institutions like the Westminster Foundation for Democracy in Britain, the National Endowment for Democracy in the USA, the Swedish International Liberal Centre and the Foundation Jean Jaurés in France – western governments sought to promote democratic processes directly by supporting legislatures, helping to frame electoral laws, assisting at election times, assisting political party development, and enhancing public policy formation and civic education (for example, workshops for student leaders in Nigeria or

seminars for potential parliamentary candidates in Indonesia), especially
for the excluded or disadvantaged (Westminster Foundation for Democracy, 1999).

The problem (and it was of course a political one) was that although 'this
covered a wide range of institutions and purposes . . . much of it brought no
direct benefit to the poor' (Short, 1997: 5). Accordingly, while concerns
with governance remain central, as does the promotion of human rights and
political stability, strategy has now been refocused, at least in the case of
British policy, so that services for the poor can be delivered by a wider
combination of decentralized government, local government, municipal
government and private-sector providers such as community and non-
government organizations in order to help achieve the OECD target of halv-
ing world poverty by 2015. In some fundamental respects there is nothing
much new here, for in the focus on the 'poor and disadvantaged', including
especially women, the new strategy for the first decade of the twenty-first
century is essentially that of basic human needs, plus human rights and
democracy (Short, 1997: 10–11; DfID, 1997). Much of the rhetoric echoes
the concerns of the 'basic human needs' and 'redistribution with growth'
strategies of the 1970s (see chapter 3).

Implications and conclusions

Whatever the merits and limitations of the commitments to some of the
grander liberal-democratic and capitalist objectives that have more or less
openly underpinned the good governance agendas of the 1990s, who could
possibly be against good governance in its limited *administrative* sense?
For that reason, it is important to welcome the belated but on-going interest
that western governments and international development institutions have
taken in questions of governance, however broadly or narrowly defined.
For is it not the case that any society – whether liberal or socialist – must be
better off with a public service that is competent, efficient, reliable and hon-
est as well as open and accountable, and with a judicial system that is speedy,
independent and fair? In this sense, at least, the narrowly administrative
conception of good governance is unexceptional. It re-identifies precisely
the principles of administration that have long been argued as being of benefit
to developing countries, just as the Northcote–Trevelyan reforms (Dearlove
and Saunders, 2000) may be said to have been in and for Britain in the mid-
nineteenth century in their emphasis on eliminating 'old corruption' and on
creating an independent career civil service imbued with the values of hon-
esty, economy and neutrality in politics. They are impeccably Weberian in
spirit, if not letter (Weber, 1964: 329–41). And even in the most unpromising

third-world circumstances, good governance in this limited administrative sense must be better for development than its opposite, bad governance. Accordingly, the work done in promoting 'good governance', 'institution-building' and 'capacity-building' is important (World Bank, 1991a: 84–5; 1997b: 79–98).

However, many of the prescriptions for good governance have been naive and the prognosis is not good because of the fundamental failure to recognize that success in instituting and sustaining good governance is ultimately and irreducibly a function of politics as expressed through the capacity of states to establish and maintain such principles and processes. Evacuated from the political context, no amount of institution-building or heavy doses of training, desirable and valuable as they may be in their own right (World Bank, 1991a: 84–5; 1997b: 79–98), will induce a framework, let alone a regime, of good governance. Furthermore, no sophisticated institutional innovations nor the best-trained or best-motivated public service will be able to withstand the withering effects of corruption or resist the developmentally enervating pulls of special or favoured interests if the politics, autonomy and authority of the state do not sustain and protect them. Even the establishment (or return) of formal representative democracy in the Philippines after 1986 was no guarantee of good governance or the extrusion of corruption or 'cronyism' from the political process (Hutchcroft, 1991; Moran, 1999). And to expect that stern conditionality will yield good governance and hence development in, say, Haiti, Zaire or Myanmar, without recognizing the enormity of the political change that is required for it to happen, is to commit the ultimate technicist error.

The fate of the Civil Service Reform Programme in Ghana is a case in point. The programmes which ran from 1987 to 1992 as part of the World Bank's Civil Service Reform Programme, and supported by the British government, sought to rationalize and make more efficient a civil service that was chronically bloated. The reform programme was only a partial success, for reasons given in a Foreign and Commonwealth Office evaluation report:

The project has been *partially successful*. Achievements have been significantly less than were expected at appraisal as many components have taken considerably longer to achieve than planned and many reforms have not yet been implemented. The fact that the reforms were essentially externally driven, and lacked the full commitment of some senior members of the Ghana Civil Service, is important in explaining the level of success achieved. (Foreign and Commonwealth Office, 2000)

In short, the simple political resistance of those who were to be most affected reduced the efficacy of the project dramatically. Likewise, the response of the former President of Sri Lanka to a researcher's query as to why civil service reform was not initiated illustrates graphically my central thesis here about the primacy of politics in an even broader setting:

with an ethnic civil war in the North, a youth uprising in the South, my neighbour (India) rattling her sabre and plummeting commodity prices, do you think I need to set the civil service on fire?' (Turner and Hulme, 1997: 235–6)

A final example may be drawn from Zimbabwe where, at liberation from minority white rule in 1981, the new government inherited an efficient, if exclusive and racist, civil service, but one not normally thought of as incompetent or corrupt. Within a decade, the revamped bureaucracy operating under the new government in the structure of the new state had become mired in escalating elite corruption as a direct consequence of the political change brought about by liberation, and the consequential eruption of new social and political forces into the political process, which located themselves in and around the new state (Meldrum, 1989; Weiss, 1994; Dashwood, 1996). Government reluctance to implement court decisions requiring the ending of illegal land occupations have been described by a British Foreign Office minister as further evidence of the 'downward spiral of governance' in the country. This illustrates how new political forces can rapidly corrode even moderately secure institutions and rules of governance.

I have tried to show in this chapter that the origins and varying influences on the conception of governance, and good governance in particular, have been political, as are the factors that will shape, and have shaped, success or failure in its implementation. Training, institution-building and capacity enhancement are all to the good, and it is unquestionable that individual participants and even individual institutions can benefit from this. But it is appropriate to be sceptical as to whether such initiatives can have any impact on the overall political culture and political process, especially where the funding involved is generally so limited. In the case of Britain, the Department for International Development (DfID) in 1998/9 committed only about £229 million, worldwide, to projects having 'good governance' or the improvement of human rights as their principal objective (mainly in Africa and Asia), though considerably more was committed to other projects in which good governance and human rights were important but not primary reasons for the programme (DfID, 1999). Spread over the developing world as a whole, the impact of this cannot be very significant and as yet there is little published evaluation of its democratic or governance value added. The Westminster Foundation for Democracy has a very small annual budget of about £4 million from the Foreign Office and its projects, worthy as they are in their own right, can have very little effect on political structures and processes in developing countries. Moreover, research into twenty-nine cases of political conditionality deployed in aid programmes by Britain, Sweden, the USA and the European Union between 1990 and 1995 to promote democratization and greater respect for civil and political rights found in general that aid sanctions 'had only been effective in a minority of cases' (Crawford, 1997: 103 and passim).

In general, therefore, without the absolutely essential condition of political will and political capacity in recipient countries, it is inconceivable that this level of public and quasi-public aid and projects could make any significant impact on the indigenous dynamics and immense complexities of, say, Indonesian or Nigerian politics, or on the cultures of corruption in, say, Kenya or India. And if overcoming the continuing offence of poverty, ignorance and disease is the *real* objective, as the British white paper of 1997 declares (DfID, 1997), then calling sternly for good governance in states that cannot sustain it is not likely to help much in many parts of the developing world, where the tidal politics of powerful social forces can easily undermine, overwhelm or simply evade the formal requirements of rules and institutions, as has been so common in efforts to implement effective land reform (Lipton, 1974). This is especially so in states whose politics have not concentrated sufficient power, probity, autonomy and competence at the centre to shape, pursue and encourage the achievement of explicit and nationally determined developmental objectives, whether by establishing and promoting the conditions of economic growth, by organizing it directly, or by a varying combination of both.

So what could hold good governance in place? As I indicated earlier, there was a second string to this particular bow and that was the call for *democratic* good governance. Democracy was to be the glue that would hold good governance in place. For although the World Bank could not make such a call, individual western governments and their collaborative organizations could – and did. Democracy therefore came to be seen as the political process that would institute and sustain good governance, hold the state and its officials accountable and demand the best and the highest standards of public service from the lot, while ensuring an improving standard of human rights.

Who could be against that? Who could be against democracy any more than one would be against virtue? Who could be against the aim of spreading 'the values of civil liberties and democracy, rule of law and good governance, and foster[ing] the growth of a vibrant and secure civil society'? (DfID, 1997: 69). Moreover, looking around the world in the late 1980s and early 1990s, democracy seemed once again to be everywhere on the march (Huntington, 1991; Diamond, 1999). But the question that has rarely been posed, let alone faced, is whether the glue itself would hold; that is, whether democracy can be viable in the conditions prevailing in much of the third world? And it is to that question I turn in the next chapter.

6

The Politics of Democratic Governance in the Third World

Introduction

At the core of the new orthodoxy that came to dominate official western aid policy and development thinking in the 1990s was the confident assertion that 'good governance' and democracy are not simply desirable but essential conditions for development in all societies. Taken together, 'democratic good governance' came to refer generally to a political regime based on the model of a representative, liberal-democratic polity, which protects human and civil rights, combined with a competent, non-corrupt and accountable public administration (Chalker, 1991a). Such political systems, the argument goes, are functional for competitive, free-market economies, and *vice versa*. Proponents of this new orthodoxy claim that such democratic capitalist systems promote a prosperous and peaceful world because they are best able to generate economic growth and do not go to war with each other (Doyle, 1983; Hurd, 1990). As a whole, this view rests on the crucial but often unspoken assumption that although the formula is essentially western in origin, it has universal developmental relevance for all cultures and societies in the modern world. In short, good governance and democracy are intimately related and, together, constitute the essential conditions for 'development'.

Such ideas are of course not altogether new. They echo and elaborate aspects of modernization theory of the 1960s, which held that western economic and political liberalism represented 'the good society itself' (Lipset,

1960: 403), and that it constituted the broad historical convergence point of diverse developmental trajectories (Lerner, 1958; Rostow, 1960; Almond, 1960; Eisenstadt, 1966; Kerr et al., 1973). And it needs of course to be said that in the post-war world, under US leadership, the West has long maintained a formal commitment to promoting democracy and human rights as one of its foreign policy goals (Whitehead, 1986). This reaches back at the very least to President Truman's programme of assistance for Greece and Turkey in 1947 as part of the evolving policy of promoting democratic regimes against the communist challenge (Packenham, 1973: 25–49). Later, in the early 1960s, President Kennedy sought to give this concrete expression in Latin American through the Alliance for Progress (Furlong, 1980). But it is important to note that even in this programme it was assumed that socio-economic growth was the essential basis for a secure democratic politics, and it was recognized that democratization without well-distributed economic and social development would have little chance of success.

But in the event, the democratic commitment was 'one of words rather than actions or deeds' (Furlong, 1980: 181). The policy goals of the Alliance failed as a rash of military governments took over in Latin America from the mid-1960s (there were fewer democracies by 1980 than there had been in 1960). Moreover, as the Cold War intensified and the fear of communism grew, the USA and western governments seemed oblivious to the abuses and incompetence of many non-democratic governments in the developing world. Aid and support continued to flow to them so long as they remained loyal to US interests. In acknowledging American support for such friendly but odious regimes, one US president made the essential political point when he was alleged to have said: 'They may be sons of bitches but at least they are *our* sons of bitches'.

Indeed, throughout the 1970s and 1980s, official development assistance (ODA), not to mention military aid, flowed freely to non-democratic regimes such as El Salvador, Honduras, Zaire, Kenya, Pakistan and the Philippines under Marcos, most of them with appalling human rights records. Calculated as a percentage of their GNP, total ODA (from both bilateral and multilateral sources) to those countries, even as late as 1986, was as follows: El Salvador (9.2%), Honduras (8.5%), Zaire (8.0%), Kenya (6.9%), Pakistan (2.9%), and the Philippines (3.2%) (OECD, 1984; Humana, 1987, 1992; World Bank, 1988: table 22).

So although western commitment to democracy and improving human rights is not new, it is clear that it has always been provisional and conditional, and always subject to considerations of the national interest, defined in terms of regional or global security and economic interests. 'The essential point, so easily obscured by abstract theory or by official rhetoric, is that at best the "promotion of democracy" will never be more than one foreign policy objective in competition with others' (Whitehead, 1986: 44). This analysis was again confirmed in the early 1990s by a research assessment of the effectiveness of political conditionality in foreign aid, which showed 'a clear pattern of subordination of human rights and democracy to other dominant foreign policy concerns, especially economic self-interest' (Crawford, 1997: 71).

However, what *was* new in the 1990s was the proposition that democracy is a necessary *prior or parallel* condition of development, not an outcome of it. In this respect the new orthodoxy turned on its head earlier claims of modernization theory that stable democracy presupposed prior economic and social development, as had been the case in much (but not all) of the now developed world, where advancing industrialization normally preceded democratization. Moreover, contrary to the best analytical work on development by political scientists of different persuasions (Hyden, 1985; Huntington, 1987; Sandbrook, 1990), the new orthodoxy seemed to assume that there were no inherent tensions, conflicts or difficult trade-offs over time between the various goals of development – such as growth, democracy, stability, equity and autonomy. In the rhetoric and policy announcements of many western governments in the 1990s it also appears to have been assumed that no special preconditions were necessary for stable democracy and that it could (and should) be instituted at almost any stage in the developmental process of any society, where it would enhance, not hinder, further development. In the 1990s that assumption was made explicit through increasing insistence by western governments that recipient countries would have to show moves towards democratization and improvement in human rights records as an essential condition of aid, as discussed in the previous chapter.

The urgent question, therefore, is not simply whether democratic politics – as part of the wider notion of democratic good governance discussed above – can promote development in the third world and elsewhere but, more fundamentally, whether the most recent 'third wave' (Huntington, 1991) of democratization, itself, can and will last?

In this chapter I shall suggest that the celebration of a victorious worldwide democratic revolution, which commenced at the 1990 Houston summit of industrialized nations (the G7), was hopelessly premature. Few of the third-world elites who dominated formerly non-democratic political systems (on left or right) have embraced democracy with either enthusiasm or commitment. And even where popular domestic protests have prised democratization out of authoritarian regimes, few third-world societies as yet exhibit the conditions that will sustain democracy, even in its most basic electoral or representative sense (Diamond, 1999: 8–9). A further central thesis of this chapter is therefore that political turbulence must now be expected in many new democracies, that growth and development will be undermined and executive or military coups are bound to follow in the course of the opening decade of the twenty-first century. In short, we are about to enter an era that will be characterized as much by democratic reversal as by democratic consolidation. But it is first necessary to explain this sudden western conversion to the support of democracy in the developing world.

Democracy: from outcome to condition of development

In many fundamental respects, the new orthodoxy turns on its head an older view, which prevailed in the bulk of western social theory and also in much of its imperial practice as indicated in the discussion of development as 'modernization' in chapter 2. This older view held that many parts of what used to be called the 'undeveloped', 'backward' or colonial world were not 'ready' for democracy and that a considerable amount of economic and social progress, plus political tutelage, was required before the institutions and processes of democracy would stick (Lee, 1967: 171–3; Larrain, 1989: 22–7). Patronizing and self-serving as many such political and theoretical arguments may have been, their influence continued to be expressed well into the 1960s and beyond in some of the best political science of the times. Indeed, in the 1960s it was widely assumed in comparative politics that democracy was a concomitant of 'modernity' and hence an *outcome* of socio-economic development, not a condition of it (Lipset, 1960; Cutright, 1963; Needler, 1968). Democracy, it was argued, required a high level of literacy, communication and education; an established and secure middle class; a vibrant civil society; relatively limited forms of material and social inequality (Dahl, 1971: 103), and a broadly secular public ideology. All this, it was held, was a function of prior economic development, which would yield these necessary, though not sufficient, conditions for sustainable democracy. 'The more well-to-do a nation, the greater the chances that it will sustain democracy' was Lipset's classic summary of his research findings (Lipset, 1960: 49–50). More recently it has been argued that a well-organized working class (itself a product of industrial growth) was equally important for promoting and defending democracy. For the struggle for democracy is best seen as a struggle for *power*, since workers need democracy as a means to both protect and advance their interests in the course of industrialization (Rueschemeyer, Huber Stephens and Stephens, 1992: 140, 77).

Evidence from the West and elsewhere can certainly sustain this view. Liberal-democratic institutions, declining social inequalities, a flourishing civil society, a widening policy consensus, a secular public and bureaucratic ideology and the extension and institutionalization of civil and human rights have seldom *preceded* economic development based on industrialization and urbanization. Indeed, the foundations of most modern advanced industrial economies were laid under non-democratic or highly limited democratic conditions – as in Britain (1750–1850), much of Western Europe (Tilly, 1975a, 1975b) and especially Bismarckian Germany and Meiji Japan. Moreover, most major post-1960 'success' stories of economic growth in the third world – Brazil, South Korea, Taiwan and, more recently, Thailand and Indonesia – have not occurred under conditions remotely approximating continuous and stable democracy but quite the opposite.

Even in the developmentally successful democratic societies – such as Botswana, Malaysia and Singapore – *de facto* one-party rule has been the norm for many years. In all these societies there have been powerful internal demands for the further extension of democratic practices, and dominant parties in these *de facto* one-party democracies have come under pressure from intellectuals and middle- and working-class groups, as evidenced in the outcome of the Taiwanese presidential election of March 2000. All this has served to underline the view that democracy is a consequence of development and hence sustain the earlier arguments in modernization theory.

An even stronger argument has traditionally been that the 'premature' introduction of democracy may actually hamper development in its early stages when there is 'a cruel choice between rapid (self-sustained) expansion and democratic processes' (Bhagwati, 1966: 204), and when there is the greatest need for effective state action or direction (Adelman and Morris, 1967; Hewlett, 1979; Cotton, 1989). This is because the early stages of development require capital accumulation for infrastructure and investment before advanced welfare systems or high wages can be afforded. Democratic systems, the argument goes, are likely to curtail processes of accumulation in favour of consumption.

But even from the 1960s, these arguments were challenged (McCord, 1965; Goodin, 1979; Kohli, 1986; Sklar, 1991) and have stimulated a debate which has regularly been reviewed (Huntington and Dominguez, 1975: 47–66; Sirowy and Inkeles, 1990; Diamond, 1992; Przeworski and Limongi, 1993). The critics argue that democracy and development are both compatible and functional for each other. If there is a trade-off between development and democracy, they claim, a slightly lower rate of growth is an acceptable price to pay for a democratic polity, civil liberties and a good human rights record. This was, allegedly, the Indian model adopted by Nehru in which democracy and development were equally important values (Kaviraj, 1996). They point out that there have been many more non-democratic than democratic regimes that at various times have had dismal or disastrous developmental records, such as Romania, Argentina, Haiti, Ghana, Mayanmar, Peru, Ethiopia and Mozambique. In these, neither growth nor liberty have prospered. And, as table 6.1 shows, while some third-world

Table 6.1   Selected average annual rates of growth of GNP per capita, 1965–1990 (%)

Democratic regimes		Non-democratic regimes	
Jamaica	−1.3	Zaire	−2.2
Trinidad and Tobago	0.0	Nigeria	0.1
Venezuela	−1.0	Zambia	−1.9
Senegal	−0.6	Libya	−3.0
India	1.9	South Korea	7.1
Sri Lanka	2.9	Taiwan	7.0
Malaysia	4.0	Indonesia	4.5
Costa Rica	1.4	Brazil	3.3
Botswana	8.4	China	5.8
Mauritius	3.2	Algeria	2.4
Singapore	6.5	Thailand	4.4

Source: Council for Economic Planning and Development (1992); World Bank (1992a)

democracies had stagnant or even negative average annual growth rates between 1965 and 1990, others performed very respectably when compared with non-democratic states.

But despite these counter-arguments, and despite the public announcements of the 1960s, it was never a significant operational plank of western development thinking or aid policy to make democratization a major condition of aid until the early 1990s. Why then did it change?

Reasons for change

It changed for the same essentially political reasons that brought the question of governance on to the agenda, as detailed in the previous chapter, not because of a new scientific discovery that democracy was a necessary condition for good governance and development. In fact, the evidence on that point has consistently remained entirely ambiguous: 'the simple answer to the question . . . is that we do not know whether democracy fosters or hinders economic growth' (Przeworski and Limongi, 1993: 64). As indicated above, some democracies do and some democracies do not, a point to which I return in chapter 8. No, the reasons for the change in western policy were the experience of structural adjustment, the rise of the neo-liberal orthodoxy, the collapse of official communism and the growth of pro-democracy movements in the developing world. To this must be added the considerable public outrage in many western countries at the accumulating evidence in the 1970s and 1980s of widespread and often brutal human rights abuses in non-democracies in the developing world (Nowack and Swinehart, 1989). In Latin America, Argentina, Brazil and Chile had especially bad records under their military dictatorships; in Africa, South Africa was a major focus of concern, as was the powerful Nigeria; and in Asia, the situation in Indonesia, Cambodia and Burma (Myanmar) drew considerable attention, as did the impact of the massacre in Tiananmen Square in Beijing, China, in the summer of 1989.

But the 'third wave' of democratization (Huntington, 1991) was already well under way by the time that western pressure began to mount on developing countries to put their democratic houses in order. Commencing in Portugal and Spain in the mid-1970s, this new wave of democratization gave rise to new or born-again democracies from the Philippines to Chile. In the 1990s it reached Africa and Eastern Europe (Potter et al., 1997).

One should not under-estimate how substantial the increase in the number of formal democracies has been during this period. Using Schumpeter's classic definition of electoral or representative democracy (Held, 1996: ch. 5; Diamond, 1999: ch. 1) as the 'institutional arrangement for arriving at political decisions in which individuals acquire the power to decide by means of a competitive struggle for the people's vote' (Schumpeter, 1943: 269), the number of electoral democracies increased from 39 in 1974 to 117 by 1998. The number of countries in the world that were formally democratic had more than doubled to over 60 per cent (Potter, 1997: 38; Diamond, 1999: 24).

These data and table 6.1 suggest that, contrary to confident official claims of the 1990s, there is no necessary relationship between democracy and development nor, more generally, between any regime type and economic performance. Rather, a more complex conclusion is appropriate. This starts, first, with the fact that *both* democratic *and* non-democratic third-world regimes have been able to generate high levels of economic development, although there are fewer formal democracies amongst them (Botswana, Malaysia, Singapore and Mauritius). However, second, there are many more non-democratic regimes with both very poor developmental achievements and appalling human rights records. Finally and emphatically, *no* examples of good or sustained growth in the developing world have occurred under conditions of uncompromising economic liberalism, whether democratic or not. From Costa Rica to China and from Botswana to Thailand, the state has played an active role in influencing economic behaviour and has often had a significant material stake in the economy itself.

Crucially, then, it has *not* been regime type but the kind and character of the *state* and its associated politics that has been decisive in influencing developmental performance. This in turn highlights the primacy of *politics*, not simply governance, as a central determinant of development. In short, the combination of democratic politics and economic liberalism has rarely been associated with the critical early breakthroughs from agrarianism to industrialism, either now or in the past. As Weiss and Hobson put it: 'the relative strength of states has been and continues to be one of the major mechanisms for determining the comparative industrial position of countries within the international economy' (1995: 3).

There can be few people who do not welcome the rise in the number of formally democratic states in the world, especially if this leads to an improvement in human rights records, which democracy usually brings (Humana, 1987, 1992). Nonetheless, the crucial question remains: will these new or born-again democracies survive and will they promote growth? And if good governance is best assured when situated within democratic polities, what is the prognosis for the latter?

I want to suggest that the opening decades of the twenty-first century will yield a very mixed pattern in which not all of the new democracies will survive. But each outcome will depend on the way in which the continuing costs and benefits of economic liberalization – 'adjustment', in the technical language – are distributed, on the one hand, and the way in which democratic openings will be used by the excluded or oppressed to attempt to correct past inequalities or new hardships. That is to say, it is not the *combination* of liberal economies and the politics of democratic governance that will determine developmental outcomes, but the *manner of their interaction*. Under many circumstances such interactions will constitute explosive and anti-developmental mixtures. Such a prognosis, however, depends on a view of the conditions that ensure democratic survival, to which I turn now.

Democratization and consolidation distinguished

The evidence from previous breakdowns in the twentieth century (Linz, 1978; Huntington, 1991) suggests some important conditions for enduring democratic politics, as do the patterns in the post-war years of democratic collapse in the third world. But, first, we must consider some context for this discussion.

In considering the prospects for democratic survival, it is important to make a clear distinction between the processes that lead up to and bring about the transition to democracy, on the one hand, and the conditions making for 'democratic consolidation' on the other (Mainwaring, O'Donnell and Valenzuela, 1992: 3). The point is that it is one thing for a democratic transition to take place; it is altogether another matter for democracy to survive (Potter et al., 1997). All the main schools of democratization theory acknowledge this explanatory distinction, for 'one must be prepared to distinguish the causal conditions of the first installation of democracy from those that maintain it after consolidation' (Rueschemeyer, Huber Stephens and Stephens, 1992: 76), while the doyen of democratization studies, S. M. Lipset, argued that 'new democracies must be institutionalized, consolidated and become legitimate' (1994: 7). And there are enough examples of both new and born-again democracies that have collapsed or failed to show that this is an important distinction.

But what is to count as 'consolidation'? When is democracy secure? The most obvious single defining feature of a consolidated democracy is where 'all major political actors take for granted the fact that democratic processes dictate government renewal' (Mainwaring, O'Donnell and Valenzuela, 1992: 3). To elaborate, democratic politics may be said to be consolidated where people, political parties and groups pursue their interests according to peaceful, rule-based competition, negotiation and cooperation, and where there is agreement that the succession of one government by another is decided by these means.

An important illustrative point to make here is that in the USA, Britain, France, Scandinavia and the Benelux countries liberal democracy *did* survive through the 1930s, despite the battering its institutional arrangements received from the economic crisis and the socio-political distress of the inter-war years (Bessel, 1997). But such survival was rare when compared with the widespread collapse of democracy in Europe in that period, the chronic instability of democracy in much of Latin America in the twentieth century, and the general pattern of democratic demise after 1960 in many former colonies which were granted independence on a democratic basis in Huntington's 'second wave' from the end of the second world war (Huntington, 1991). And, although there have been important examples of democracy withstanding the onslaught of anti-democratic pressures (often within the state itself), as in India and Jamaica, there have already been reversals of the 'third wave' of democratization. For instance, by the end of 1999, democracy had already failed, or been renewed and failed again, in a number of sub-Saharan African states. These included Lesotho, Nigeria, Sierra Leone, The Gambia and Niger, while in Algeria democratization was suspended in the middle of the electoral process at the end of 1991, though renewed again later. In Pakistan, democracy was again dismissed by the military in a coup in late 1999.

Given that it is clear that the establishment of democratic political systems in the past has in no way meant that they will survive to become consolidated, it is appropriate therefore to ask: will recently established democracies survive? In order to answer this question I offer a set of five conditions, which the comparative evidence suggests are necessary for democratic consolidation to take hold.

Five conditions for democratic survival

I suggest that there are five main conditions for democratic consolidation, which, taken together, illustrate the centrality of politics for development. They also highlight the utility of bringing important general theoretical questions in political science (and the findings of comparative politics) to bear on developmental issues; that is, placing political science at the heart of development studies, and vice versa.

Legitimacy

Legitimacy is a notoriously difficult concept to define and measure, especially in authoritarian political systems in which opinion is suppressed. Elusive as the concept is, its most simple meaning is *acceptability*. But, as Held (1996: ch. 5) points out, people may accept a political system (or, rather, not challenge it, which is different) for many reasons; and it is probably quite rare that positive informed acceptance is the basis of legitimacy. People may acquiesce out of fear or as a result of traditional compliance (deference); or they may give only resigned acceptance or conditional agreement. It has been argued, for instance, that the ability of the Indonesian government after 1966 to promote economic growth and still distribute its benefits widely has been one of the factors that secured its legitimacy, despite its sternly authoritarian rule (Putzel, 1997). What has been described as widespread legitimacy, even popularity, of Soeharto's New Order in Indonesia between 1965 and 1998 (Liddle, 1992: 450) has been said to have been conditional upon sustained economic growth, but this came under serious pressure when the Asian financial crisis brought that to a halt in the late 1990s.

Despite these problems with the concept it is clear that no democratic polity can survive and become consolidated unless it enjoys some form of legitimacy, whether of the passive acceptance kind or whether of the uncommon positive kind. However, the concept of legitimacy might be better understood and operationalized if it is broken down into three components: geographical, constitutional and political legitimacy.

Geographical legitimacy means that those who live within the state accept its territorial definition and the appropriateness of their place within it or, at least, they do not positively oppose it, except by constitutional means. Where, for instance, people do not consider the state to be legitimate in this respect, democratic politics comes under threat. In the extreme case, the threat might take the form of a secessionist or irredendist movement, where a group or region wishes to break away and establish its own state or join another. Where people have no political means for achieving secession from the state, they are unlikely to abide by democratic processes and violence is almost inevitable. Democratic politics (at the very least in the disputed region, and often beyond it) is very difficult, if not improbable. Examples of such situations include the Basque region of northern Spain; Eritrea, which was formerly part of Ethiopia; northern Sri Lanka, where the Tamil community has been fighting for an independent state; and it has been dramatically illustrated by the struggle of Chechnya for independence from the new post-Soviet Russian Federation.

Constitutional legitimacy refers to acceptance of the constitution – that is, the formal structure of rules whereby political power is competed for, organized and distributed. One of the toughest parts of the process of democratization lies precisely in establishing such a constitution, as the complex negotiations in the case of South Africa between 1990 and 1994 illustrate. As democracies emerge from the political darkness of authoritarian rule, a whole range of interests erupt into the more open but *less predictable* political space or stand exposed in it. Some may be powerful or rich and fear change; some may be poor and hitherto weak, and demand change. There may be economic interests (landowners), political or institutional interests (political parties and legislatures), functional interests (bureaucracies or armies, especially in Latin America), class interests (organized workers, as in Brazil), 'ethnic' interests (Afrikaners in South Africa or Indians in Fiji), regional interests (a province or sub-national area), or a mix of some of them. Each will want to have a shrewd idea how the new distribution of power in the constitution will affect it, and each will want to ensure that their interests will be protected. To some extent constitutions can do that (Przeworski, 1986: 60), which is why negotiation and bargaining is normally so tough as groups seek to influence the shape of the constitution and what goes in it. Will it be a parliamentary or presidential system? If the latter, how powerful will the presidency be in relation to the legislature and what will the role of political parties be? How many sequential terms may a president serve? How will the army be controlled? What powers will be reserved to the centre (in a federal structure, for instance) and how much power – and resources – will the regions or sub-national regional governments have? Will there be a Bill of Rights? What will go in it? How difficult will it be to change it? For instance, will private property be protected? If so, then the constitution places immediate and far-reaching constraints on government options in aspects of, say, economic policy.

Even in established and long-consolidated democracies (such as Britain, or the somewhat younger and less consolidated case of India), regional or ethnic interests can intensify over time and put pressure on the central state for constitutional reform: unsatisfied, this can extend into violence. In Britain, the debate about devolution of power to Scotland and Wales – which has waxed and waned – is a good example (Nairn, 1977). In India, demands for greater autonomy for the Punjab, even independence, have placed considerable stress on the Indian state (Singh, 1983), as has the rising tempo of Hindu nationalism (Corbridge and Harriss, 2000: chs 8 and 9). So, assuming people regard the geographical definition of the state as legitimate, they must also regard the formal constitution as legitimate for consolidation to have a chance to settle and be sustained.

Finally, there is *political legitimacy*. This refers to the extent to which the electorate (or, more realistically, organized parties in it, or other institutions like the army) regard the government in power as being entitled, procedurally, to be there. That is to say, for present purposes a government may be said to be politically legitimate when the outcome of the election reflects voting preferences according to the rules and that the results have not been rigged. In Haiti, for instance, there has been persistent and widespread rigging of the votes and violence in elections since the mid-1980s, after the overthrow of the Duvalier regime, coupled with army intervention to cancel the democratic result (Derbyshire and Derbyshire, 1996: 230–2). These have been just some of the factors reducing the political legitimacy and status of democracy in that country to such a low point. In Kenya, after the first multi-party election in 1992, many members of the opposition parties (which lost) claimed that there had been widespread irregularities and that the outcome of the election – and hence the new democracy itself – was in jeopardy (Holmquist and Ford, 1994), though the Commonwealth election observer mission concluded that, despite irregularities, the overall result reflected the will of the electors. In the event, it was accepted, but an uneasiness has remained in Kenya. In short, confidence in the *process* and confidence in the *outcome* of democratic electoral politics is crucial for democratic consolidation.

But the central point here is that, for all the difficulties with the concept, *geographical, constitutional and political forms of legitimacy* are necessary conditions for a democratic polity to survive, although they are not sufficient conditions. However, these basic conditions are not easy to obtain in many of the new democracies, where legacies of hate, mistrust and conflict remain, and where fear of the consequences of losing power is matched only by attraction to the prizes of winning.

Adherence to the rules of the game

For democracies to survive, there needs to be agreement or acquiescence about the rules of the political game and loyalty to those rules; that is, to the democratic process itself, especially amongst the political elites (Mainwaring, 1992: 309). The distinguished American political scientist Adam Przeworski has theorized democratization as 'a process of institutionalizing uncertainty, of subjecting all interests to uncertainty' (Przeworski, 1986: 58; 1988). By this he means that because democratic politics involves open competition for power, no group can be certain of winning. Indeed, the shift from authoritarian rule to democracy means precisely that the group that has held power (such as the military in Latin America, the Party in the former communist bloc or whites in South Africa) abandons effective control over outcomes and thus has to embrace 'uncertainty' (Przeworski, 1986: 58). This uncertainty has at least two dimensions, both understandably threatening to the group that is giving up control: (i) that it may not win the election and hence would lose power; and (ii) that the policy changes introduced by a new government would damage its interests – a point I shall return to shortly.

But, assuming that the constitution is agreed by the major political groups, even in the most limited and conditional sense, and assuming that an election has been judged to have taken place fairly according to the rules, then for democracy to work the *losers* must abide by the result, thereby showing commitment to the democratic process itself. They must not defect to antidemocratic forces, as happened in Mrs Aquino's troubled post-Marcos administration, or threaten to use democracy to suspend it, as the Islamic Salvation Front (FIS) did in Algeria in 1991/2, or resort to violence, as after the 1992 Angolan elections. *Winners*, on the other hand, must know that they are not in power for ever and will have to compete again and put their record to the test in the next election, which they cannot suspend.

The 'losers' might be the party representing the former authoritarian regime or it might be one of the groups that has fought for democracy and was suppressed by that regime. In both Myanmar and Nigeria in the early 1990s the military regimes refused to accept that 'their' parties had lost and cancelled the result of the elections. In Algeria, in late 1991, for somewhat different and more complex reasons, the government suspended the democratic electoral process when it became clear that the FIS was about to win and might itself abolish democratic procedures (Mortimer, 1991). In Angola, one of the main political parties (UNITA), which had been engaged in a long civil war with the governing party (MPLA), immediately took up arms after losing the election, claiming that the ballot had been rigged. In all these instances, democracy was simply overturned. By contrast, in both Zambia and Malawi, the leadership of the old regimes (of Presidents Kaunda and Banda) went quietly when they lost, as did communist parties in many parts of Eastern Europe and the former Soviet Union.

Generally, stable democracy also requires that there be no serious threat to the authority and power of the state (Linz, 1978), such as private armies (as in Peru, Colombia, Northern Ireland, the Philippines and Somalia). Where democracy emerges (or re-emerges) from right-wing authoritarianism (as in much of Latin America, the Philippines and South Korea), the political forces associated with the old regime must commit themselves to democratic practices. Crudely, the troops which held the old regime in power must return to the barracks – and stay there. If and when democracy returns to Myanmar, this will have to happen there too. But, equally, military groups that emerged in the struggle for democracy, such as the former Zimbabwe African National Union (ZANU) and African National Congress (ANC) guerrillas in Zimbabwe and South Africa or the Nicaraguan Sandinistas, have had to commit themselves to effective demobilization or incorporation in the armed forces of the new state, and to the ballot-box and committee rooms in their struggle for power or for influence over policy. In passing – and to illustrate the point that the problem of democratic consolidation is not confined to the third world – the problem (perhaps the final major stumbling block) in Northern Ireland over the decommissioning of arms illustrates this precisely, which is why some people are so fearful that a democratic settlement, achieved in the committee rooms of Whitehall, Dublin and Stormont, will not hold.

Policy restraint by winning parties

However, it is unlikely that any group or party would accept the rules of the electoral game if losing meant that it or the interests it represented would lose *too* much. It follows that while losers must accept the outcome, winners must also accept that there are significant limits to what they can do with their newly won power. This third condition means that democratic consolidation also depends on victorious parties exercising restraint when in government, although the temptation (and sometimes need) is often to rewrite the policy book. That is to say, new or born-again democracies are more likely to consolidate and prosper if the new government does not pursue highly contentious policies too far or too fast, especially when these policies seriously threaten other major interests.

Indeed, such agreed limits on policy change are often established *before* democratization is completed, in the course of negotiations (whether secret or otherwise), and are thus part of that process itself (Huntington, 1991/2: 609–15). This shows that while the distinction between democratization and consolidation is conceptually important, there are also very important continuities between them. In short, what happens in the course of democratization has important consequences for what happens afterwards.

The case of Venezuela sharply illustrates the long-term salience of this principle of policy self-restraint as a condition for democratic consolidation, precisely because it sustained democratic governance for more than thirty years after 1958 – completely against the run of politics in Latin America. In 1958 two extraordinary pacts were agreed in Venezuela (McCoy,

1988). The first was a Worker–Owner Accord by which, in effect, 'capitalists accepted democratic institutions as a means for workers to make effective claims to improve their material conditions, while workers accepted private appropriation of profit by capitalists as an institution in expectation of further gains from production' (ibid.: 86). What this meant was that 'workers accepted capitalism and capitalists accepted democracy, *each foregoing a more militant alternative*' (ibid.: 86; emphasis added). It is the final point that is central here. The second agreement was the so-called Pact of Punto Fijo, signed by the three major political parties (but excluding the Communist Party). According to the pact, the three dominant parties would each have a share of government posts, irrespective of who won in the elections; they would pursue agreed national development goals and would keep the communists out (ibid.: 88; Przeworski, 1992: 124). Venezuela has of course been fortunate in having a steady stream of oil revenues to help fund the politics of these pacts by paying for social and economic reform. These pacts came under immense pressure from the end of the 1980s and into the early 1990s and Venezuelan democracy came very close to collapsing – but did not, and its elites have been able to renegotiate the compacts that keep its democracy going (Coppedge, 1992; Romero, 1996; Ellner, 1997). However, despite these threats to its democracy, the central point is that for thirty years from 1958 these pacts framed the limits of policy change and effectively tied the major parties into the democratic process by guaranteeing that they would all have a stake in the government and that neither they nor their supporters would ever lose too much. I return to explore the developmental implications of this kind of 'pacted' democracy in chapter 8.

Another good recent illustration of this comes from South Africa, where the ANC government since 1994 has thus far been extremely careful not to threaten white economic interests or the interests of capital more generally (Lodge, 1995). And in Mauritius, in a highly plural society consisting of Christians, Muslims and Hindus, where there has been a bewildering pattern of fusion and fission in party alliances, democratic consolidation has also been secured by comparable means. In the Mauritian case, however, this has largely been due to the acceptance by all parties that government can only be by coalition and because 'on core values (religious and linguistic toleration, parliamentary democracy . . . and . . . a development strategy based on a mixed economy but with concern for all) there has been a national consensus' (Bowman, 1991: 101).

There is, however, at least one major problem that makes achieving such agreements about policy constraint so difficult in post-transitional democratic polities. This is that the followers of some newly elected democratic regimes not unreasonably expect rapid and often radical policies of redistribution. After all, they might argue, they represent the majority (as in post-apartheid South Africa), and have they not fought and suffered for this for many years? Yet the new government is likely to find that it cannot meet their demands (which may be for jobs, better wages, houses, health care, land reform), at least not immediately and at least not until sustained economic growth has generated the resources to pay for this. Also, for all the reasons given above, the government dare not dispossess the wealthy if they wish to sustain the political agreements that will keep the new democracy going. This is especially the case if there has been some form of 'pact' between the elites on the limits of policy change under the new democratic auspices; these may even have been written into the constitution. It is also especially the case if the new government seeks not only goodwill but also foreign aid and investment from major western institutions and companies. Such assistance might be threatened if government policies were thought to be too radical or unfriendly to the operation of free markets, a feature of new democracies that illustrates both the continuing salience of external factors even after democratization has been completed and also the role that national and international factors play in the politics of development.

But if the new government does *not* then satisfy the demands of its militant followers, it is open to them to use their newly won democratic rights to the full in the political space now provided by democracy. How far they go will vary from place to place. They may turn against 'their' government; take to the streets; organize demonstrations, strikes, go-slows and perhaps even more violent forms of protest, as have occurred in many parts of Latin America since the new democracies have been established (Cammack, 1991). If these escalate, the danger is obvious. Not only may this destabilize democracy (hence tempting the army to storm out of the barracks again to re-impose 'order', or more), but it may undermine the economy and hence damage the new government's strategy for growth.

In short, while policy restraint by winners appears to be an important operational condition of democratic consolidation, it is not something that all new democratic regimes can willingly, easily or always ensure, given their domestic political situations and also external demands, conditions and expectations.

Poverty as an obstacle to democratic consolidation

Until the most recent phase of the 'third wave' of democratization – that is, after about 1990 – consolidated democracies have seldom been found in really poor societies. On the contrary, there has been a strong positive correlation between the wealth of a country and democracy (Huntington, 1984: 198–9; Lipset, Seong and Torres, 1993: 156), though India has remained the most important exception among liberal democracies. This is not to say that more wealthy societies will *automatically* be able to consolidate democracy, as the more deterministic interpretations of modernization theory suggest. The evidence from oil-rich Middle Eastern countries shows that this is simply not the case. Wealth is not a sufficient condition for democracy.

Nonetheless, most societies in the developing world with a per capita income of less than $600 per annum in the 1990s (World Bank, 1997a) had not been successful in consolidating liberal democracy before 1990. There are, of course, a few exceptions, such as The Gambia (until 1994, at least) and especially India (allowing for its state of emergency between 1975 and 1977), though a few more have attained the status of partial (non-liberal) democracy. Pakistan and Egypt are both intermittent and borderline cases in point. By contrast, it has generally been the case that those developing countries (India apart) that have consolidated liberal or partially democratic politics since the 1960s (such as Venezuela, Costa Rica, Jamaica, Botswana, Mauritius, Singapore and Malaysia) have for some time achieved per capita incomes in excess of $600 per annum, a point I shall return to shortly.

One reason why serious poverty seems to restrain democratic consolidation is that in profoundly poor countries, the struggle for scarce resources, and the enormous advantages that permanent control of the state may bring to a party or faction, makes democracy very unlikely. Incumbents holding state power will be reluctant to engage in compromise and will be very unwilling to lose control. Suspending democracy is a good way of staying in power. This has been very much the case in sub-Saharan Africa (Wiseman, 1997), where poverty has given rise to the situation discussed in chapter 4 and described as the 'politics of the belly' (Bayart, 1993). Moreover, poverty is often accompanied by relatively low levels of literacy, formal education and communication, none of which have historically been associated with stable democracy.

While a large number of very poor countries have recently democratized, and hence have considerably eroded the (up till now) positive correlation between wealth and democracy, the issue is not settled by any means. For if these new poor democracies fail to consolidate into the twenty-first century, this particular correlation will, again, be strong. But if this most recent tranche of especially poor countries are able to consolidate their democracies, the salience of this point about the relationship between affluence and democracy will be greatly diminished.

Ethnic, cultural or religious cleavages as constraints on democracy

Sharp 'national', ethnic, cultural or religious differences (especially where they overlap with material inequalities between the groups) make both transition *and* consolidation difficult. Of course, they are not impossible to overcome in consolidating democracies, as in the multi-cultural, multi-ethnic or multi-religious examples of Switzerland, Canada, Mauritius, Trinidad and even – for long periods – in the Lebanon. Carefully crafted constitutions, coalitions or inter-elite pacts can keep democracies going by binding or buying groups into the institutional structures of democracy. But without such countervailing conditions, divisions of this kind have never made it easy to sustain democracy. This was illustrated by some of the problems that conflicting national and ethnic groups in Europe posed for democracy between the wars, as in Poland, Czechoslovakia and especially Yugoslavia (Bessel, 1997: 86–9).

There are many other more recent illustrations of this. Severe conflict between the Chinese and Malays in Malaysia in the 1960s and in Fiji between native Fijians and Indians in the late 1980s, and in 2000, ended with the suspension of democracy. Open tensions between Muslim, non-Muslim and Chinese groups in the vast sprawl of Indonesia surface regularly in bitter violence. The African continent provides some of the sharpest modern examples of such ethno-cultural conflicts, as in the continuing instability in Nigeria, Angola and Sudan, not to mention the recent (but not new) bloodshed in Rwanda. In Kenya, barely contained ethnic divisions in a context of looming land shortages, a bulging demographic pattern and massive social and regional inequalities place immense stress on the born-again democracy urged on that country by western donors in the early 1990s. Closer to Western Europe, the grim spectacle of Yugoslavian disintegration, in the 1990s, with its special contribution of 'ethnic cleansing', illustrates the point graphically.

Elsewhere, intense religious conflict can erode the prospects of a consensual basis for democratic politics. This is best illustrated by the increasingly hostile and sometimes violent confrontations within Islam, as in Algeria, Egypt and even Bangladesh. In India democracy has looked increasingly shaky as it has been threatened, first, by regional tensions and, more recently, by mounting religious conflict and Hindu fundamentalism (Kaviraj, 1996; Corbridge and Harriss, 2000).

In all these examples, ethnic or religious differences become the contours along which political mobilization flows, often with uncompromising and therefore anti-democratic consequences. Perhaps not until the salience – that is, the pull – of ethnic, religious or cultural loyalty is confined to the private sphere and hence disarmed and dispersed in favour of a widespread commitment to a common, public and above all secular citizenship, will democratic political processes be consolidated. It certainly seems to be the case in Islamic countries that the strongest supporters of democratic processes come from the more secular sections of the societies, as in Turkey, Egypt and Algeria (Bromley, 1997). And in Israel those most determined to undermine the democratic traditions, and who are least likely to accept the legitimacy of the state, may be found amongst Jewish fundamentalists.

Democratic endurance

So, if legitimacy, acceptance of the rules of the game, policy restraint and the absence of gross poverty in a minimally plural cultural, ethnic and religious context are critical structural conditions that make for democratic stability, what wider factors enable these essentially political conditions to take hold?

In a comprehensive review of the survival and death of 224 political regimes in 135 countries between 1950 and 1990, four American political scientists (Przeworski, Alvarez, Cheibub and Limongi, 1996) found a number of conditions that had been critical for democratic endurance.

First, apart from the obvious but important fact that the longer a democracy exists and the more democracies there are around it, the greater are the chances of survival, they found that the level of affluence was a critical predictor of democratic survival. For no democratic system in their survey has collapsed in a society where per capita income has been above $6000 per annum. Not one 'third-wave' democracy in Africa meets this condition; only Argentina and Uruguay do so in Latin America (though Chile is close) and only a handful (such as Slovenia and Korea) do so in Eastern Europe and Asia. Of course, poor democracies have survived below that level: Jamaica, Costa Rica, Botswana and Venezuela are good examples, as is India (notwithstanding the emergency in the mid-1970s), but most have not.

Second, poor democracies are only likely to survive if their economies do not stagnate or contract. Growth, that is, can compensate for poverty. But many of the new or born-again democracies (in the East and the South) have had very weak, if not negative, rates of growth through the 1990s and they, as with others, are highly vulnerable to the threat of recession. 'After plunging in 1998, developing country growth will slow further in 1999, but then begin to recover. However there is substantial danger: the world economy could still fall into a serious recession' (World Bank, 1999c: 183).

Third, they found that poor democracies are more likely to survive where their income inequalities are either moderate or declining. In practice, the widespread effects of continuing 'adjustment' through the 1980s and 1990s has meant that the opposite is happening and some new democracies remain amongst the most grotesquely unequal societies in the world – notably Brazil, Chile, Colombia, Kenya and South Africa (World Bank, 1998b: 198-9). As economic decline afflicts them, unemployment grows and inequality deepens, thus placing yet further pressure on their new democratic systems.

Fourth, where democracy has previously been overthrown, then new democracies in these economic circumstances are more vulnerable – a bleak consideration for many African and Latin American countries where the coup culture has been deeply entrenched, as Nigeria has repeatedly illustrated, and as has once again been demonstrated in Asia by the military coup in Pakistan in 1999.

Fifth, parliamentary democratic regimes seem to last much longer than presidential ones (Riggs, 1991). There are complex reasons for this but the two major ones appear to be that presidential systems can often lead to a deadlock between an executive presidency and the legislature, and hence paralysis (something that it is tempting for the army to break), while a parliamentary system generates an executive that reflects the dominant party or a coalition of parties in the legislature.

In short:

Democracies can survive in even the poorest nations if they manage to generate development, if they reduce inequality, if the international climate is propitious and if they have parliamentary institutions. (Przeworksi et al., 1996: 49)

Nothing illustrates this better than the circumstances that gave rise to a serious challenge to Venezuelan democracy in the late 1980s and early 1990s: a concatenation of profound economic crisis (brought about by falling oil prices through the 1980s), which saw wages drop by almost 45 per cent and hence brought about increasing inequality, in a context where the presidential system of power was faced by very strong parties in the legislature (Coppedge, 1992; Romero, 1996).

A final critical factor promoting the endurance of democratic politics is a rich and pluralistic civil society (Rueschemeyer, Hubert Stephens and Stephens, 1992: 6; Diamond, 1999: 239–60). Civil society consists of those cultural, political or economic 'areas of social life . . . which are organised by private or voluntary arrangements between individuals and groups outside the *direct* control of the state' (Held, 1987: 281; Diamond, 1999: 221). These may be youth groups, trade unions or business organizations, religious or professional associations, independent media, as well as consumer or interest groups, which may serve to exercise pressure and restraint on the state and thereby strengthen the assumptions and practices of democratic self-management in complex societies (Dahl, 1985; Held, 1990; Diamond, 1999: 222). However, though organizations in civil society have commonly proliferated where urbanization and structural change have occurred in the economy (notably Latin America, where they have been immensely influential politically), the richness of civil society varies greatly from society to society, especially in Africa (Bratton and van de Walle, 1997: 147).

One feature of many third-world societies is that the institutions of civil society, to the extent that they have been allowed to exist, have been penetrated and 'captured' by dominant one-party states and thus transformed into agencies of the regime. But equally, as Sklar (1991, 1996) has perceptively pointed out, there may be some realms or 'estates' within civil society where (despite or perhaps even because of repression) democratic practices are advancing and some realms where they are not. This is a theme taken up by Diamond (1999) in his conception of 'developing democracy', which I discuss below.

Conclusions and implications

A variety of theories seek to explain the paths to democracy (Potter, 1997; Leftwich, 1997). Modernization theorists (Lipset, 1960) emphasize the political effects of economic growth over time as a major secular process which generates political forces with strong democratic interests within societies. Transition theorists (Rustow, 1970) stress the roles of elite negotiations and compacts in the democratization process, while structural theorists (Moore, 1966; Rueschemeyer, Huber Stephens and Stephens, 1992) focus on the shifting balances of class forces. Others give some weight to the effects of international factors and pressures (Whitehead, 1986; Przeworski et al., 1995). Whatever the precise balance or mix of these factors, the point remains that democracies need to be consolidated if they are to endure. And if, as the current orthodoxy has it, democracy is the guarantor of good governance and democratic good governance is what will produce development (and the elimination of world poverty), then the opening question of this chapter remains central: will the new democracies survive?

There are three main points to make here. First, the historical and comparative record suggests that the presence of only one or two of the various conditions outlined above is unlikely to ensure democratic consolidation, while the presence of all will make it much more probable. The absence of some conditions may also be compensated for by the effectiveness of others. For instance, the effects of sharp ethnic or cultural cleavages may be mitigated by careful constitutional design, by policy restraint or broadly-based coalition-building. The problem, however, is that few of the new democracies appear to have many of these conditions (Leftwich, 1993a). As a consequence, the prognosis for widespread democratic consolidation is not good, and it would therefore be prudent to expect democratic reversals during the first decade of the twenty-first century. Though there will be international pressure against it, and though it may happen first in small or partial democracies, it would only take a few 'big' reversals to establish a climate for others to follow.

It is of course possible that 'pseudo-democracies' may continue, for they are not democratic at all. They are characterized by a facade of democratic institutions that can easily disguise the reality of non-democratic and authoritarian rule. The term 'pseudo-democracy' is used to distinguish such 'democracies' from genuinely electoral democracy or, more fully, liberal democracy. Examples might include Mexico, Uganda, Algeria and Indonesia, as well as Peru, Jordan and Zimbabwe (Diamond, 1999: 15).

Second, it is important to remember that, historically speaking, it has been largely from within a western perspective that democracy has been assumed to be a good thing. For instance, in the late 1950s, S. M. Lipset wrote that

democracy is not only or even primarily a means through which different groups can attain their ends or seek the good society; *it is the good society itself in operation.* (Lipset, 1960: 403, emphasis added)

And although it is true that today there are voices and groups demanding democracy in almost every country in the world, it is important to remember that this view is not universally held. Some traditional elites within parts of Islam, for example, hold that democracy is a western institution and hence inappropriate for a non-western society (Bromley, 1997). Such views can also be found in the South Pacific where a *Fiji Times* editorial in 1992 described democracy as a 'foreign flower', unlikely to take root in Fijian soil (Larmour, 1995: 230). Moreover, there is a view, the so-called 'Lee thesis' (often associated with Lee Kuan Yew of Singapore), that the kind of self-focused (if not self-obsessed) individualism that underpins electoral democracy, and liberal democracy in particular with its adumbration of rights rather than responsibilities, is essentially a western phenomenon and one that is ill suited to non-western cultures (Zakaria, 1994). Elsewhere, determined modernizing elites have argued that democracy can hinder the urgent tasks of economic transformation and that it would be both 'premature' and dangerous to allow liberal democracy to flourish in the volatile conditions of rapid economic change. Germany under Bismarck in the late nineteenth century, Japan after the Meiji 'revolution' of 1867, Korea after 1960 and the People's Republic of China since 1980 are good examples of this. Indeed, both the Cuban and Chinese governments have regarded the post-Soviet Russian experiment (of combining political democracy with economic liberalization) with undisguised horror. Both Cuba and China have themselves embarked upon wide-ranging programmes of economic liberalization, but have done so under strictly non-democratic conditions (Howell, 1993; Duckett, 1998; Cole, 1998).

Third, this last point raises a final and uncomfortable paradox about democracy in general and about liberal democracies especially. This paradox is that democracies may be thought of typically as *simultaneously* radical and conservative. They can be considered as radical in that no other political systems have promoted and protected individual *political rights and civil liberties* to the same extent (Gastil, 1986; Humana, 1992). In their struggles to define, win or protect such rights in the political domain, countless millions of people have died or suffered appallingly at the hands of authoritarian regimes. These are the human dramas that illustrate so powerfully the 'narrative' of the struggle for democratization in the nineteenth and twentieth centuries.

But 'social and economic conservatism may be the necessary price for democracy', suggests Przeworski (1988: 80), because, radical as it may be in the above respects, democracy may be considered 'conservative' in another respect. The key point here is that while they have established the principle of various rights in their constitutions (where they have them), and sought to institutionalize them in their political systems, democracies have not, to the same extent, been able to institutionalize social and economic rights, such as job security, minimum incomes and access to health and welfare systems (although their record in these matters is generally better than authoritarian regimes). Of course, many liberal democrats, and neo-classical economists too, would argue that these provisions (what the Chinese describe as subsistence rights), desirable as they may be, are not rights but the products of economic growth, which democracy will promote – in the long run. And without growth, they are simply undeliverable by any regime.

Democracy may be considered 'conservative' in another more troubling sense, too; that is, in the difficulties it faces in taking rapid and far-reaching steps to reduce inherited structural inequalities (which may be necessary for growth), for all the reasons given in chapter 1. For although new democratic governments (like the ANC in South Africa) or older ones (as in India) may be committed to poverty reduction and promoting the welfare of the masses, it is often the case that radical and essentially *non-consensual* steps are necessary for this. The difficulty is that such steps could easily breach the formal or informal 'pacts' that may have helped to bring democratization about in the first place.

The profound dilemma raised by this last point is that, in laying the foundations for growth, such non-consensual and non-democratic measures may often be essential in the early stages of developmental sequences, and also for sustainable democracy in the long run. To extend the brief illustration from chapter 1, land reform is a good example, since it is widely recognized that this can be an important condition for agricultural and rural development, for the economic and social welfare of rural people and hence for democratic stability. But landowners in general do not consent to land reform! As in Latin America and Asia, they often constitute a very powerful interest with intimate connections to the state. In consequence, democratic third-world governments have seldom been effective in overcoming such vested rural interests to achieve the restructuring of rural wealth and power, which land reform is designed to bring about, as in the Philippines after the restoration of democracy in 1986 (Kerkvliet, 1974; Moran, 1999: 581) and in Pakistan under the Bhutto regime in the 1970s (Herring, 1979). Indian democracy, too, has had very little success in pushing through land reforms; landlessness and appalling rural poverty remain, though some state governments in India, as in Kerala, have been more successful. Moreover, at a more general level of redistributive policy and practice, there has been 'hardly any significant taxation of agricultural income and wealth' (Bardhan, 1984: 46 and ch. 6).

In short, and uncomfortably, democratic politics is seldom the politics of radical economic change. Yet radical change may be precisely what is required at key points in developmental processes, and this is one of the key reasons why the relationship between democracy and development is so tense. Consolidated democratic politics is, rather, the politics of accommodation, compromise and the centre. Given a diversity of interests in society, this is inevitable. For this reason, democracy is improbable in highly polarized societies, whether divided by income, class, ethnicity, religion or culture. Whether liberal or socialist, the logic of democratic politics is necessarily consensual, conservative and incremental in the change it brings about. For many that is its virtue: for others, its vice. For precisely these reasons, as E. M. Forster first put it in a different context, the best we may be able to say right now for many countries that have democratized in the course of the current 'third wave' is 'two cheers for democracy'.

But it may be that democracy needs to be thought of as developmental, as 'democracy in parts' (Sklar,1996: 40), rather than as a 'whole system' phenomenon, involving democratic movement in some areas of society though not simultaneously in all. It may be thought of as developing in another sense, whereby partial pseudo-democracies, if they endure, may become truly electoral democracies and, in time, fully liberal democracies (Diamond, 1999). Moreover, if and when the new democracies consolidate they may also accumulate the political means and capacities for a slow and steady reduction in such inequalities of access to economic resources and opportunities. This has been the slow, uneven and secular trend in most of Western Europe as some social and economic rights were added to political and civic ones during the twentieth century (Marshall, 1950). But the enduring paradox is that such changes may be too slow for democratic consolidation to occur, especially where democracy is being attempted 'on top of a minefield of social apartheid' (Francisco Weffort, cited in Lipset, 1994: 17).

What all this suggests, finally, is that there are many goals of development, or of progress, of which democracy is only one. More to the point here, it is not proven at all that democratic regimes always promote economic development better than non-democratic ones, as the contrasting cases of India and China between 1950 and 1980 illustrate so graphically. But some democratic states, even though they may have fallen far short of being liberal democracies, have promoted development much more effectively than non-democratic ones. Botswana and Singapore, for instance, contrast radically with, say, Burma and Zaire between the mid-1960s and the end of the twentieth century. In short, there have been some democracies *and* some non-democracies that have been developmentally successful, and it is therefore crystal clear that regime type (that is, democratic or not) has had little to do with it.

So what, then, is the explanation? The answer, I suggest, lies in the character and capacity of their states, whether democratic or not, and in particular in that form of state now widely recognized as the 'developmental state'. What are these states? How do they arise? What are their structural and political characteristics? How do non-democratic and democratic developmental states differ? And what are the different developmental implications of different forms of democratic politics and the democratic state? Those questions constitute the substance of the next two chapters.

7

Developmental States: Bringing Politics Back In

Introduction

As I suggested in the opening chapter of this book, a major deficiency in both development studies and the discipline of political science (Politics) over the last thirty years of the twentieth century has been the *de facto* separation of each from the other, to the detriment of both. In the field of development policy and practice, especially, all major international agencies (like the IMF and the World Bank), as well as most national aid and overseas development ministries, have largely ignored politics in their analytical work and rarely employ political scientists. Until recently, there was barely a handful of studies amongst the literally hundreds of official publications from such institutions that in any way addressed key issues in the *politics* of development (Lamb, 1987; Gulhati, 1988, 1989). Even the World Bank's conversion in the 1990s to the importance of 'governance' in development, as discussed in chapter 5, has been presented primarily as a matter of administrative enhancement and public-sector management, in which 'good governance' is equated with 'sound development management'.

As I also pointed out in chapter 1, the discipline of Politics as a whole has, professionally and pedagogically, paid scant attention to the field of development, apart from the relatively small number of dedicated analysts, some of whose outstanding work was discussed earlier. There have, of course, been other important accounts, which include: O'Donnell's analysis of the provenance and features of bureaucratic authoritarian states of Latin America

(1973); Stepan's work on state and society in Peru (1978); Trimberger's comparative political analysis of 'revolutions from above' in Japan, Turkey, Peru and Egypt (1978); Wade's account of Taiwanese state development strategy (1990) and Evans's analysis of the state and industrial transformation (1995). Yet despite these and other important contributions, the dominant preoccupations in the mainstream of the discipline of Politics have remained resolutely parochial in their reach, when in fact the processes of development (or lack of it) provide some of the best recent and contemporary illustrations of the fundamental and universal concerns (both normative and analytical) of the discipline of politics. These include the character, role and capacity of the state (especially the bureaucracy); the sources, forms, distribution and control of power in a society; the principles of coalition fusion and fission; the relationship between state, economy and civil society; the problem of reconciling or accommodating diverse and conflicting interests; the tension between democracy and development, and – especially and most recently – the conditions for democratic survival. Indeed the contemporary work on democratization in the developing world will make an enormous contribution to our understanding of the nature of, and conditions for, democracy, but little of it has been assimilated back into the major spheres of democratic theory. Indeed, if the debates and findings about these central political issues in non-western developmental contexts were recycled back into the mainstream of Politics, the discipline would be profoundly enriched, as Richard Sklar has pointed out in relation to African political studies (Sklar, 1993: 83–6). This would also help to reduce the remaining aspects of institutional, philosophical and theoretical parochialism of the discipline, and it would improve the prospects for a unified and comparative political science, applicable to developed, developing and underdeveloped societies alike.

In the light of these considerations, this chapter examines one central area where fundamental issues in the disciplines of Politics and development studies converge directly: the forms and features of the 'developmental state'. But first, some background is necessary.

States of development

Between 1965 and 1997 many developing countries (mainly but not only in Africa) registered negative average annual rates of growth in their GNP per capita (World Bank, 1999c: table 1.4). A considerably smaller number have had moderate rates of growth (between 1.5 and 3.5%). But only a handful of developing countries achieved average annual rates of growth in their GNP per capita in excess of 4% over that period. Within the latter category are Botswana (7.7%), South Korea (6.7%), Taiwan (7.0%), Singapore (6.3%), China (6.8%), Indonesia (4.8%), Thailand (5.1%) and Malaysia (4.1%) (Council for Economic Planning and Development, 1992; World Bank, 1999c). By world standards, these are remarkable achievements.

Yet apart from their geographical concentration in East and South-east Asia, these societies have little in common. Some, like China and Indonesia, have huge populations; others, like Botswana and Singapore, do not. Some have valuable and exportable raw materials, like Indonesia (oil) and Botswana (diamonds); some, like Korea and Thailand, do not. Economic policy and practice have varied widely between them: contrast China with Singapore, or Korea with Malaysia. Some may be thought of as 'plural' in their socio-cultural or ethnic structures, as in Malaysia and Indonesia; others are culturally more homogeneous (though not entirely so), like Taiwan, Botswana and Thailand. A few have sustained democratic or quasi-democratic politics, like Botswana, Malaysia and Singapore; but most have not.

What then explains their success? I suggest that they all share versions of a type of state that has been capable of generating sustained developmental momentum. This is the 'developmental state', which, in its origins, is a function of the politics of these societies and their politico-economic relations with the international system and, especially, key players within it. To this larger extent, as Pempel has argued (1999), developmental states may be thought of as part of wider 'developmental regimes' involving principles of power and action. Nonetheless, the state is at their core. Before outlining the essential elements of the developmental state, I deal first with the provenance and meaning of the concept itself.

The developmental state: conceptual provenance and meaning

For preliminary purposes, the distinguishing characteristic of developmental states is that their political purposes and institutional structures (especially their bureaucracies) have been developmentally driven, while their developmental objectives have been politically driven. For at the heart of these states, fundamentally *political* factors have shaped the urgency, thrust and pace of their developmental strategies through the structures of the state (Castells, 1992; Pempel, 1999). These political factors have normally included nationalism, ideology and a wish to 'catch up' with the West. But there has also commonly been a strong 'primordial association' between the development of military capacity and the power and autonomy of the developmental state (Burmeister, 1986: 122). This has largely been a consequence of their need to respond to regional competition and external threat, and this point underlines and extends Tilly's (1975a) claim (for Europe) about the link between state formation and war-making. In short, nationalism lies at the heart of the developmental state regime (Woo-Cumings, 1999b: 8).

A more detailed account of the central characteristics of the developmental state comes later. For the present, an operational definition of developmental states identifies them as those states whose *politics* have concentrated sufficient power, autonomy, capacity and legitimacy at the centre to shape, pursue and encourage the achievement of explicit developmental objectives, whether by establishing and promoting the conditions of economic growth (in the capitalist developmental states), by organizing it directly (in the 'socialist' variants), or a varying combination of both. Such states are not common.

In a variety of implicit and explicit forms, the basic idea and concept of the developmental state can be traced back a long way. It may be found, for instance, in Friederich List's mercantilist arguments about the need for 'less advanced nations' to use 'artificial means' (the state) to catch up with the advanced nations in order to 'accomplish the economical development of the nation and to prepare it for admission into the universal society of the future' (List, 1885/1966: 175). Explicitly (and presciently, remembering Japan and Korea in the twentieth century), List claimed that

a perfectly developed manufacturing industry, an important mercantile marine, and foreign trade on a really large scale, can only be attained by means of the interposition of the power of the State. (ibid.: 178)

Marx, too, in the second of his major theories of the state, may be interpreted as having had a rudimentary notion of the capitalist developmental state when he referred to the 'completely independent' position of the state in France under Louis Bonaparte, which had thoroughly consolidated the strength of its position against civil society (Marx, 1852/1958a: 333). Although such a state arose from the balance of class forces in society, and might have been able to break free from the specific interests of particular classes, it was not a free-floating state. It still had as its fundamental objective the furthering of capitalist interests in general. Jon Elster holds that this version of the autonomous capitalist state in Marx was 'the cornerstone of his theory' after 1850 (Elster, 1985: 426), and was later developed by European Marxists, such as Poulantzas (1973). Moreover, Elster argues, this theory corresponds well with the actual historical development of the capitalist state in European development

as an active, autonomous agent from the sixteenth century onwards, pursuing its own interests by harnessing those of others to its purposes. (Elster, 1985: 426)

In the 1930s and beyond, weak aspects of the idea and limited practice of a developmental state lay at the heart of some of the colonial welfare and development policies of the imperial powers, as discussed in chapter 2 (Lee, 1967). Though none referred to the idea or concept of the developmental state as such, theorists like Gerschenkron (1962) after the second world war recognized the need for a state with developmental functions in the context of late development, a belief that became an article of faith among economic planners and development economists alike (Robertson, 1984). Fred Riggs's notion of 'the bureaucratic polity' in Thailand (1966) also contained seeds of the idea of the developmental state. This notion was later applied to Indonesia and defined as

the political system in which power and participation in national decisions are limited almost entirely to the employees of the state, particularly the officer corps and the highest levels of the bureaucracy, including especially the highly trained specialists known as the technocrats. (Jackson, 1978: 3)

S. P. Huntington also stressed the critical developmental importance of concentrating power in a 'bureaucratic polity' (1968: 167) as a modernizer and innovator in socio-economic development. To be successful such a state would also need to undertake the political destruction of those existing 'social forces, interests, customs and institutions' which have held back development and which continue to oppose modernization (ibid.: 141–2), a task which, in practice, has defeated many states. And in the 1970s, Cardoso and Faletto deployed the notion of a 'developmentalist state' to describe the attempts by the Mexican and Chilean states in the inter-war and immediate post-war years to promote industrialization (Cardoso and Falleto, 1979: 143–8).

As discussed earlier (pp. 80–3), Myrdal (1968, 1970) drew the elementary distinction between 'soft' and 'hard' states in the third world, and others have built on that since then, offering accounts of 'bureaucratic authoritarian' and 'strong' states in the third world (O'Donnell, 1973; Migdal, 1988; Leftwich, 1993b). But it was only in the last twenty years of the twentieth century that political scientists began to look more closely at the precise conditions for effective developmental action by states and at some of their characteristics (Nordlinger, 1987). Ellen Kay Trimberger (1978) sought to explain how autonomous and developmentally progressive bureaucratic states emerged in the third world. Focusing comparatively on Japan, Turkey, Egypt and Peru, she argued that a bureaucratic state apparatus achieved relative autonomy when, first, those holding high civil and military office were not drawn from dominant landed, commercial or industrial classes; and, second, where they did not *immediately* form close relations with these classes after achieving power (ibid.: 4). And although her primary interest lay in theories of revolution, her account provided important insights into historical and structural conditions of developmental states. About the same time, A. J. Gregor depicted Italian fascism as a 'developmental regime' in respect of its modernizing role. Seeing their main task as 'the rapid modernization and industrialization of a retarded socio-economic system' (Gregor,1979: 311), the fascists stressed the expansion and importance of the 'state as a centralizing, integrative and managerial agency' (ibid.: 304).

Thus, some of the ideas of the developmental state – both as a concept and practice – may be found in a number of antecedent sources and histories, but in none of these accounts (apart from that of Cardoso and Faletto) was the concept of the 'developmental state' explicitly used, nor was there ever any attempt to elaborate it by specifying its preconditions, characteristics or constitutive elements. As in much development economics (see Gillis et al., 1992: 25), a major role for the state was announced, but the political and institutional conditions for its effective discharge of that role were never identified (Green, 1974). Even after calls were made to 'bring the state back in' (Evans, Rueschemeyer and Skocpol, 1985), there was still no full engagement with the political determinants of state autonomy and capacity. This failure to analyse and understand the political anatomy of the developmental state has been a major limitation in post-war development theory and policy. For the absence of a theory of the developmental state has allowed anti-statist theorists to berate all planned developmentalism (rather than discriminate between the successful and unsuccessful), denounce state failure as inevitable and seize both the theoretical and policy initiatives in the 1980s (Lal, 1983).

It was only with the publication of Chalmers Johnson's seminal work on East Asian developmental states, and Japan in particular (Johnson, 1981, 1982, 1987, 1995, 1999), that the phrase 'developmental state' made its formal debut and that a serious attempt was made to conceptualize it. Crucially, Johnson distinguished the 'developmental orientation' of such a 'plan-rational' state from the 'plan-ideological' state in the Soviet-type command economies on the one hand, and from the more familiar 'regulatory orientation' of typical liberal-democratic or even social-democratic states, on the other hand. A crucial feature of the developmental state was the intimacy of its relationship with the private sector and the intensity of its involvement in the market (Johnson, 1981: 9–10). The Japanese developmental state was pre-eminent in 'setting . . . substantive social and economic goals' (Johnson, 1982: 19) for the private sector to meet, whereas the regulatory state merely established the framework for components of this sector to set their own goals. The Japanese formula for this has been 'a plan-oriented market economy'.

Just as Gregor (1979: 308) had claimed for Italy, Johnson argued that a further feature of the developmental state was the power, continuity and autonomy of its elite bureaucracy, which has remained a defining feature of the species. In the case of Japan, this was centred in key ministries, notably the Ministry of Finance and the Ministry of International Trade and Industry (MITI). The developmental state in Japan was also characterized by agreed policy goals, largely determined by the bureaucratic elite, which has been far more the epicentre of decision-making than the political or legislative elites. As Johnson put it: 'the politicians reign and the state bureaucrats rule' (1981: 12). And his answer, fourteen years later, to the question 'Japan: Who governs?' has remained consistently simple: 'Who governs is Japan's elite bureaucracy' (Johnson, 1995: 13). Finally, he stressed that the Japanese developmental state must first and foremost be understood *politically*, for its provenance lay in the essentially political and nationalist objectives of the late developer, concerned to protect and promote itself in a hostile world.

It arises from a desire to assume full human status by taking part in an industrial civilization, participation in which *alone* enables a nation or an individual to compel others to treat it as an equal. (Johnson, 1982: 25)

In respect of this kind of deep nationalist purpose, Johnson echoed precisely the point made by List about Germany, almost 150 years before; by Mussolini about Italy in the inter-war years (Gregor, 1979); by Stalin in 1931 about the urgency of Soviet economic development (Deutscher, 1966: 328); by the leadership of the Chinese Communist Party before and after 1949 (White, 1985), and by President Park Chung-hee in Korea in 1963 (Lim, 1985: 73). Nationalist momentum for economic development is not new; countless leaders of developing countries have announced precisely such objectives . The point, however, is that few have had the political capacity to be able (or, perhaps, also be willing) to drive through these objectives, whereas developmental states *have* been able to do so, and we need to understand that difference politically. For instance, the 'failed developmental state' in India (Herring, 1999) was hamstrung not only by the size of the country but by the particular interests whose political access and relentless pressures sapped the Nehruvian vision. Likewise, the *desarrollista* states of Brazil and Mexico never attained the level of coherence and autonomy of the East Asian developmental states. This was largely as a consequence of their politics and especially the politics of their systems of bureaucratic appointments, which made for discontinuity and uncertainty in their bureaucratic capacity, hence undermining the achievement of stated developmental goals (Schneider, 1999).

By contrast, East Asian and other developmental states have been able to

extract capital; generate and implement national plans; manipulate private access to scarce resources; coordinate the efforts of individual businesses; target specific industrial projects; resist political pressures from popular forces such as consumers and organized labour; insulate their domestic economies from extensive foreign capital penetration; and, most especially, carry through a sustained project of ever-improving productivity, technological sophistication, and increased market shares. (Pempel, 1999: 139)

Gordon White's important account of the developmental state and socialist industrialization (1984) isolated three political variables in order to construct a preliminary classification of what he saw as its three main types: state capitalist, intermediate and state socialist. First, he highlighted the nature of the social forces and interests that shaped the state and its purposes (that is, the political sociology of the state). Second, he underlined the state's political, administrative and technical capacities as crucial factors. The third variable, he argued, was the mode of the state's involvement in economic activity, whether 'parametric' (framework-setting) or 'pervasive' (substantive involvement). The way in which these variables combined in any given state determined its broad position in the classificatory scheme.

Since then, there have been a number of valuable interpretations of particular developmental states, or comparisons of them (for instance, Evans, 1985; White and Wade, 1985; Deyo, 1987; Johnson, 1987; Wade 1990; Woo-Cumings, 1999a), and a few important attempts to develop the concept further (Burmeister, 1986; Evans, 1989; Önis, 1991; Castells, 1992; Hawes and Liu, 1993). In the light of these contributions, it is the purpose of the remainder of this chapter to sketch a wider general model of the developmental state, drawing on both the insights of theorists already mentioned and on the rich empirical detail now available about a number of such states. With the exception of the contributions to a recent volume on the subject (Woo-Cumings, 1999a), almost every account of the developmental state has remained focused on East Asia, with a few minor concessions to South-east Asia (Haws and Liu, 1993). Some even argue that the developmental state is *sui generis* to East Asia, a product of 'its unique historical circumstances' (Önis, 1991: 113). But I argue that this is far too narrow, and my account includes not only Malaysia, Thailand and Indonesia but Botswana as well. Though I shall elaborate the point later, it is important to stress here that while all these states do not share all characteristics of the type in equal measure, and that they vary with respect to both 'structures and strategies' (Pempel, 1999: 149), I shall suggest that they share enough of them to be deemed part of the category.

Towards a model of the developmental state

A model in this sense represents an attempt to extract common general properties from a set of sometimes diverse concrete forms, and this is no exception. I suggest that there are a number of major components of the developmental state model (Leftwich, 1995). These are: a determined developmental elite; relative autonomy of the developmental state; a powerful, competent and insulated economic bureaucracy; a weak and subordinated civil society; the capacity for effective management of private economic interests; and an uneasy mix of repression, poor human rights (especially in the non-democratic developmental states), legitimacy and performance.

Developmental elites

First and foremost, all developmental states have been led by determined developmental elites, which have been relatively uncorrupt, at least by comparison with the pervasive corruption so typical of, say, Haiti, Zaire and the Philippines (under Marcos). These elites have often been associated with founding figures, such as Lee Kuan Yew in Singapore, Sir Seretse Khama in Botswana, General Park Chung Hee in Korea and President Soeharto in Indonesia. Moreover (though Soeharto came close), no developmental state has exhibited the one-man 'sultanism' (Weber, 1964: 346–7) of many African states (Sandbrook, 1986). On the contrary, they have often been run by shifting coalitions of diverse interests and, as socio-economic change has occurred, all such states have experienced (sometimes severe) intra-elite political and policy conflict, often intensifying over time.

Often, the core policy circle surrounding the leadership has been quite small. For instance, even in Indonesia, with a vast population of 170 million, it was estimated for the 1970s that the small ruling group responded primarily to the values and interests of less than 1000 persons in the bureaucratic, technocratic and military elite of the country (Jackson, 1978: 3–4). What seems to characterize developmental elites such as these is their developmental determination, their commitment to economic growth and transformation and their capacity to push it through. This contrasts starkly with, say, the incompetent and 'predatory' state of Haiti (Lundahl, 1992) or the corrupt 'cronyism' of the Marcosian Philippines (Hawes, 1992), or even the relative developmental immobilism of the Indian state, given its control by three dominant 'proprietary classes' (Bardhan, 1984: 54).

A further feature of these developmental elites has been the dense traffic between top levels of the civil and military bureaucracies and high political office, something that is very rare in western liberal democracies, and indeed frowned upon. Such elites have in general also been highly nationalistic – a major impetus for economic development, often responding to internal or regional security threats and thus underlining and extending Tilly's thesis (for Europe) about the importance of war-making in state formation (Tilly, 1975a).

Corruption is notoriously difficult to define, identify and measure comparatively (Ward, 1989), and developmental states have certainly not been immune from it. In rapidly growing economies, sudden wealth (and tidal flows of aid or investment) can generate huge temptations, especially so, perhaps, in cultures where patron–client relations are deeply embedded, and where the role of the state in economic life is intense. Hence the politics of developmental transition in some of these states has displayed extraordinary mixtures of patrimonialism, centralization, technocratic economic management, coercion and corruption. Thailand and Indonesia are examples where there have been cases of spectacular high-level corruption, but none are without it. For instance, the Soeharto regime was described as 'a giant patronage machine with a network extending from Jakarta to the provinces' (Crouch, 1984: 82). Yet it has also been argued that in using a whole range of what might be termed 'corrupt' measures, Soeharto was consolidating his power (notably over the army and bureaucracy) to consolidate an Indonesian developmental state by winning over support and buying off opposition. In the case of Korea, corruption 'functioned as a dynamic part of the developmental process' and, in effect, was 'nationalized' as the state used it to promote policies it favoured and to reward corporations it favoured and which delivered good results (Moran, 1999: 571–2). However, corruption, even of this allegedly developmental kind, can go badly wrong and, in Korea, it did ,as democratization and liberalization of the state proceeded (Johnson, 1998; Moran, 1999: 575–6), thereby reducing state supervision and hence 'privatizing' corruption, a process which the contemporary state is seeking to reverse (Moran, 1999: 576).

Nonetheless, as a general pattern, these states have not manifested the corrupt and developmentally corrosive patrimonialism of non-developmental states, like the Philippines under Marcos, or Haiti or Zaire (Young, 1978), or many others, where pervasive corruption in conjunction with coercive states combined to produce economic stagnation, chronic political instability, endemic poverty and gross inequality.

Relative state autonomy

A shared aspect of all developmental states has been the relative autonomy of the elites and the state institutions which they command. By 'autonomy' is meant that the state has been able to achieve relative independence (or insulation) from the demanding clamour of special interests (whether class, regional or sectoral, where they exist) and that it can and does override these interests in the putative national interest (Nordlinger, 1987: 369–71). It is important to note that 'autonomy' in this sense does not mean isolation from the society. On the contrary, as Evans (1989) describes it, the reality is more like 'embedded autonomy'. This means that the autonomy of the well-developed bureaucracies has been embedded in a dense web of ties with both non-state and other state actors (internal and external) who collectively help to define, re-define and implement developmental objectives. Indeed, in the capitalist developmental state, on the Japanese template, it has been this intimacy between the key bureaucracies and the economic agents in the private sector that has made the combined public–private drive to attain development goals so powerful and effective. Here, state and market are, in theory, pulling in the same direction, though in Wade's terms it is the state that is the senior partner, actively involved in 'governing the market' (Wade, 1990).

In non-democratic or intermittently democratic states, the source of this autonomy has commonly been revolution or the military seizure of power – as in China, Taiwan, Korea, Thailand and Indonesia. In democratic (or partially democratic) developmental states, the key factor making for this autonomy appears to have been the dominance of single-party rule brought about by repeated victory in elections since the 1960s, as in Singapore, Malaysia and Botswana. I explore this more fully in the next chapter.

In almost all cases, the inflow of foreign aid, loans and state-directed investment has been substantial. Korea and Taiwan in the 1960s, Thailand and Indonesia in the 1970s and Botswana in the first decade after independence saw huge inflows of such financial support, thereby reducing state dependency on locally generated revenue and giving it a much freer hand to direct the resources (Leftwich, 1995: 411).

Bureaucratic power

Both the developmental determination of the elite and the relative autonomy of the state have helped to shape very powerful, professional, highly competent, insulated and career-based bureaucracies with authority to direct and manage the broad shape of economic and social development. MITI, in Japan, might be thought of as the ideal example of this (Johnson, 1982, 1995), but in all developmental states comparable institutions have existed. These included institutions such as the Economic Planning Board in Korea, the Economic Development Board in Singapore and the Ministry of Finance and Development Planning in Botswana. What differentiates these economic high commands (or 'pilot agencies', as Johnson calls them) in developmental states from the generality of planning institutions in so many developing countries is their real power, authority, technical competence and insulation in shaping the fundamental thrusts of development policy.

The difference between these states and the typical pattern of predatory and patrimonial states in much of sub-Saharan Africa will be obvious.

But it is also important to note the key bureaucratic differences between developmental states and Latin and Central American states, even under authoritarian rule in the latter. The absence of this kind of power and authority – and especially continuity – in the Latin American state bureaucracies has been one of the major factors limiting their developmental capacity, largely due to the very considerable number of bureaucratic appointments (especially top ones) that incoming presidents can make. Estimates for Brazil and Mexico suggest that the number of such appointments in each is about 50,000 and 'all positions with any real power are open to appointment and subject to immediate dismissal' (Schneider, 1999: 292). These conditions have worked against the emergence of either stable, career-oriented bureaucracies in Latin America (which might have formed the backbone for state capacity) in the classical Weberian tradition, or the developmental state model of autonomous, determined and dynamic planners, pushers and policy-makers of industrial policy, on the East Asian model.

Furthermore, in Latin America, powerful (and often violently opposed) class forces and organizations (both rural and more recently urban) have been active, either as dominant influences on the state apparatus or as threats to it, and often both. Their power has produced major crises for the regimes and precluded the emergence of developmental states with either autonomy or capacity (O'Donnell, 1973; Hamilton, 1981; Rueschemeyer, Huber Stephens and Stephens, 1992: ch. 5), even in the case of Brazil after the military coup (Hagopian, 1994). Comparing East Asia with Latin America, one observer noted: 'the absence of rural elite influence from the formation of state policy unites the East Asian cases and separates them from those of Latin America' (Evans, 1987: 215).

There has been some decline in the power of the developmental state bureaucracies and, especially, increasing complexity and difficulty in their management of economic affairs, as either or both liberalization or democratization have occurred (Muramatsu and Krauss, 1984; Amsden, 1985; Picard, 1987; Ahmad, 1989; Wade, 1990; Johnson, 1998; Weiss, 1998; Chang, Park and Yoo, 1998; Yong-duck Jung, 1999). Nonetheless, the authoritative and pivotal influence of the bureaucracy in making development policy at the height of their developmental trajectories was pre-eminent, commonly at the expense of both political and legislative elites. Already there is evidence (from Korea) of efforts to re-empower the bureaucratic institutions (Yong-duck Jung, 1999).

Weak civil society

In all developmental states, civil society has experienced weakness, flattening or control at the hands of the state. Either the institutions of civil society (or the classes which have generated them) have been negligible at the inception of the developmental state, as in Botswana (Molutsi and Holm, 1990: 327), or they have been smashed or penetrated by it, as in Korea, Indonesia and China (Moon and Kim, 1996; Sundhaussen, 1989: 462–3; Gold, 1990: 18–25). And it seems that this weakness or weakening of civil society has been a condition of the emergence and consolidation of developmental states. Later (for instance in Korea in the 1980s), as the pressures for democratization emerged, they have often come from those groups in society – students, professionals, managers – who would normally have formed the core of civil society institutions and who, when democracy arrives, move quickly to do so. But what is fundamental here is that such political forces only emerge as serious challengers to non-democratic rule where and when significant changes have occurred in the socio-economic structure of the society.

The developmental state and economic interests

The power, authority and relative autonomy of these developmental states was established and consolidated at an early point in their modern developmental history, well *before* national or foreign capital became important or potentially influential, or previously dominant classes were destroyed or subordinated (Castells, 1992: 65). This is interestingly demonstrated in China, now, as foreign capital is beginning to become important and, no doubt in due course, as will local capital. The power and authority of the state appears well enough established to deal with this. It is for this reason, as well as many others, that China since 1979 may be seen as having begun to move clearly in the direction of a typical developmental state (White, 1991, 1996) or a 'market-facilitating' state, as some call it (Howell, 1993: 2), or even an 'entrepreneurial state' (Duckett, 1998), a process that will accelerate if economic liberalization continues.

This consolidation of state power and authority before national or foreign capital has begun to grow in importance has greatly enhanced the capacities of developmental states *vis-à-vis* private economic interests, whether internal or external. It has enabled these states to have much greater influence in determining the role that both foreign and national capital have played in development and has also enabled the state to set the terms for this. All developmental states established a battery of instruments which they have been able to use to bend capital to their developmental purposes (Mardon, 1990; Pempel, 1999: 175). The liberalization of financial control measures in the 1990s, in relation to both local and foreign capital (Chang, Park and Yoo, 1998: 737) was one of the major factors creating the Korean crisis of 1997.

However, the important comparative point to note here is that the earlier capacity to control capital sharply differentiates these developmental states from the generality of Latin American states, where historically powerful landed interests, an emerging bourgeoisie and foreign capital were deeply entrenched (Evans, 1987). This seriously compromised the capacity and restrained the autonomy of Latin American states to achieve balanced national industrial modernization.

Developmental states and human rights

Whether democratic or not, there is little doubt that developmental states have not been particularly attractive states, at least not by either western liberal or socialist standards. The treatment of some individuals and organizations (student, labour, political and religious) has often been atrocious. Even in the softer and quasi-democratic Singapore, official attitudes to opposition and dissent have hardly been tolerant, as Lee Kuan Yew indicated in 1982:

Every time anybody starts anything which will unwind or unravel this orderly, organized, sensible, rational society, and make it irrational and emotional, I put a stop to it and without hesitation. (cited in Harris, 1986: 61)

This is especially true for the non-democratic developmental states, where human rights records have been very poor and, sometimes, appalling (Bello and Rosenfeld, 1992). Opposition has not been tolerated and, as would be expected from the earlier point about civil society, any organization or movement that looked as if it would challenge the state and its developmental purposes has been swiftly neutralized, penetrated or incorporated as part of the ruling party. But despite this, most developmental states have had better records (which may not be saying much) than many non-developmental states, as table 7.1 shows. It is based on Humana's work for the 1980s (1987), which offers a percentage mark for human rights records. It is worth noting that Humana calculated that the world average was 55 per cent.

While the human rights records of Taiwan, Indonesia and China have been very poor, the others are about average, or better, on a global basis, and (in 1987) were better than South Africa, the former Soviet Union, Iran, Albania and the Central African Republic. By the early 1990s, these records had not changed much, most of them having improved slightly (Humana, 1992).

Table 7.1   Human rights records of developmental states, 1987

Country	Score (%)
Botswana	71
Singapore	59
South Korea	59
Thailand	57
Malaysia	53
Taiwan	47
Indonesia	30
China	23

Source: Humana (1987), which explains how the percentages are calculated.

Developmental states: legitimacy and performance

As mentioned in the previous chapter, legitimacy is notoriously difficult to measure, especially under non-democratic conditions. Nonetheless, despite often poor human rights records, case studies suggest widespread support for the regimes and considerable legitimacy, even in Indonesia as late as the early 1990s (Liddle, 1992: 450). This is not to say that these states have been without internal opposition. On the contrary, they have all experienced often persistent (and sometimes violent) opposition, as in Korea, Indonesia and Thailand (Bello and Rosenfeld, 1992). Despite this, and especially in the course of their most dynamic periods of growth, few developmental states appear to have had their fundamental constitutional or political legitimacy seriously threatened.

It is probable that this strange mixture of repression and legitimacy is best explained by the manner in which these states have been able to distribute the benefits of rapid growth, at least in terms of schools, roads, health care, public housing and other facilities, to an expanding circle of people. Using the Human Development Index (HDI) of the United Nations Development Programme (UNDP, 1998: 2), it would seem that most developmental states have done remarkably well. The HDI measures progress in human development by combining indicators of per capita income, life expectancy and educational attainment, and it ranks countries from best (1) to worst (174). In this ranking, Korea, Singapore and Malaysia fall broadly in the top 30 per cent, while the others are all in the top 60 per cent – ahead of, say, India, Pakistan, Vietnam, Egypt, Kenya, Brazil, Zimbabwe or Bolivia. For example, in the developmental states referred to here, life expectancy (in 1997) as a key social indicator was nowhere lower than 65 years of age (Indonesia) and was as high as 74 in Singapore. In the others, it was as follows: Korea (72), Malaysia (70), Botswana (51) and Thailand (69). This compares favourably with, say, Tanzania (48), Zaire/Democratic Republic of Congo (51), India (3), Peru (69) and Bolivia (61) (World Bank, 1999c). In some (Malaysia, Korea, Indonesia and Taiwan in particular) levels of social inequality, measured by distribution of income, have been relatively mild, compared to some Latin American societies such as Brazil or Chile and some African societies like Senegal, Zimbabwe or Kenya (World Bank, 1998b: table 5).

Conclusions

In the light of the foregoing, it is now possible to offer a more comprehensive definition of the developmental state.

- The developmental state is a transitional form of the modern state which has emerged in late developing societies, from the nineteenth century to the present. It is a state whose political and bureaucratic elites have generally achieved relative autonomy from socio-political forces in the society and have used this in order to promote a programme of rapid economic growth with more or less rigour and ruthlessness.
- The developmental state is typically driven by an urgent need to promote economic growth and to industrialize, in order to 'catch up' or to protect or promote itself, either economically or militarily or both, in a world or regional context of threat or competition, and to win legitimacy by delivering steady improvement in the material and social well-being of its citizens. Developmental states in the modern era have thus commonly been associated with a high degree of both economic and political nationalism and have been able to generate an average annual rate of growth in GNP per capita of 4 per cent, at least, over the last few decades of the twentieth century.
- Though the Soviet and Chinese states are sometimes represented as the socialist variants of the non-democratic developmental state, most (and the most successful) developmental states have been those that have thrived in mixed capitalist economies, since one of the key characteristics of this state type is its determination and ability to stimulate, direct, shape and cooperate with the domestic private sector and arrange or supervise mutually acceptable deals with foreign interests. The Soviet developmental state, such as it may have been, no longer exists. However, in both China and Cuba at the present (2000) we are seeing

profound changes occurring in developmental state–society relations as economic liberalization promotes a greater role for the private sector, while state power in, and influence over, the economy remains, though weaker than before.

- Developmental states are constituted by particular political forces and processes, which are not found, nor can they be easily replicated or created, in all developing societies. These politics have given rise to two broad types of developmental states: non-democratic and democratic ones.

- Finally, developmental states are not static. They are transitional forms of the modern state in that their success in promoting economic growth has often had the effect of creating interests and organizations in an increasingly complex economy and civil society. These organizations and interests, plus external pressures, may then successfully challenge the power, authority and autonomy of the state, and hence produce further political and economic change. Thus most developmental states, whether democratic or not, go through a life-span that commences with origins, progresses through consolidation, and continues with metamorphosis as other state forms may emerge.

This brief account suggests a number of important conclusions, which underline the central arguments of the book. The first is that the developmental state, as a sub-type of state in the modern world, has not been confined to Confucian East Asia, as is sometimes suggested (Önis, 1991: 124). Developmental states, even in their East Asian forms, vary considerably (Pempel, 1999: 161). Versions of this type of state, often much weaker versions, have been found in Islamic and Buddhist South-east Asia, as well as in Africa. Above all, developmental states have been dominated by fiercely nationalistic and determined developmental elites. Combining varying degrees of repression and legitimacy, where civil society is weak or weakened, these states have concentrated considerable power, authority, autonomy and competence in the central political and especially bureaucratic institutions of the state, notably their economic bureaucracies, and they have generated pervasive 'infrastructural capacity' (Mann, 1986) to achieve their developmental objectives. This has enhanced the capacity of these states to deal authoritatively and not dependently with both domestic and especially foreign economic interests in pursuit of national developmental objectives.

Second, it should be clear that developmental states are not easily located within either of the two main traditions of state theory, stemming from Marx and Weber, discussed in chapter 4. These states have been neither the creatures of dominant classes nor even the product of balanced class struggles (as in Marx's second formulation). The political and bureaucratic elites have also not been typically patrimonial in their behaviour, and they have certainly not exhibited the division of labour between policy-makers and policy-implementers, implicit in modern liberal-democratic forms of the state and theorized in the tradition that derives from Weber (Beetham, 1974: 72–9). On the contrary, especially in their formative periods and their prime, developmental states have been essentially mobilizing states. They have virtually fused political and bureaucratic elements to utilize and orchestrate all the public institutions of state (and many of society) to promote a particular vision and strategy of development whose provenance and urgency of attainment can be traced to the political struggles and histories that constituted the formative processes of these states.

Third, these considerations underline the main point of the book: the primacy of politics in development and the centrality of the state. Wherever one looks it has been the political context, the political dynamics and the political purposes that have shaped the structure of these states, fashioned their developmental aims and determined their remarkable outcomes. Politics has also been central in the reforms and changes that have occurred in these states in the course of the 1990s, and that have had contradictory consequences (Moon and Kim, 1996; Johnson, 1998; Wade, 1998). Their futures are open. But in each instance, as recent experience worldwide has shown, the particular outcome will depend on the constellation of political forces within the society – and beyond it.

Fourth, two seemingly contradictory conclusions follow. On the one hand, it seems unlikely that it is possible in the modern world for any society to make a speedy and successful transition from poverty without a state that in some respects corresponds to this model of a developmental state – and it may be that the dominant industrial societies will need to borrow elements from the model to craft increasingly 'catalytic' states (Lind, 1992).Without it, a society may possibly do it slowly, but at the cost of continuous and immense human suffering, as demonstrated over the last few decades of the twentieth century in India, Nigeria and Brazil and many more societies with non-developmental states. In short, contrary to the current orthodoxy, development requires not less state but better state action (Sandbrook, 1990: 682), and that action is most likely from developmental states. Calls for good governance, which focus exclusively on managerial good practices, and which may be justified in their own right, entirely miss the point that such virtues can only be instituted and sustained by politics. Such narrowly administrative models of development simply evacuate politics from the heart of developmental processes.

But on the other hand, precisely because of the primacy of politics, developmental states can not be had to order. If the politics is not appropriate, such states are highly unlikely to emerge. So concerns to promote good governance or democratization largely avoid the central political issue. Moreover, it is not the alleged trade-off between 'democracy' and development that is crucial, nor even whether democracy is a necessary condition of development, but the *type of democracy* and its developmental capacity that needs to be the starting point. For different forms of the democratic state will generate different levels of development. What these forms are and what their developmental capacity may be, is the subject of the next chapter.

8

Democracy and the Developmental State: Democratic Practices and Development Capacity

Introduction

This chapter develops a number of issues that were raised but not fully pursued in earlier chapters. In particular, it explores the problems and paradoxes of democracy as a 'conservative' system of power (see chapter 6), especially when it is also expected to be developmentally effective or, as at present, when it is held to be a necessary condition for economic development. Two related questions flow from this issue. What has enabled some democratic states to be 'developmental' and how have the different politics of democracy in these 'democratic developmental states' influenced the pattern and level of their developmental performance? In short, the issue is not so much concerned with whether 'democracy' – as a general category – is a necessary condition for development. Rather, the issue is concerned with the way in which different kinds of democracy promote differentially developmental democratic states.

Although we have yet to see how many of the new 'third-wave' democracies will last, the fact remains that few states in the developing world were able to sustain even the most basic elements of democracy in the second half of the twentieth century. The few that have been able to do so include Venezuela, Costa Rica, Jamaica, Botswana, Mauritius, Malaysia, Singapore and India. Even so, many analysts baulk at calling Singapore and Malaysia 'democratic' (Ahmad, 1989; Diamond, 1999) and hence refer to them as only 'partially democratic' states (Potter, 1997: 38). But, that aside, only a few states from this broad democratic or quasi-democratic category have been able to generate high annual average rates of growth in their GNP per capita and hence begin to lift the bulk of their people out of poverty, hardship and vulnerability. Those that have been able to do so include Botswana, Singapore, Malaysia and Mauritius. Though each is very different with respect to key variables such as physical size, population, history, resource endowments, ethno-cultural and class structures, they have all generated political elites and state structures with the determination and capacity to preside over economic growth and welfare. Instead of describing these as democratic developmental states, which is the conventional label (Robinson and White, 1998), I refer to them, I think more accurately, as *developmental democratic states*. This is partly to make the distinction with non-developmental democratic states more semantically and substantively sharp, but equally to stress that what differentiates this broad group of states is not so much their democratic credentials or practices (though these differ) but their developmental capacities.

On the other hand, while *non-developmental democratic states* may have satisfied basic democratic criteria, they have not performed nearly as well in terms of developmental criteria. This applies very much to the other third-world democracies named above (Costa Rica, Venezuela, Jamaica and India), whose states have not been able to manage comparable levels of growth and where, by contrast, sluggish or even negative annual average rates of growth in GNP per capita have prevailed (at least until fairly recently).

This distinction between developmental and non-developmental democracies is in some respects misleading. For instance, although Botswana and Mauritius have had faster growth rates than both Venezuela and Costa Rica, the latter score better on the human development index (HDI) discussed in chapter 3 (UNDP, 1996). And while Jamaica and India have performed weakly in respect of *both* growth and the HDI, they score better in terms of income distribution than Venezuela, Costa Rica or Botswana (World Bank, 1992b, 1996; Good, 1993). And although I shall use these particular developmental and non-developmental democracies as examples that will serve to highlight important distinctions, it may be useful to think of all these democratic states as being ranked as 'high' or 'low' developers along a variety of related but not identical continua, with some performing better on the growth continuum and others performing better on the human development and distributional continua. Nonetheless, growth is such a crucial precondition for other developmental goods that it must remain a critical indicator of developmental performance and promise.

The previous chapter made it clear why some (largely) *non-democratic* political systems, such as South Korea, Taiwan and Indonesia, have been able to manage rapid and sustained economic growth over time

(Rueschemeyer and Evans, 1985; Diamond, 1992; Leftwich, 1995; Weiss and Hobson, 1995). But it is much less clear why some *democratic* states have also been able to do so. More crucially, what explains the difference between developmental and non-developmental democratic states? In short, what conditions enable a democratic state to generate the capabilities that transform it into a successful *developmental* democratic state?

The 'third wave' of democratization (Huntington, 1991) has added a very considerable number of states to the current list of full or partial democracies and, by 1998, had confined authoritarian rule to a minority of states in the modern world, whereas twenty-five years earlier they constituted a significant majority (Potter, 1997: 1–10; Diamond, 1999: 25). But few, if any, of these new democracies in the developing world may *yet* be called effective developmental democratic states. Given this, and contemporary official concerns to treat or promote democracy as a condition of development, it is crucial to see what prospects there may be for the new democracies to become developmental. For while the transition to democracy is clearly a necessary condition for the emergence of developmental democratic states, it is not a sufficient condition. More centrally, democratic states come in a variety of types, each of which embodies a different form of democratic politics and each of which, I argue, contains a different potential for developmental capacity.

Using a comparative analysis of these older third-world democracies, the main aim of this chapter is to underline the major argument of the book about the primacy of *politics* in development. In particular, I argue that the explanation for the different developmental capacities of different types of democratic state turns crucially on the primary role of politics in shaping the character and capability of their *states*, and this in turn reflects far more complex legacies in their economic, social, class and ethnic structures.

Theory and argument

The problem for developmental democratic states is that they must satisfy two sets of independent criteria to qualify as being both developmental *and* democratic. The primary developmental criterion that I use here is an annual average rate of growth in GNP per capita of at least 4 per cent over a period of twenty-five or thirty years. And for present purposes I use the term 'democracy' in its minimalist (electoral) Schumpeterian sense to refer to a national political system in which people, political parties and groups are free to pursue their interests according to peaceful, rule-based competition, negotiation and cooperation within an 'institutional arrangement for arriving at political decisions in which individuals acquire the power to decide by means of a competitive struggle for the people's vote' (Schumpeter, 1943: 269). In practice this means free and regular elections, plus peaceful succession where governments change; low barriers to political participation, and the protection of civil and political liberties (Diamond et al., 1989: xvi).

At the heart of the argument here are two propositions. Taken together, they define the central structural contradiction that makes developmental democratic states so difficult to establish and sustain and that constitutes the starting point for explaining their diverse types and capacities.

The first proposition (which I raised in chapter 6) is that *democracy*, once consolidated and stabilized, especially in its minimal representative form, is a conservative system of power. By this I mean that both the decision-making processes and policy output in consolidated democracies are generally 'conservative' in that they normally involve inter-elite accommodation, compromise, consensus and incrementalism, and seldom entail much popular participation (as Schumpeter recognized). As I pointed out in chapter 6, for many that is the virtue of democracy; for others, its vice.

The second proposition is that *development* is both by definition and in practice a radical and commonly turbulent process which is concerned with often far-reaching and rapid change in the use and distribution of resources, and which – if successful – must transform the fundamental structures of economic and social life, thereby generating new political interests and challenging established ones. For many, too, that is the virtue of development; for others, that is its vice.

The problem, of course, is that the perceived vices and virtues of democracy and development rarely coincide. This is not to say that democratic politics cannot be turbulent, but that where the fundamental basis of consensual and accommodational politics breaks down, or is put under severe stress, democracy itself may be overturned or be put under threat (as occurred in Chile and Jamaica in the early and mid-1970s).

In having to fulfil both democratic and developmental objectives, the contradiction that democratic developmental states have therefore to contain and resolve is that, under *most* circumstances, the rules and hence the practices of stable democratic politics will tend to restrict policy to incremental and accommodationist (hence conservative) options. On the other hand, developmental requirements (whether liberal or radical) will be likely to pull policy in the direction of quite sharp (and unpleasant) changes affecting the economic and social structure of the society, and hence important interests within it. It is this structural contradiction between the conservative requirements of stable democratic survival and the transformative logic of economic growth that new or old democracies must survive and ultimately transcend if they are to become effective developmental democracies. This is especially so if they are to avoid a 'vicious spiral' of economic and political decline (White, 1998: 21). For it is not only the case that poor developmental performance can undermine the consolidation of democracy (as in the case of Venezuela, as mentioned in chapter 6, and which I shall elaborate on shortly), but also that unconsolidated and unstable democracy has a high probability of restraining or undermining economic growth.

In what follows I explore these issues using a preliminary classification of the various types of developmental and non-developmental democratic state. The central point here is that each of these types represents the particular *local* political resolution of the fundamental contradiction referred to above, and that each form broadly defines the possibilities and limits of its developmental capacities. Throughout, I draw comparatively on the practices of the democratic and partially democratic states mentioned above – mainly Botswana, Singapore, Malaysia, Mauritius, Venezuela, post-apartheid South Africa, Jamaica and Costa Rica – but I also make passing reference to the example of what is still the largest democracy in the world, India. In linking discussions of democratization and developmental states in this way, I hope too that this will help to bring the discipline of political science more directly to the core of development theory and practice, for no topic lends itself better to this task than that of the developmental democratic state.

Before proceeding into the empirical material, it is worth summarizing the argument thus far. The conditions promoting the consolidation of democracy are likely to impose various structural constraints on the developmental capacity of new or born-again democratic states. But the problem, as Gordon White argued (1998), is not whether democracy is good or bad for development. Rather, the problem is to recognize that the kinds of formal or informal pacts and agreements that underpin the different forms of democratic politics will have very different implications for the developmental autonomy, capacity and performance of the state.

Forms of developmental democratic states: a preliminary classification

In the previous chapter I suggested some central defining features of developmental states which, in their more extreme manifestations, have been most clearly expressed in non-democratic developmental states (both capitalist and socialist). It is important to note, however, that milder versions may be found in the structure and politics of various developmental democratic states. These features include:

1   a dedicated developmental elite;

2   relative autonomy for the state apparatus;

3   a competent and insulated economic bureaucracy;

4   a weak and subordinated civil society;

5   the capacity to manage effectively local and foreign economic interests;

6   a varying balance of repression, legitimacy and performance, which appears to succeed by offering a trade-off between such repression as may exist and the delivery of regular improvements in material circumstances.

Now the central political and institutional features of third-world democratic states do not come in a standard form. Using as examples the list of third-world democracies referred to above, I therefore suggest a preliminary and simple classification of four broad types of democratic state *in descending order of developmental capacity* (see figure 8.1). They are of course only ideal types since there are no pure examples in practice. Each concrete instance represents only a major tendency in one direction. Yet what each example typically reveals is the way in which political factors shape the relationship between democratic practices and developmental capabilities. India is not included on this list because, as I shall discuss later in the chapter, it illustrates how it is possible for a democratic state to shift categories in the course of democratic consolidation.

Developmental democratic states

1   Dominant-party developmental democratic states: Botswana, Singapore (Malaysia)

2   Coalitional or consociational developmental democratic states: Mauritius, Malaysia

Non-developmental democratic states

3   Class-compromise non-developmental democratic states: Venezuela, South Africa

4   Alternating-party developmental democratic states: Jamaica, Costa Rica

Figure 8.1   A classification of democratic states in terms of developmental capacity

Type 1: Dominant-party developmental democratic states

This type in some respects approximates most closely to the non-democratic developmental state in many of its features since the unity, authority and relatively unchallenged central power of a single and overwhelmingly dominant party distinguishes it decisively from the other types and goes a long way to explain its autonomy and developmental success. The paradigm case here was of course Japan, where the Liberal Democratic Party held power without a break from 1955 to 1993, which ensured policy continuity buttressed by the strength and influence of the bureaucracy (Johnson, 1982). But these central characteristics have also been found in Singapore and Botswana, two of the most remarkable of the developmental democratic states, although their resource endowments and associated economic strategies and trajectories could not be more different.

In Singapore, the People's Action Party (PAP) has dominated politics, economy and society from before independence in 1965, as has the Botswana Democratic Party (BDP) since independence in 1966. The strength of these dominant parties originates in the pre- and early-independence period of democratization when they and the rules of the political game in the new states were established. In the case of Singapore, leftist groups were effectively eliminated (Bradley, 1965; Bellows, 1970) and much of the local political talent was co-opted into the party, with its power base built on labour unions and worker constituencies (Chan, 1978; Sours, 1997), making it a dominant multi-class party from the start. Moreover, and in contrast with both Venezuela and South Africa at the time of their transitions to democracy (1958 and 1992–4, respectively), Singapore and Botswana inherited no legacy of established parties representing old and powerful interests. Nor was there a proliferation of new parties or splits in old ones (as there was in Mauritius).

In short, socio-economic structures in Singapore and Botswana (though very different) generated little serious or lasting contestation over the distribution of power, the rules of the game, the shape of new constitutions or the broad direction of development strategy. Moreover, social and demographic structures in both societies (and tough political action by party and government in the case of Singapore) meant that no major regional, ideological, class or ethnic cleavages existed, or were allowed to exist, as poles around which powerful contending parties could have mobilized (as they have in Fiji and Nigeria). Civil society was clearly weak, or weakened, from the start (and kept that way in Singapore). Where (as in the case of Botswana) new and independent organizations (farmers, parent–teachers, cooperatives) came into existence in the post-independence years, they were quickly absorbed by the BDP or financed by the state (Molutsi and Holm, 1990).

Furthermore, again unlike Venezuela after 1958 or democratic post-apartheid South Africa, the structure of the Singaporean and Botswanan economies during democratic consolidation meant that no significant institutionalized economic interests had become established prior to these parties consolidating their power in the democratic state structures. Thus the playing field was not so much level as it was *open*, and the dominant feature within it was the more-or-less unopposed but formally democratic party-controlled state. Moreover, unlike those societies where authoritarian regimes have long been the norm (typically, in Latin America), the military apparatus was not only new but had no historical association with older established classes or ethnic groups (as in South Africa), and hence was far less of a threat (Trimberger, 1978).

Taken together, therefore, the combination of a relatively undeveloped economy, few organized interests and a weakly differentiated class structure, relative socio-cultural homogeneity and no long-standing military apparatus that had to be controlled or conciliated enabled dominant parties to emerge and to have a relatively clear run. These circumstances enabled power to be concentrated at the political centre and enhanced the relative but 'embedded' autonomy of the state (Evans, 1989: 575–81). This provided the conditions under which determined leaderships were able to enhance state developmental capacity. They did so, especially, by creating and promoting key economic developmental bureaucracies, and were able to protect them from politicians and from the clamour of other special interests and to keep a sharp eye on the development of the economic and political institutions of civil society.

In Singapore this was the powerful Economic Development Board (Haggard, 1990a; Low et al., 1993; Huff, 1995), and in Botswana it was the Ministry of Finance and Development Planning (MFDP) (Raphaeli et al., 1984; Holm, 1988; Charlton, 1991). Using these institutions, the PAP and the BDP (as dominant developmental parties) have been able to pursue consistent, coherent and continuous developmental policies without fearing seriously that the allegedly 'uncertain' outcomes of democratic electoral politics would derail their strategies or that losers in repeated electoral contests could or would threaten the stability of the polity. They have helped to generate powerful private-sector interests, but have been able to work with them in pursuing developmental goals. The formal procedures of democratic electoral politics have imposed few restraints on developmental policies and programmes: on the contrary, they have repeatedly legitimized them. In short, and paradoxical as it may seem, democracy has been dependent on the unchallenged hegemony of these parties. And while satisfying formal democratic criteria, the hegemony of those parties has bestowed a degree of relative autonomy on the state that has led both to be independently described as 'administrative states' (Crouch, 1984: 11; Picard, 1987:13).

Given these politics, the contradiction I have suggested between the re-straining and consensual logic of democratic bargaining, on the one hand, and the conflictual logic of transformative developmentalism, on the other hand, in these dominant-party developmental democratic states has been resolved in favour of the latter. And while their growth performances have been remarkable, they raise very uneasy implications for both the theory and practice of liberal (or social) democracy and the protection of civil rights, as the Singaporean case graphically illustrates. Rates of raw economic growth have been high in Singapore. And while this has also been accompanied by relatively uneven patterns of income distribution, by comparison with other high-income economies (World Bank, 1996: table 5), it has nonetheless enabled the Singaporean state to maintain low unemployment and to fund far-reaching social welfare programmes, which have in turn sustained the hegemony of the party and the legitimacy of the state. Similarly, in Bot-swana, while capital accumulation and economic growth have been rapid, social inequalities have begun to sharpen and environmental decline has occurred (Good, 1993; Yeager, 1993).

Type 2: Coalitional or consociational developmental democratic states

What of those situations where there is or can be no single dominant party? The political resolution of the contradiction of developmental democracy is very different in such societies for there has been no single party to domi-nate. In these societies the developmental autonomy of the state is accord-ingly relatively reduced. If democracy is to survive under these circumstances then the solution lies in political coalitions. And if developmental momen-tum is to be established and maintained, a broad agreement must be negoti-ated between all major participating parties about the direction, shape and pace of development strategy, so that whatever may be the composition of the coalition of the day, the strategy is kept on course (or altered or renewed by agreement).

In coalitional (or consociational) developmental democracies, the two prime political conditions for democratic consolidation (agreement about the rules of the game and, commonly, about the distribution of the spoils of power and about the limits of policy) are *much* more important than in the first model, and *need to be* if democracy is to be consolidated and if devel-opmental continuity is to be ensured. Under these circumstances, more-over, the political vision and skills of elites play a very important role. The origin, structure and role of coalitions is not a new theme in mainstream political science, where theories of consensual or consociational democratic forms are well established (Lijphart, 1974, 1984; Lane and Ersson, 1994).

But what is important here is to see the connections between the insights of political science and these developmental issues.

Societies still predominantly characterized by sharp and primary vertical cleavages in ethnicity, culture or religion – even where this is compounded by regional focuses or horizontal cleavages in class – are the most obvious candidates for the emergence of coalitional developmental democracy. Class-compromise developmental democracies (see Venezuela, in type 3, below) are inappropriate since class formation in such plural societies is usually rudimentary and unconsolidated. The alternating-party model is also inappropriate for two reasons: first, because it requires clear (and changing) majorities, which individual parties in these societies cannot muster (as in Mauritius); and, second, because even if they can muster such majorities (as with the United Malays National Organization – UMNO – in Malaysia), the suspicion and unease with which significant excluded minorities would view their stranglehold on power could easily provoke violence and would deprive the ruling party of precisely the cooperation it needs for developmental effectiveness. This is especially the case where a community holding the majority of *political* resources needs the cooperation of a community controlling a majority or major part of *economic* resources (as in Malaysia and, also, South Africa).

Coalitional developmental democracies do not arise easily or quickly. However, where they do emerge, they are likely to be the product of economic or political crises that led at least one major party (or all) to recognize the political and economic virtues of settling down to forge (and perhaps formalize) the new rules of the political game and a workable policy compromise and consensus about development. The case of Mauritius fits the parameters of the model very closely.

An intricately plural society, Mauritius has produced what has been described as an almost 'seamless web of consolidation and fragmentation' amongst the political parties (Bowman, 1991: 68). This is hardly surprising, given the heterogeneous complexity of the society drawn from Indian, French, African, Chinese and British antecedents, of which the Indo-Mauritians constitute nearly 70 per cent. But these ethno-cultural groups are further divided by religion: some 51 per cent of the population is Hindu, 30 per cent Christian and 17 per cent Muslim (Bowman, 1991: 44; Derbyshire and Derbyshire, 1996: 382). Linguistic subdivisions have complicated the picture further, as have caste and class divisions within and across communal boundaries.

From the time of its independence in 1968, the history of Mauritian politics has been characterized by a kaleidoscopic pattern of coalitional fusion and fission both within and between parties. But during the first fifteen years or so, this was also accompanied by much deeper economic and political crises, stemming from the structural legacies of the colonial plantation economy and its associated social structure (Bowman, 1991; Pandit, 1995). Described as 'the perfect worst case', Mauritius in the 1960s was a poor, typical, sugar-dependent plantation economy with limited land and high rates of population growth and unemployment, coupled with the pluralism described above (Beckford, 1972; Lempert, 1987; Wils and Prinz, 1996: 220). It is hardly surprising that by the late 1960s these circumstances had given rise to a sharp ideological cleavage with the rise of the Mouvement Militant Mauricien (MMM), which challenged the hitherto communal bases of coalition politics in Mauritius with a class analysis and appeal. This led to widespread industrial disturbance, political instability and the suspension of democracy and emergency rule from 1972 to 1975.

Escalating economic crises from the mid-1970s (declining sugar prices, negative balance of payments and trade deficits, mounting debt and swelling unemployment), compelled the major parties on left and right to realize that their welfare objectives (such as unemployment benefits), not to mention job creation and wage increases, were simply unattainable without rapid economic growth. By the early 1980s, with a series of IMF and World Bank austerity and structural adjustment programmes in place, the economy began to boom. New economic policies involved the modernization of the sugar sector, diversification of agriculture, tourism and especially the promotion of exports through a major extension of the Export Processing Zone, originally established in the early 1970s (Minogue, 1987; Bowman, 1991; Pandit, 1995).

But crucially underpinning all this was an emerging political consensus about development strategy, which the multiple economic and political crises of the 1970s and early 1980s had precipitated, cemented by a commitment to both toleration in communal, religious and linguistic matters and to the democratic process. This has distinguished Mauritius sharply from what has occurred in the not entirely dissimilar plural society of Fiji, where native Fijian claims to exclusive and dominant status in the political domain have undermined democracy (Carroll, 1994).

Thus while fusion and fission of alliances have remained the central features of Mauritian politics, the underlying stability of this fluid coalitional democracy since the early 1980s has rested on two key pillars: first, on a fundamental political and policy consensus about a national development strategy that has successfully generated an annual average growth of GNP per capita between 1985 and 1994 of almost 6 per cent (World Bank, 1996); and, second, on respect for the constituents of its pluralist social structure.

Although Malaysia has certain features of the dominant-party type, because of the supremacy of UMNO, it is better thought of as a further example of the kind of plural society that has successfully generated a coalitional developmental democratic state. Some 58 per cent of the population is Malay (and primarily rural), 32 per cent is Chinese (and primarily urban) and 9 per cent originated in the Indian sub-continent; 54 per cent of the population is Muslim, 19 per cent Buddhist, 12 per cent Confucian/Daoist and 7 per cent Christian (Derbyshire and Derbyshire, 1996: 167–8). It is certainly the case that although the offices of head of state and prime minister are open only to Malays, and although UMNO has been the dominant political party, its power and authority have been mediated and refracted through a complex ruling coalition (now called the Barisan Nasional) and a federal structure against a background of historically sensitive and often tense cultural pluralism. This places Malaysia in the coalitional category discussed here.

The tensions between (primarily) the Malay and Chinese communities exploded in 1969 and brought about the suspension of democracy. But this in turn led to a new consensus, embodied in the dominant coalition, the Barisan Nasional, which pursued a broadly agreed development strategy (based on the New Economic Policy) through a constitution and political deal that has concentrated considerable power and developmental direction at the centre. This in turn has invested the politico-bureaucratic elite with relative developmental autonomy to develop or amend strategy and the role of the state in it (Ahmad, 1989; Bowie, 1991). Malaysia has generated a remarkable record of growth, which has yielded an average annual rate of growth in GNP per capita since the mid-1980s of 5.6 per cent (World Bank, 1996).

Thus while coalitional democracies clearly satisfy the formal democratic criteria, their political resolution of the structural contradiction of developmental democracy involves agreement and compromise about a common denominator of development policy, which is likely to be lower than some would hope for and higher than others would want. And while the relative autonomy of the state appears less than that found in the dominant-party model, the democratic consolidation that such a political agreement can achieve produces stability, which naked majoritarian politics of the dominant-party model would simply not allow in these contexts.

Turning now to the non-developmental democracies, what is it that has sapped them of developmental capacity?

Type 3: Class-compromise non-developmental democracies

Though it is not altogether inaccurate, there is something inappropriate about referring to this type (and the alternating party type) as 'non-developmental'. But the term is used here, first, to exaggerate the differences between the dynamic growth achievements of dominant-party and coalitional democracies in the first two categories and the relatively sluggish (or sometimes negative) rates of growth of those in the latter two categories; and, second, to highlight the policy and developmental implications of different patterns of democratic politics, something that is graphically illustrated in these democratic class-compromise states, a notion admirably pioneered in political science by Przeworski and Wallerstein (1982) and applied to Venezuela by Jennifer McCoy (1988).

The class-compromise democratic state is most likely to be the best – or *only – democratic* political resolution attainable in those societies where (i) class is the dominant cleavage, though not the only one; where (ii) the major political forces and interests ranged on either side of the central class rift have come to recognize that while successful revolution (the seizure of state power) is impossible, continued repression has profound economic costs and is thus counter-productive; and (iii) where, even if one party can gain a large enough majority to push through its policies, radical and sectarian changes (however necessary they may be from a developmental point of view, or however desirable from a social justice point of view) will threaten other interests (internal and external) so fundamentally that those interests are likely to adopt non-democratic means to protect themselves, thereby destroying democracy (as occurred in Chile). Furthermore, formal or informal coalitions (as in Venezuela and in the initial phase of South African democratization) within or between parties are a likely means of institutionalizing and monitoring the fundamental agreement that underpins this type of class-compromise democratic state.

However, although they have some elements in common, two major factors differentiate the class-compromise type from the coalitional type. First, the fundamental assumption underlying democratization in these class-compromise states has been *that the practices of democratic politics should not be used to undermine the essential principles of capitalist economic life, even where the state is allotted a significant role.* Second, there have been clear (and, so far as possible, constitutional) agreements on the limits of policy. There is no better illustration of this type of non-developmental democratic state than that provided by the case of Venezuela, which I discussed briefly in chapter 6 and which I expand here.

The political history of Venezuela from the nineteenth century to the mid-twentieth century may be summarized crudely as a history of uprisings, revolts, regional *caudillos* and dictatorial military regimes, most notably and recently those of General Gomèz between 1909 and 1935 and General Marcos Pérez Jiménez between 1948 and 1958 (Levine, 1989; Kornblith, 1991). The relatively stagnant agrarian economy at the time of independence in 1830 was given some stimulus by the emergence of the coffee export economy in the mid-nineteenth century. But it was the growth of the oil industry from the 1920s that transformed Venezuelan society by 'destroying agriculture; spurring massive internal migration; and funding an active state' (Levine, 1989: 250). These developments stimulated profound political and civil change, which frightened the economic and social elites and which the military sought to repress. In particular, it spurred the growth of powerful trade unions (though heavily repressed) and other organizations in civil society. Some liberalization under the Medina government from 1943 allowed the emergence of the Acción Democrática (AD) party, which, with the help of young military officers, overthrew the regime and established democracy, but it was only to last for three years, the so-called *trienio*.

During the *trienio* the AD was largely unassailable politically, at least in formal democratic terms, and hence (inadvisedly, as it turned out) ruled without consultation or conciliation as a dominant party, attacking established interests head-on. Its pro-peasant, pro-worker and anti-Church educational reform policies threatened both materially and symbolically many established interests (rural landowners, oil, business and Church) (Karl, 1986: 72–6). This brought into being a conservative opposition, notably the Comité de Organización Política Electoral Independiente (COPEI), and in November 1948 finally provoked a military coup. This instituted a further decade of brutal military rule under General Marcos Pérez Jiménez, which proceeded to reverse the major policy reforms of the *trienio*. However, over the next decade, despite severe suppression by the security apparatus, there was again a build-up of opposition, including the Catholic Church. This led to popular protests and demonstrations, which ultimately brought down the military regime in January 1958 and initiated the democratic system that has lasted until now.

What is crucial to note here, however, is that the AD and other major parties had learned from the experience of the *trienio* that if democracy was to survive, politics would have to be based on 'conciliation, compromise and prudence', and *serious reform would have to be postponed* (Levine, 1989: 257, 265). The 'political class' had learned that in the context of sharp class and ideological cleavages, Venezuelan democracy could *only* survive on the basis of elite pacts and coalitions, a *limited* programme of reform, controlled and channelled participation in politics and the exclusion of the revolutionary left (ibid.: 257), in short, *a very 'conservative' programme*.

To this end, a set of negotiated compromises was embodied in a series of remarkable pacts, which aimed to 'establish political rules of the game for competition among elites . . . institutionalize the economic boundaries between public and the private sectors, provide guarantees for private capital and *fix the parameters of future socio-economic reform*' (Karl, 1986: 66; emphasis added). These pacts, concluded in 1958, were the Pact de Punto Fijo, a Worker–Owner Accord and the Declaration of Principles and Minimum Program of Government, which set down the common economic and political programme to be followed by all parties and which was later incorporated in the constitution (McCoy, 1988). What did they amount to?

Politically, it was agreed by the three major parties that they would keep the communists out and that each party was guaranteed a share of government posts and patronage, irrespective of which party won the presidential election (McCoy, 1988: 88; Przeworski, 1992: 124). Moreover, the military received an amnesty for earlier abuses and the promise of improved salaries and new equipment (Levine, 1989: 258). Economically, they agreed to a national development strategy involving a significant role for the state but which was nonetheless 'based on local and foreign capital, subsidies to the private sector, principles of compensation for any land reform, and a generally cautious approach to economic and social reform' (ibid.).

What is important here – and illustrates the thesis about one aspect of the conservatism of democracy outlined earlier – is that these pacts and accords meant in practice that 'capitalists accepted democratic institutions as a means for workers to make effective claims to improve their material conditions, while workers accepted private appropriation of profit by capitalists as an institution in expectation of further gains from production' or, in short, that 'workers accepted capitalism and capitalists accepted democracy, *each foregoing a more militant alternative*' (McCoy, 1988: 86).

Three factors made this particular resolution of the contradiction of developmental democracy both possible and workable. First, so long as the oil revenues continued to flow, especially in the boom years of the 1970s when the price of oil rocketed from $2 to $14 per barrel, the state was able to fund this deal and the state bureaucracy expanded to provide basic services (health, housing, education, welfare) to a wider section of the population, thereby consolidating the legitimacy of the pact settlement (McCoy and Smith, 1995: 122). However during this time the state proved developmentally ineffective in 'sowing the oil'; that is, in using the oil revenues to promote diversification, productivity, employment and wages in the non-oil sector of the economy (ibid.:127). Second, although a federal state, Venezuela had always been highly centralized (for instance, until recently state governors and city mayors were appointed from the centre). This enabled the dominant political elites to extend and maintain control nationally, from the centre (unlike in India). Third, while the power, autonomy and developmental effectiveness of the state was clearly limited by the class-compromise pacts and coalitions, this was compensated by cooperation between the two highly centralized and elite-run political parties (AD and COPEI), which achieved institutional expression in the wide use of relatively autonomous policy-making commissions. These commissions were largely appointed and used by the executive to hammer out developmental policies (within the terms of the agreed principles of the Minimum Programme). Moreover, they were effectively insulated from popular participation and legislative control, thereby serving to institutionalize inter-elite compromises and deals while restricting participation (Crisp, 1994).

It is clear that these politics in Venezuela were initially far better at

protecting and consolidating democracy than either stimulating growth outside the oil sector or promoting greater socio-economic equality and opportunity. Thus the relative decline of its oil revenues in the 1980s and escalating
external public debt severely limited the Venezuelan state's ability to continue to fund the fundamental compromise implicit in the pacts, and the
legitimacy of the political system itself went into decline. This was has-
tened by the effects of austerity programmes imposed by the IMF, to which
Venezuela had to turn in the late 1980s. These programmes exaggerated
already sharp inequalities and deepened poverty: the number in poverty
jumping from 32 per cent in 1981 to 53 per cent in 1989 (McCoy and Smith,
1995: 124–5). Unsurprisingly, this led to massive protests (*caracazo*) and
two attempted coups in 1992. Although the Punto Fijo consensus held the
line against a descent into military rule, it would appear that until and unless Venezuelan democracy is able to 're-equilibrate' its politics (ibid.: 156)
around a new set of political, economic and social agreements, which, unlike the circumstances of the 1970s, would have to be take account of the
significantly reduced oil revenues, both its democratic and developmental
prospects will remain strained.

The situation in South Africa suggests parallels and places that country
in the same category of non-developmental democracy. For although it is
too early to predict the outcome, the problems of achieving successful developmental democracy in South Africa are not entirely dissimilar to those
of Venezuela (Lodge, 1995). The ending of apartheid clearly involved a
class compromise, profoundly complicated by ethnic legacies (unlike in
Venezuela). The new democratic state has three major tasks to achieve.
First, it has to correct the gross inequalities of the past by undertaking redistribution. But in order to do so, it must (second) also promote rapid economic growth of the private sector, attracting foreign investment and aid.
Finally, it must maintain democratic political stability. Whether these tasks
can be achieved simultaneously, and whether such essentially centrifugal
objectives can be held together, not only poses the central problem for democratic development in polities constituted by democratic class compromises
but also defines the multiple forms that the contradiction takes in such democracies (Sisk, 1994; Adler and Webster, 1995).

These problems also illustrate why, *ceteris paribus,* class-compromise
democratic states are likely to have slow and limited developmental rates
and why the agreements comprising these democracies tend to be so conservative in practice. For while civil and political liberties are protected in
both Venezuela and post-apartheid South Africa, developmental state autonomy is necessarily limited by the pacts and agreements that underwrite
the democratic process. Both the Venezuelan and South African cases illustrate the primacy of politics in shaping the character of the state and hence
its developmental autonomy and capacity.

Type 4: Alternating-party non-developmental democratic states

The remaining alternating-party democratic state type is likely to occur where there is no single dominant party (as there is in Botswana, Singapore or even Malaysia); where ethnic, cultural or religious pluralism is not central to politics (as it is in Mauritius); and where the class-compromise solution, at least initially, has been excluded because *the main contending parties themselves* are cross-class parties, each based on the incorporation of working- and middle-class elements, each (when in power) dispensing clientelist patronage to its followers and supporters, and each differentiated from the other mainly by a combination of historical association, personal loyalties, anticipation of patronage prospects and (at times) ideological policy orientations (Stone, 1980; Stephens and Stephens, 1986; Edie, 1991).

The alternating-party type can only secure democratic stability where the major multi-class parties have reached a broad consensus about development policy – and Costa Rica is a good example of this. There, in a unitary state where there was no legacy of typical Latin American rural inequality or a powerful class of landholders (Cammack, 1997: 170–1), and where the standing army was abolished, two dominant and multi-class parties, the National Liberation Party (PNP) and the (now) Christian Socialist Unity Party (PUSC) have alternated in power since 1949. Both have adopted a strongly anti-communist line (as in Venezuela) and both have also been committed to a mixed economy, the extension of public welfare and the reduction of inequality based on the belief that 'unfettered capitalist development causes undesirable and destabilizing socioeconomic dislocations and inequalities' (Booth, 1989: 404). Costa Rican democracy has survived under these conditions, though it has presided over low rates of growth and only slight reductions in the very considerable social inequalities.

But when a major ideological divide opens up between such parties, leading to sharp shifts in policy (both internal development policy and external relations), democratic stability has come under intense pressure, which has in turn had negative implications for growth and development, as has been the case in Jamaica. The island's colonial history, dominated by its plantation economy (Beckford, 1972), had produced little industrialization by independence in 1962 and had given rise to high levels of unemployment and sharp income inequality: even in the early 1990s the top 20 per cent took 47 per cent of income and the bottom 20 per cent took less than 6 per cent (World Bank, 1996). The two main parties, the Jamaica Labour Party (JLP) and the People's National Party (PNP), have dominated Jamaican politics since its largely peaceful 'constitutional decolonization' (Munroe, 1972). Both parties have been multi-class parties and both have been committed to a mixed economy. However, the PNP has historically been a much more left-of-centre party, while the JLP has always adopted a more centrist position, being more sympathetic to private (especially foreign) capital and emphasizing cooperation with the USA.

Until the early 1970s, under the first JLP government, these differences remained relatively subdued, though inequality was sharp and unemployment high (23 per cent in 1972). Political violence, especially around election times, became common (Stephens and Stephens, 1986: 42–4). In the 1972 election, the PNP won power after a decade of JLP government and embarked on a more radical programme, aiming to reduce economic dependence, increase the role of the state (including nationalization of utilities and greater control of the bauxite industry), promote more equal distribution, achieve political independence from the West and establish better relations with Cuba (Stephens and Stephens, 1986: 101; Huber and Stephens, 1992: 63–5). The net effect was to shatter whatever tacit accord had existed between the state and the private sector, thereby making it difficult for the mixed economy to work and provoking capital flight. Political and civic instability mounted and violence escalated, leading to a state of emergency in 1976 and in 1980 the threat of a military take-over (Stephens and Stephens, 1986: 231). As the PNP ran into even more difficulties with an increasingly hostile USA and a severe balance of payments crisis, it was compelled to turn to the IMF. When it failed to meet the IMF terms, the PNP was ejected from government in the election called in 1980 and Edward Seaga's JLP took office again.

Another shift in policy now occurred as the JLP shelved the PNP's democratic socialist objectives in favour of policies that were more in line with IMF thinking and the conventional battery of structural adjustment programmes. But these, in turn, though helping to promote growth by the late 1980s, were unpopular, and the PNP again won power in 1989. This time there was greater continuity in policy for the PNP 'has essentially followed the JLP's model of the 1980s' involving 'liberalization, privatization, austerity policies and export promotion' (Huber and Stephens, 1992: 79). Clientelism and patronage have remained central to the inner dynamics of Jamaican politics (Stone, 1980; Edie, 1991).

Nonetheless, it appears that Jamaica is, for the moment, moving closer to the more stable Costa Rican version of the alternating-party democratic state around a broadly common (if reluctant) development consensus, from which there appears no escape. The parties are becoming essentially competing management teams, with relatively minor differences in emphasis and style, while still allowing the government of the day to reward its followers and supporters with the accepted prizes of patronage and perks.

Both the Jamaican and Costa Rican examples illustrate very clearly a central point in the earlier argument, that the consolidation of democratic politics can only be achieved in these alternating party democracies where a broad consensus and continuity in development policy have been achieved, often (as is increasingly the case) when internal economic circumstances and external conditionality shape its dominant features.

Indian exceptionalism

Before concluding it is worth adding that I have excluded any detailed discussion of India from this account, largely because of its size and daunting complexity. India does not fall easily into any one of these categories, but seems to have moved through them and, in this respect, its political history is instructive. For Indian democracy started life as a rather short-lived dominant-party type under the Congress Party. But Congress was a party waiting to self-destruct. For unlike dominant parties elsewhere, it soon began to disintegrate and the consolidation of Indian democracy in the first two decades was won at the price of the developmental ineffectiveness of the Indian state (Nayar, 1976). Holding democracy together in India was brought about by factionalism, patronage politics and the attempt to incorporate, reconcile and placate contradictory interests and expectations in and around the party, all of which led to 'incoherence at the level of policy formulation and implementation and . . . intra-party dissidence' (Kaviraj, 1996; Mitra, 1996: 709; Herring, 1999; Corbridge and Harriss, 2000). The three decades since then have seen the dissolution of Congressional dominance and the emergence of coalition politics in the context of increasing regional, religious and class conflicts. Holding such coalitions together in the face of such multiple pulls will become increasingly difficult, raising further doubts about the capacity of the central state to manage the urgency and immensity of India's developmental needs.

Conclusions

I argued in the previous chapter that developmental states can not be had to order. This is even more true of developmental democratic states because of the intensely political implications of the divergent pulls of the conditions for democracy, on the one hand, and the requirements of development, on the other. However nice it might be to think of democracy and development as two entirely compatible values, I hope I have at least been successful in suggesting that the 'conservative' structural features of the politics of democracy (consensus, containment, incrementalism) may be in sharp conflict with the often radical and transformative structural requirements of 'development'. And it has been one of my aims here to emphasize the *primacy* of politics in shaping not only the forms of democracy and the developmental possibilities of the state but also the tensions between them. However, I am not arguing for the *autonomy* of politics. For it is clear that in each instance the political and hence democratic possibilities are a function of internal structural legacies in the history, economy and social structure of the society in question. However, it is also clear that the multiple effects of external factors, through the impacts of globalization, constitute another set of factors (McGrew, 1997).

Again, the issue is not whether democracy will promote development or hinder it – it is clear that some democracies and some non-democracies *have* been able to promote rapid and moderately egalitarian social and economic development, and some have not. The issue is really what type of democracy is possible in societies with very different economic and social-structural properties and how far and to what extent each type allows the emergence of a developmentally democratic state. In short, the kind of developmental democracy that is possible is a direct and political function of the kind of democracy itself that is possible.

It is clear, therefore, that the gross concept of the democratic developmental state needs to be dis-aggregated and the various forms and possibilities dissected and classified, as I have proposed in a preliminary way here. For just as the main third-world democracies discussed here may be ranked as 'high' or 'low' developers along a series of developmental continua, they may also be ranked as 'high' or 'low' in terms of their democratic characteristics. Arguably, coalitional or alternating-party democracies are *more* democratic than dominant-party democracies, but they may have considerably less developmental momentum – as the contrasting cases of Costa Rica, Jamaica and Singapore illustrate.

Only the simple-minded can now believe that 'democracy' is a sufficient condition for development or that 'development' is incompatible with democracy. The fact of the matter is that different kinds of democracy both allow and shape different kinds of developmentalism, and the product of the interaction between them is expressed in the character and capacity of the state.

9

Conclusions

The main theme of this book has really been quite simple: politics matters because politics shapes states, and states shape development. But I argue that politics matters not simply as one amongst many complementary variables in the complex practices of development; but, rather, it matters because it is the fundamental and decisive process that has shaped the definitions, designs, implementation and outcomes of 'development' everywhere. This why I refer to the 'primacy of politics' in the subtitle and opening chapter of the book.

Politics, as defined in chapter 1, is of course not an autonomous or independent realm of activity in a society but is a function of its history, social and economic structures and culture or cultures. To that extent, it is 'superstructural' in the narrowly Marxist sense in that it reflects and expresses these processes. But my thesis here of course is that politics in practice also shapes history, social and economic structures and culture through, and beyond, the state. To that extent it is not so much sub-structural as *intrastructural*. More to the point, the politics of any society is decisive in shaping the fundamental character and capacity of the state, and different kinds of politics give rise to different kinds of state. For example, different kinds of democratic politics (chapter 8) have generated different kinds of democratic states. But *whether democratic or not*, different politics produce states with different developmental purposes and capacities.

That is the key point. For it has been the character of the state, not the regime type, that has been decisive in differentiating the developmental

from the non-developmental, and four broad types of state may be identified. Within the category of democratic (or partially democratic) states there
are both developmental and non-developmental variants. For instance, the
sluggish and so-called 'Hindu rate of growth' in 'democratic' India contrasts sharply with rapid growth in 'democratic' Malaysia or Singapore.
Likewise, the non-developmental and predatory ruthlessness, patrimonial
or 'cronyist' elitisms of non-democratic states – like Haiti under the
Duvaliers, Zaire under Mobuto, Nigeria under the military, the Philippines
under Marcos and his cronies – all stand in sharp contrast to the developmental transformations of non-democratic Korea, Taiwan and (intermittently) Thailand. But the central point here is that each particular example –
whether democratic or not, whether developmental or not – is the product
of its distinctive history and politics. Given this primacy of politics in development, it is one of the major tasks of modern political science to map
these patterns of politics and states and to identify their developmental implications. In this respect political science should be far more central in the
study and promotion of development than it is, and issues pertaining to the
politics of development should be far more central to the empirical and
theoretical concerns of the discipline, for such an engagement would be
greatly beneficial to both.

Yet despite a small but insightful and sometimes brilliant academic literature on the *politics of development*, some of which I have discussed earlier, this primacy of politics is rarely acknowledged in the official litanies
and lines of development. Part of the problem has been that economists
have largely dominated the field. With the greatest respect to their discipline, economists generally find it either distasteful or difficult to deal with
the immensity of social forces and political interests that shape societies
and which, in third-world contexts, have the habit of sweeping off course
the carefully modelled 'solutions' for development that they devise and that
have been built into the thousands of projects and programmes deployed
worldwide by national governments, non-governmental organizations
and international agencies. Of course many of these programmes and projects have worked; they have improved the lot of the recipients and have
initiated important changes. But many have not, or have only partly achieved
their objectives, as wave after wave of different developmental fashions
have shown – from growth, through social development and basic needs,
through structural adjustment, good governance and the promotion of non-
governmental organizations.

Where political factors have belatedly been acknowledged, two broad
but inappropriate approaches have recently come to be used. One is of the
largely *de-politicized* type, associated with the neo-classical economics of
politics, or rational-choice, school. Much of it is theoretically inventive, but
anodyne, because in practice it ignores, or avoids, the intensity and immen-

sity of the dramas of politics. Though rational-choice models may indeed be helpful in generating explanatory ideas about how, in pursuit of their goals, conflicting interests (including the state or different parts of it) shape or hinder the achievement of developmental goals, their analytical frameworks are largely oblivious to the complexity, depth and dimensions of these interests and to the ferocity with which they interact in contexts as diverse as Tiananmen Square or the forests of the Amazon basin in the conflicts between loggers and indigenous inhabitants. In evacuating intensity from interests, rational-choice theory simply mis-measures or fails to measure them and therefore often appears to be in a state of mild surprise – or even detachment – when these forces act, react or erupt in what appear to be unpredictable and model-threatening ways.

The other approach to 'politics' tends to be the recent 'official' one, which emphasizes technical innovation and improvement through better governance, public-sector management, institution-building, capacity-enhancement and – in some instances – democratization and the improvement of human rights and environmental conditions. While few would object to such aims, there are also many who view such stated goals with cynicism. This is partly because over the second half of the twentieth century such worthy objectives have been overridden by other national and foreign-policy priorities on the part of the dominant western countries, and there is little reason to believe that this has changed. But, equally, for reasons given here, it is naive to believe that calling for such improvements, or using aid to reward or punish those who do or do not implement them, can seriously transform the character of the state. No doubt there will be benefits for individuals and individual institutions (often at elite levels), but to believe that these changes can significantly alter the ebb and flow of politics in such societies is part of what I have called the 'technicist illusion' (chapter 5), because these efforts do not seriously impact upon the social and economic structures and forces shaping the tides of politics and, in turn, shaping the character of the state. The ease, apparent impunity and popular support with which the Pakistani military once again seized power in 1999 illustrates that sharply. And it will only take recession, disturbance and a coup in one of the big Latin American polities (Brazil, for instance), and elsewhere, for others to follow suit.

There is another view of politics that is equally naive. Those who oppose the prevailing discourses of development, as explained in chapter 3, also stress the need for 'another development' and hence another politics, or imagine a 'post-development' era (Escobar, 1995a, 1995b). This politics of development, they argue, will be local, indigenous, based on grass-roots social movements, democratic and directly reflecting the priorities and purposes of the participants, who will need to wrest some control from national governments and also international agencies and aid donors. Although these approaches may appear to be radical politically, they can often be as idealistically apolitical as the rational-choice theorists or the technicians of governance – but for different reasons. There is, at least, a strong implication in many (Esteva, 1987) that somehow the politics of community action for development will be a different politics, a new politics, another politics – democratic, participatory, humane, egalitarian and environmentally friendly. But this, too, is an illusion – though one that many might find attractive. For if my fundamental assumption about what politics is and why it happens is correct (see chapter 1), then such local-level, culturally specific, self-organizing development can not be, and is not, immune from the universal processes of politics everywhere. Anyone who has worked with or studied self-organizing groups or communities will know just how vibrant and positive they can be, how much dignity and empowerment they can generate, but also how active and pervasive their politics can be, and how easily – sometimes – some such groups can explode in conflict and mistrust and, now and again, self-destruct. But even if their fate is not by any manner of means always so bleak as this suggests (and it is not), as time passes and complexity evolves, all such groups will inevitably have to discover and deal with the universal matters of politics, which are found everywhere. Politics is about differences, conflict, resources, power and control, as I have argued in chapter 1 and elsewhere (Leftwich, 1983). The point is that it is not possible, really, to evacuate politics from politics. And it is only realistic to believe that wherever people live, there will always be different ideas, preferences and interests about how, for what and by whom resources should be used, and that these differences interact in the context of diverse structures of inequality and opportunity. And it is these relations of people, resources and power that politics is about, anywhere, and it is that which makes developmental processes, especially, so political. What is crucial to understand is whether and how these interests, ideas and preferences can be reconciled, and what happens if they can not.

This brings us back to the centrality of the state and its role in development, and hence to states of development. For despite the appeal of the local level and the self-organizing community group, and despite inroads on state sovereignty brought about by globalization, the state remains a major and decisive force in the politics of development, whether democratic or not, and always has been (Weiss and Hobson, 1995; Weiss, 1998; Held et al., 1999). It can no more be avoided than can politics. And as I have show in the preceding chapters, the character and performance of states has varied greatly and that, too, is a function of their national, regional and international politics. Given its importance, only a clear understanding of the political basis of any state will yield understanding of its developmental potential and prospects.

This recognition, then, must be the starting point for developmental questions in the new century. For too long politics has been extruded from the study and promotion of development, and it is time to bring it back in – not disinfected notions of management, governance or administration, but politics. Understanding the importance of getting the politics right is developmentally prior to getting the prices right. Without this, the prospect of reducing world poverty by half by the year 2015 is a commendable but wholly unrealistic goal. However, getting the politics right is something that can usually only happen indigenously, within societies, unless – as the Japanese did effectively in both Korea and Taiwan – colonialism largely restructures social, economic, political and state processes. There is a long way to go; it will take time and is likely to be complex, sometimes violent – and always difficult. But whoever thought that development – and hence the politics of development – would not be?

References

Abrahamsen, R. (1996) 'Economic liberalization, civil society and democratization', in M. H. Hansen and A. E. Rund (eds) *Weak? Strong? Embedded? New Perspective on State–Society Relations in the Non-Western World* (Oslo, Centre for Development and the Environment), pp. 15–26.

Adelman, I. and Morris, C. (1967) *Society, Politics and Economic Development* (Baltimore, MD, Johns Hopkins University Press).

Adler, G. and Webster, E. (1995) 'Challenging transition theory: the labour movement, radical reform and transition to democracy in South Africa', *Politics and Society* 23(1), pp. 75–106.

Ahmad, Z. A. (1989) 'Malaysia: quasi democracy in a divided society', in L. Diamond et al. (eds) *Democracy in Developing Countries, vol. 3, Asia* (Boulder, CO, Lynne Rienner), pp. 347–82.

Akamatsu, P. (1972) *Meiji 1868* (London, George Allen & Unwin).

Ake, C. (1991) 'Rethinking African democracy', *Journal of Democracy* 2(1), pp. 32–44.

Alavi, H. (1972) 'The state in post-colonial societies: Pakistan and Bangladesh', *New Left Review* 74, pp. 59–81.

Albrow, M. (1970) *Bureaucracy* (London, Macmillan).

Alford, R. R. and Friedland, R. (1985) *Powers of Theory: Capitalism, the State and Democracy* (Cambridge, Cambridge University Press).

Allen, G. C. (1981) *A Short Economic History of Modern Japan* (Basingstoke, Macmillan).

Almond, G. A. (1960) 'Introduction: a functional approach to comparative politics', in G. A. Almond and J. Coleman (eds) *The Politics of the Developing Areas* (Princeton, NJ, Princeton University Press), pp. 3–64.

Almond, G. A. and Powell, G. B. Jr (eds) (1996) *Comparative Politics Today*, 6th edn (New York, Harper Collins).

Amin, S. (1976) *Unequal Development* (New York, Monthly Review Press).

Amsden, A. (1985) 'The state and Taiwan's economic development', in P. B. Evans et al. (eds) *Bringing the State Back In* (Cambridge, Cambridge University Press), pp. 78–106.

Apter, D. (1965) *The Politics of Modernization* (Chicago, IL, University of Chicago Press).

Apter, D. (1980) 'The passing of development studies: over the shoulder with a backward glance', *Government and Opposition* 15 (3/4), pp. 263–75.

Arndt, H. W. (1978) *The Rise and Fall of Economic Growth* (Chicago, IL, University of Chicago Press).

Arndt, H. W. (1987) *Economic Development: The History of an Idea* (Chicago, IL, University of Chicago Press).

Avineri, S. (1969) *The Social and Political Thought of Karl Marx* (Cambridge, Cambridge University Press).

Axford, B., Browning, G. K., Huggins, R., Rosamond, B. and Turner, J. (1997) *Politics: An Introduction* (London, Routledge).

Bagchi, A. K. (1982) *The Political Economy of Underdevelopment* (Cambridge, Cambridge University Press).

Baran, P. A. (1957) *The Political Economy of Growth* (New York, Monthly Review Press).

Bardhan, P. (1984) *The Political Economy of Development in India* (Oxford, Basil Blackwell).

Barrett, R. E and Whyte, K. M. (1982) 'Dependency theory and Taiwan: analysis of a deviant case', *American Journal of Sociology* 87(5), pp. 1064–89.

Barya, J.-J. B. (1993) 'The new political conditionalities: an independent view from Africa', *IDS Bulletin* 24(1), pp. 16–23.

Bates, R. H. (1981) *Markets and States in Tropical Africa* (Berkeley, CA, University of California Press).

Bates, R. H. (1983) *Essays on the Political Economy of Rural Africa* (Cambridge, Cambridge University Press).

Bauer, P. T (1981) *Equality, The Third World and Economic Delusion* (London, Methuen).

Bayart, J.-F. (1993) *The State in Africa: The Politics of the Belly* (Harlow, Longman).

Beckford, G. L. (1972) *Persistent Poverty* (New York, Oxford University Press).

Beetham, D. (1974) *Max Weber and the Theory of Modern Politics* (London, George Allen and Unwin).

Bell, C. L. G (1974) 'The political framework', in H. Chenery et al. *Redistribution With Growth* (London, Oxford University Press), pp. 52–72.

Bello, W. and Rosenfeld, S. (1992) *Dragons in Distress: Asia's Miracle Economies in Crisis* (Harmondsworth, Penguin).

Bellows, T. (1970) *The People's Action Party: The Emergence of a Dominant Party System*, Southeast Asia Studies Monograph 14 (New Haven, CT, Yale University Press).

Ben-Ami, S. (1983) *Fascism from Above: The Dictatorship of Primo de Rivera in Spain, 1923–1930* (Oxford, Clarendon Press).

Berman, B. (1984) 'Structure and process in the bureaucratic states of colonial Africa', *Development and Change* 15, pp. 161–202.

Bernstein, H. (1971) 'Modernization and the sociological study of development', *Journal of Development Studies* 7(2), pp. 141–60.

Bessel, R. (1997) 'The crisis of modern democracy', in D. Potter et al. (eds) *Democratization* (Cambridge, Polity), pp. 71–94.

Bhagwati, J. (1966) *The Economics of Underdeveloped Countries* (London, Weidenfeld and Nicolson).

Birnie, P. (1993) 'The UN and the environment', in A. Roberts and B. Kingsbury (eds) *United Nations, Divided World* (Oxford, Clarendon Press), pp. 327–83.

Blundell, S. (1986) *Greek and Roman Thought* (London, Croom Helm).

Bock, K. (1979) 'Theories of progress, development, evolution', in T. B. Bottomore and R. Nisbett (eds) *A History of Sociological Analysis* (London, Heinemann), pp. 39–80.

Boone, C. (1994) 'States and ruling classes in Africa', in J. S. Migdal, A. Kohli and V. Shue (eds) *State Power and Social Forces* (Cambridge, Cambridge University Press), pp. 108–42.

Booth, J. A. (1989) 'Costa Rica: the roots of democratic stability', in L. Diamond et al. (eds) *Democracy in Developing Countries, vol. 4, Latin America* (Boulder, CO, Lynne Rienner), pp. 387–422.

Bottomore, T. B., Harris, L., Kiernan, V. G. and Miliband, R. (eds) (1983) *A Dictionary of Marxist Thought* (Oxford, Basil Blackwell).

Bowie, A. (1991) *Crossing the Industrial Divide* (New York, Columbia University Press).

Bowman, L. (1991) *Mauritius: Democracy and Development in the Indian Ocean* (London, Dartmouth).

Bradley, C. P. (1965) 'Leftist fissures in Singapore politics', *Western Political Quarterly* 18(2), pp. 292–308.

Bratton, M. and van de Walle, N. (1997) *Democratic Experiments in Africa* (Cambridge, Cambridge University Press).

Brewer, A. (1980) *Marxist Theories of Imperialism: A Critical Survey* (London, Routledge and Kegan Paul).

Bromley, S. (1997) 'Middle East exceptionalism: myth or reality?', in D. Potter et al. (eds) *Democratization* (Cambridge, Polity), pp. 321–44.

Bryant, R. L. and Bailey, S. (1997) *Third World Political Ecology* (London, Routledge).

Burmeister, L. L. (1986) 'Warfare, welfare and state autonomy: structural roots of the South Korean developmental state', *Pacific Focus* 1(2), pp. 121–46.

Bury, J. B. (1932) *The Idea of Progress* (New York, Dover).

Callaghy, T. M. (1984) *The State-Society Struggle: Zaire in Comparative Perspective* (New York, Columbia University Press).

Callaghy, T. M. (1987a) 'Absolutism, Bonapartism, and the formation of ruling classes: Zaire in comparative perspective', in I. L. Markovitz (ed.) *Studies in Power and Class in Africa* (Oxford, Oxford University Press), pp. 95–117.

Callaghy, T. M (1987b) 'The state as lame Leviathan: the patrimonial administrative state in Africa', in Z. Ergas (ed.) *The African State in Transition* (New York, St Martin's Press), pp. 87–116.

Callaghy, T. M. (1988) 'The state and the development of capitalism in Africa: theoretical, historical and comparative reflections', in D. Rothchild and N. Chazan (eds) *The Precarious Balance: State and Society in Africa* (London, Westview), pp. 67–99.

Callaghy, T. M (1989) 'Towards state capacity and embedded liberalism in the third world: lessons for adjustment', in J. Nelson (ed.) *Fragile Coalitions: The Politics of Economic Adjustment* (New Brunswick, NJ, Transaction Books), pp. 115–38.

Callaghy, T. M. (1990) 'Lost between state and market: the politics of economic adjustment in Ghana, Zambia and Nigeria', in J. Nelson (ed.) *Economic Crisis and Policy Choice* (Princeton, NJ, Princeton University Press), pp. 257–320.

Cammack, P. (1991) 'Democracy and development in Latin America', *Journal of International Development* 3(5), pp. 537–50.

Cammack, P. (1997) 'Democracy and dictatorship in Latin America, 1930–1980', in D. Potter et al. (eds) *Democratization* (Cambridge, Polity), pp. 152–73.

Cammack, P., Pool, D. and Tordoff, W. (1993) *Third World Politics* (Basingstoke, Macmillan).

Cardoso, F. H. and Faletto, E. (1979) *Dependency and Development in Latin America* (Berkeley, CA, University of California Press).

Carroll, T. (1994) 'Owners, immigrants and ethnic conflict in Fiji and Mauritius', *Ethnic and Racial Studies* 17(2), 301–24.

Carson, R. (1962) *Silent Spring* (Harmondsworth, Penguin).

Castells, M. (1992) 'Four Asian tigers with a dragon's head', in R. P. Appelbaum and J. Henderson (eds) *States and Development in the Asian Pacific Rim* (Newbury Park, CA, Sage), pp. 33–70.

Chabal, P. and Daloz, J.-F. (1999) *Africa Works: Disorder as Political Instrument* (Oxford, James Curry).

Chalker, L. (1991a) *Good Government and the Aid Programme* (London, Overseas Development Administration).

Chalker, L. (1991b) 'Practical ways to promote good government', *Conservative Party News* 25 March (London, News Department, Conservative Central Office).

Chamberlain, M. E. (1999) *The Scramble for Africa* (London, Longman).

Chan, Heng Chee (1978) *The Dynamics of One-Party Dominance: The PAP at the Grass Roots* (Singapore, Singapore University Press).

Chang, H.-J., Park, H.-J. and Yoo, C. G. (1998) 'Interpreting the Korean crisis: financial liberalisation, industrial policy and corporate governance', *Cambridge Journal of Economics* 22, pp. 735–46.

Charlton, R. (1991) 'Bureaucrats and politicians in Botswana's policy-making process: a re-interpretation', *Journal of Commonwealth and Comparative Politics* 29(3), pp. 265–82.

Chazan, N., Mortimer, R., Ravenhill, J. and Rothchild, D. (1992) *Politics and Society in Contemporary Africa* (Boulder, CO, Lynne Rienner).

Chenery, H., Ahluwalia, M. S. and Bell, C. G. (1974) *Redistribution with Growth* (London, Oxford University Press).

Chester, N. (1975) 'Political studies in Britain: recollections and comments', *Political Studies*, 23(2/3), pp. 151–64.

Clapham, C. (1985) *Third World Politics: An Introduction* (London, Croom Helm).

Coes, D. V. (1995) *Macroeconomic Crises, Policies, and Growth in Brazil 1964–1990* (Washington, DC, The World Bank).

Cohen, H. J. (1991) 'Democratization in Africa', *US Department of State Dispatch* 28 October, pp. 795–6.

Colclough, C. (1993) 'Structuralism vs neo-liberalism', in C. Colclough and J. Manor (eds) *States or Markets? Neo-liberalism and the Development Policy Debate* (Oxford, Clarendon Press), pp. 1–25.

Cole, K. (1998) *Cuba: From Revolution to Development* (London, Pinter).

Commission of the European Communities (1991) *Human Rights, Democracy and Development Cooperation Policy*, Commission Communication to the Council and Parliament, SEC (91) 61 final, 25 March (Brussels, CEC).

Commoner, B. (1971) *The Closing Circle* (New York, Knopf).

Cooper, F. (1981) 'Africa and the world economy', *The African Studies Review* 24(2/3), pp. 1–86.

Coppedge, M. (1992) 'Venezuela's vulnerable democracy', *Journal of Democracy* 3(4), pp. 32–44.

Corbridge, S. and Harriss, J. (2000) *Reinventing India: Liberalization, Hindu Nationalism and Popular Democracy* (Cambridge, Polity).

Cornia, G. A., Jolly, R. and Stewart, F. (eds) (1987) *Adjustment With Human Face*, vol. I (Oxford, Clarendon Press).

Cotton, J. (1989) 'From authoritarianism to democracy in South Korea', *Political Studies* 37, pp. 244–59.

Council for Economic Planning and Development (1992) *Taiwan Statistical Data Book* (Taipei, Republic of China).

Cowen, M. P. and Shenton, R. W. (1996) *Doctrines of Development* (London, Routledge).

Craske, N. (1999) *Women and Politics in Latin America* (Cambridge, Polity).

Crawford, G. (1997) 'Foreign aid and political conditionality: issues of effectiveness and consistency', *Democratization* 4(3), pp. 69–108.

Crisp, B. (1994) 'Limitations to democracy in developing capitalist societies: the case of Venezuela', *World Development* 22(10), pp. 1491–1509.

Crouch, H. (1984) *Domestic Political Structures and Regional Cooperation* (Singapore, Institute of Southeast Asian Studies).

Crush, J. (1995) 'Imagining development', in J. Crush (ed.) *Power of Development* (London, Routledge), pp. 1–23.

Cutright, P. (1963) 'National political development: measurement and analysis', *American Political Science Review* 28, pp. 253–64.

Dadzie, K. (1993) 'The UN and the problem of economic development', in A. Roberts and B. Kingsbury (eds) *United Nations, Divided World* (Oxford, Clarendon Press), pp. 297–326.

Dag Hammarskjöld Foundation (1975) *What Now? The Dag Hammarskjöld Report on Development and International Cooperation Prepared on the Occasion of the Seventh Special Session of the UN General Assembly* (Uppsala, Sweden, Dag Hammarskjöld Foundation).

Dahl, R. A. (1971) *Polyarchy* (New Haven, CT, Yale University Press).

Dahl, R. A. (1985) *A Preface to Economic Democracy* (Cambridge, Polity).

Dashwood, H. S. (1996) 'The relevance of class to the evolution of Zimbabwe's development strategy, 1980-1991', *Journal of Southern African Studies* 22(1), pp. 27–48.

Dearlove, J. and Saunders, P. (2000) *British Politics,* 3rd edn (Cambridge, Polity).

Demery, L. and Addison, A. (1987) *The Alleviation of Poverty under Structural Adjustment* (Washington, DC, The World Bank).

Derbyshire, D. and I. (1996) *Political Systems of the World* (Edinburgh, Chambers).

Deutscher, I. (1966) *Stalin: A Political Biography* (Harmondsworth, Penguin).

de Waal, J. (1982) *Chimpanzee Politics* (London, Cape).

Deyo, F. C. (ed.) (1987) *The Political Economy of the New Asian Industrialism* (Ithaca, NY, Cornell University Press).

DfID (Department for International Development) (1997) *Eliminating World Poverty: A Challenge for the 21st Century,* White Paper on International Development, Cm 3789 (London, The Stationery Office).

DfID (Department for International Development) (1999) *Statistics on International Development* (London, Government Statistical Service).

Diamond, L. (1987) 'Class formation in the swollen African state', *Journal of Modern African Studies* 25(4), pp. 567–96.

Diamond, L. (1992) 'Economic development and democracy reconsidered', *American Behavioral Scientist* 35(4/5), pp. 450–99.

Diamond, L. (1999) *Developing Democracy: Toward Consolidation* (Baltimore, MD, Johns Hopkins University Press).

Diamond, L., Linz, J. J. and Lipset, S. M. (1989) 'Preface', in L. Diamond, J. J. Linz. and S. M. Lipset (eds) *Democracy in Developing Countries, vol. 4, Latin America* (Boulder, CO, Lynne Rienner), pp. ix–xxvi.

Dodds, E. R. (1973) *The Ancient Concept of Progress* (Oxford, Clarendon Press).

Dominguez, J. I. (1987) 'Political change: Central America, South America and the Caribbean', in M. Weiner and S. P. Huntington (eds) *Understanding Political Change* (Boston, MA, Little Brown), pp. 65–99.

Doornbos, M. (1990) 'The African state in academic debate: retrospect and prospect', *Journal of Modern African Studies* 28(2), pp. 179–98.

Dos Santos, T. (1973) 'The crisis of development theory and the problem of dependence in Latin America', in H. Bernstein (ed.) *Underdevelopment and Development* (Harmondsworth, Penguin), pp. 57–80.

Doyle, W. M. (1983) 'Kant, liberal legacies and foreign affairs: part I', *Philosophy and Public Affairs* 12, pp. 213–35.

Duckett, J. (1998) *The Enterprise State in China* (London, Routledge).

Dunleavy, P. and Hood, C. (1994) 'From public administration to new public management', *Public Money and Management,* July/September, pp. 9–16.

Dunleavy, P. and O'Leary, B. (1987) *Theories of the State* (Basingstoke, Macmillan).

Durkheim, E. (1893/1964) *The Division of Labour in Society* (New York, The Free Press).

EBRD (European Bank for Reconstruction and Development) (1991) *Agreement Establishing The European Bank For Reconstruction and Development* (London, EBRD).

Edie, C. J. (1991) *Democracy by Default: Dependency and Clientelism in Jamaica* (London, Lynne Rienner).

Eisenstadt, S. N. (1966) *Modernization, Protest and Change* (Englewood Cliffs, NJ, Prentice Hall).

Ekeh, P. (1975) 'Colonialism and the two publics', *Comparative Studies in Society and History* 17(1), pp. 91–112.

Ellner, S. (1997) 'Recent Venezuelan political studies', *Latin American Research Review* 32(2), pp. 201–18.

Elster, J. (1985) *Making Sense of Marx* (Cambridge, Cambridge University Press).

Engels, F. (1976) *Anti-Duhring* (Peking, Foreign Languages Press).

Ergas, Z. (ed.) (1987) *The African State in Transition* (Basingstoke, Macmillan).

Escobar, A. (1984) 'Discourse and power in development: Michel Foucault and the relevance of his work to the third world', *Alternatives* 10(3), pp. 377–400.

Escobar, A. (1992) 'Reflections on "development": grassroots approaches and alternative politics in the Third World', *Futures* 24(5), pp. 411–36.

Escobar, A. (1995a) *Encountering Development: The Making and Unmaking of the Third World* (Princeton, NJ, Princeton University Press).

Escobar, A. (1995b) 'Imagining a post-development era', in J. Crush (ed.) *Power of Development* (London, Routledge), pp. 211–27.

Esteva, G. (1987) 'Regenerating people's space', *Alternatives* 12(1), pp. 125–52.

Esteva, G. (1992) 'Development', in W. Sachs (ed.) *The Development Dictionary* (London, Zed), pp. 6–25.

Evans, P. B. (1985) 'Transnational linkages and the economic role of the state: an analysis of developing and industrialized nations in the post-World War II period', in P. B. Evans et al. (eds) *Bringing the State Back In* (Cambridge, Cambridge University Press), pp. 192–226.

Evans, P. B. (1986) 'State, capital and the transformation of dependence: the Brazilian computer case', *World Development* 14(7), pp. 791–808.

Evans, P. B. (1987) 'Class, state and dependency in East Asia: lessons for Latin Americanists', in F. C. Deyo (ed.) *The Political Economy of the New Asian Industrialism* (Ithaca, NY, Cornell University Press), pp. 203–26.

Evans, P. B. (1989) 'Predatory, developmental and other apparatuses: a comparative political economy perspective on the third world state', *Sociological Forum* 4 (4), pp. 561–87.

Evans P. B. (1992) 'The state as problem and solution: predation, embedded autonomy, and structural change', in S. Haggard and R. R. Kaufman (eds) *The Politics of Economic Adjustment* (Princeton, NJ, Princeton University Press), pp. 139–81.

Evans, P. B. (1995) *Embedded Autonomy: States and Industrial Transformation* (Princeton, NJ, Princeton University Press).

Evans, P. B., Rueschemeyer, D. and Skocpol, T. (eds) (1985) *Bringing the State Back In* (Cambridge, Cambridge University Press).

Ferguson, J. (1990) *The Anti-politics Machine* (Cambridge, Cambridge University Press).

Fieldhouse, D. K. (1986) *Black Africa, 1945–1980: Economic Decolonization and Arrested Development* (London, Allen and Unwin).

Foreign and Commonwealth Office (2000) at http://www.fco.gov.uk

Foucault, M. (1972) *The Archaeology of Knowledge* (London, Tavistock).

Foucault, M. (1980) *Power/Knowledge* (London, Harvester).

Frank, A. G. (1971) *Capitalism and Underdevelopment in Latin America* (Harmondsworth, Penguin).

Freire, P. (1972a) *Cultural Action for Freedom* (Harmondsworth, Penguin).

Freire, P. (1972b) *Pedagogy of the Oppressed* (Harmondsworth, Penguin).

Friedman, M. and R. (1980) *Free to Choose* (Harmondsworth, Penguin).

Frischtak, L. L. (1994) *Governance Capacity and Economic Reform in Developing Countries*, World Bank Technical Paper 254 (Washington, DC, The World Bank).

Fukuyama, F. (1989) 'The end of history?', *National Interest*, Summer 1989, pp. 3–18.

Furlong, L. (1980) 'Political development and the Alliance for Progress', in H. J. Wiarda (ed.) *The Continuing Struggle for Democracy in Latin America* (Boulder, CO, Westview), pp. 167–84.

Furtado, C. (1964) *Development and Underdevelopment* (Los Angeles, CA, University of California Press).

Gallie, W. B. (1956) 'Essentially concepts', *Aristotelian Society*, 56, pp. 167–98.

Gandhi, M. (1909/1997) *Hind Swaraj. And Other Writings*, ed. A. J. Parel (Cambridge, Cambridge University Press).

Gann, L. H. and Duignan, P. (1968) *The Burden of Empire* (London, Pall Mall).

Gastil, R. S. (1986) *Freedom in the World* (New York, Greenwood Press).

Gerschenkron, A. (1962) *Economic Backwardness in Historical Perspective* (Cambridge, MA, Harvard University Press).

Ghai, D. (ed.) (1991) *The IMF and the South* (London, Zed Books).

Gillis, M., Perkins, D. H., Roemer, M. and Snodgrass, D. R (1992) *Economics of Development,* 3rd edn (New York, Norton and Co.).

Gills, B. and Rocamora, J. C. (1992) 'Low intensity democracy', *Third World Quarterly* 13(3), pp. 501–23.

Glewwe, P. and de Tray, D. (1988) *The Poor During Adjustment: A Case Study of Côte d'Ivoire* (Washington, DC, The World Bank).

Gold, T. (1990) 'The resurgence of civil society in China', *Journal of Democracy* 1(1), pp. 18–31.

Good, K. (1993) 'At the ends of the ladder: radical inequalities in Botswana', *Journal of Modern African Studies* 31(2), 203–30.

Goodin, R. E. (1979) 'The development-rights trade-off: some unwarranted economic and political assumptions', *Universal Human Rights* 1, pp. 31–42.

Goulet, D. (1971/1988) 'Development . . . or liberation?', in C. K. Wilber (ed.) *The Political Economy of Development and Underdevelopment* 4th edn (New York, Random House), pp. 480–7.

Green, D. C. (1986) *The New Right* (Brighton, Harvester).

Green, R. H. (1974) 'The role of the state as an agent of economic and social development in the Least Developed Countries', *Journal of Development Planning* 6, pp. 1–39.

Green, R. H. (1978) 'Basic human needs: concept or slogan, synthesis or smokescreen?' *IDS Bulletin* 9(4), pp. 7–11.

Green, R. H. (1986) *Sub-saharan Africa: Poverty of Development, Development of Poverty*, IDS Discussion Paper 218 (Brighton, Institute of Development Studies).

Green, R. H. (1988) 'Ghana: progress, problematics and limitations of the success story', *IDS Bulletin*, 19(1), pp. 7–16.

Gregor, A. J. (1979) *Italian Fascism and Developmental Dictatorship* (Princeton, NJ, Princeton University Press).

Gulhati, R. (1988) *The Political Economy of Reform in Sub-Saharan Africa* (Washington, DC, The World Bank).

Gulhati, R. (1989) *Impasse in Zambia: The Economics and Politics of Reform*, EDI Development Policy Case Series, No. 2 (Washington, DC, The World Bank).

Haggard, S. (1990a) *Pathways From the Periphery: The Politics of Growth in the Newly Industrialising Countries* (Ithaca, NY, Cornell University Press).

Haggard, S. (1990b) 'The political economy of the Philippines debt crisis', in J. Nelson (ed.) *Economic Crisis and Policy Choice* (Princeton, NJ, Princeton University Press), pp. 215–55.

Haggard, S. and Kaufman, R. R. (1989a) 'Economic adjustment in new democracies', in J. Nelson (ed.) *Fragile Coalitions: The Politics of Economic Adjustment* (New Brunswick, NJ, Transaction Books), pp. 57–78.

Haggard, S. and Kaufman, R. R. (1989b) 'The politics of stabilization and structural adjustment', in J. D. Sachs (ed.) *Developing Country Debt and the World Economy* (Chicago and London, University of Chicago Press), pp. 263–74.

Haggard, S. and Kaufman, R. R (1992) (eds) *The Politics of Economic Adjustment* (Princeton, NJ, Princeton University Press).

Hagopian, F. (1994) 'Traditional politics against state transformation in Brazil', in J. S. Migdal et al. (eds) *State Power and Social Forces* (Cambridge, Cambridge University Press).

Hailey, Lord (1938) *An African Survey* (London, Oxford University Press).

Hall, S. (1992) 'The West and the rest: discourse and power', in S. Hall and B. Gieben (eds) *Formations of Modernity* (Cambridge, Polity), pp. 275–332.

Hamilton, N. (1981) 'State autonomy and dependent capitalism in Latin America', *British Journal of Sociology* 32(3), pp. 305–29.

Harris, N. (1986) *The End of the Third World* (London, I. B. Tauris).

Harrison, D. (1988) *The Sociology of Modernization and Development* (London, Unwin Hyman).

Harrison, J. (1978) *An Economic History of Modern Spain* (New York, Homes and Meier).

Harrison, J. (1993) *The Spanish Economy: From the Civil War to the European Community* (Basingstoke, Macmillan).

Harling, P. (1996) *The Waning of 'Old Corruption': The Politics of Economic Reform in Britain, 1799–1846* (Oxford, Clarendon Press).

Hawes, G. (1992) 'Marcos, his cronies, and the Philippines' failure to develop', in R. McVey (ed.) *Southeast Asian Capitalists* (Ithaca, NY, Cornell University Southeast Asia Program), pp. 145–60.

Hawes, G. and Liu, H. (1993) 'Explaining the dynamics of the Southeast Asian political economy: state, society and the search for economic growth', *World Politics* 45(4), pp. 629–60.

Haynes, J. (1996) *Third World Politics* (Oxford, Basil Blackwell).

Haynes, J.(1997) *Democracy and Civil Society in the Third World* (Cambridge, Polity).

Hayter, T. (1971) *Aid as Imperialism* (Harmondsworth, Penguin).

Hayter, T. and Watson, C. (1985) *Aid: Rhetoric and Reality* (London, Pluto).

Healey, J. and Robinson, M. (1992) *Democracy, Governance and Economic Policy in Sub-Saharan Africa in Comparative Perspective* (London, ODI).

Held, D. (1987) *Models of Democracy* (Cambridge, Polity).

Held, D. (1989) 'Central perspectives on the modern state', in D. Held *Political Theory and the Modern State* (Cambridge, Polity), pp. 11–55.

Held, D. (1990) 'The contemporary polarization of democratic theory: the case for a third way', in A. Leftwich (ed.) *New Developments in Political Science* (Aldershot, Gower), pp. 8–23.

Held, D. (1996) *Models of Democracy*, 2nd edn (Cambridge, Polity).

Held, D., McGrew, A., Goldblatt, D. and Perraton, J. (1999) *Global Transformations* (Cambridge, Polity).

Heper, M. (1987) 'The state and public bureaucracies: a comparative historical perspective', in M. Heper (ed.) *The State and Public Bureaucracies: A Comparative Perspective* (London, Greenwood Press), pp. 9–23.

Herring, R. J. (1979) 'Zulfikar Ali Bhuto and the "eradication of feudalism" in Pakistan', *Comparative Studies in Society and History* 21(4), pp. 519–57.

Herring, R. J. (1999) 'Embedded particularism: India's failed development state', in M. Woo-Cumings (ed.) *The Developmental State* (Ithaca, NY, Cornell University Press), pp. 306–34.

Hewitt, T. (1992) 'Brazilian industrialization', in T. Hewitt, H. Johnson and D. Wield (eds) *Industrialization and Development* (Oxford, Oxford University Press).

Hewlett, S. A. (1979) 'Human rights and economic realities: trade-offs in historical perspective', *Political Science Quarterly* 943, pp. 453–73.

Heywood, A. (1997) *Politics* (Basingstoke, Macmillan).

Hobsbawm, E. J. (1964) 'Introduction', in Karl Marx, *Pre-Capitalist Economic Formations* ed. E. J. Hobsbawm (London, Lawrence and Wishart), pp. 9–66.

Hobsbawm, E. J. (1969) *Industry and Empire* (Harmondsworth, Penguin).

Hobson, J. A. (1902/1954) *Imperialism: A Study* (London, George Allen and Unwin).

Hochschild, A. (1998) *King Leopold's Ghost* (Basingstoke, Macmillan).

Holm, J. D. (1988) 'Botswana: a paternalistic democracy', in L. Diamond et al. (eds) *Democracy in Developing Countries, vol. 3, Asia* (Boulder, CO, Lynne Rienner), pp. 179–215.

Holmquist, F. and Ford, M. (1994) 'Kenya: state and civil society. The first year after the election', *Africa Today* 4th quarter, pp. 5–25.

Hoogvelt, A. (1997) *Globalization and the Post-colonial World* (Basingstoke, Macmillan).

House of Commons Debates (1990) *House of Commons Debates*, vol. 182, no. 28, cols 1235–99 (London, House of Commons).

Howarth, D. (1995) 'Discourse theory', in D. Marsh and G. Stoker (eds) *Theory and Methods in Political Science* (Basingstoke, Macmillan), pp. 115–36.

Howell, J. (1993) *China Opens its Doors* (London, Harvester Wheatsheaf).

Huber, E. and Stephens, J. D. (1992) 'Changing development models in small economies: the case of Jamaica from the 1950s to the 1990s', *Studies in Comparative International Development* 27(2), pp. 57–92.

Huff, W. G. (1995) 'The developmental state, government and Singapore's economic development since 1960', *World Development* 23(8), pp. 1421–38.

Humana, C. (1987) *World Human Rights Guide* (London, Pan).

Humana, C. (1992) *World Human Rights Guide* (New York, Oxford University Press).

Huntington, S. P. (1968) *Political Order in Changing Societies* (New Haven, CT, Yale University Press).

Huntington, S. P. (1971) 'The change to change: modernization, development and politics', *Comparative Politics* 3, pp. 283–322.

Huntington, S. P. (1984) 'Will more countries become democratic?', *Political Science Quarterly* 99(2), pp. 193–218.

Huntington, S. P. (1987) 'The goals of development', in M. Weiner and S. P Huntington (eds) *Understanding Political Development* (Boston, MA, Little Brown and Co.), pp. 3–32.

Huntington, S. P. (1991) *The Third Wave: Democratisation in the Late Twentieth Century* (Norman, OK, University of Oklahoma Press).

Huntington, S. P (1991/2) 'How countries democratize', *Political Science Quarterly* 106(4), pp. 579–616.

Huntington, S. P. and Dominguez, J. I. (1975) 'Political development', in F. I. Greenstein and N. W. Polsby (eds) *Handbook of Political Science*, vol. 3 (Reading, MA, Addison-Wesley).

Hurd, D. (1990) 'Promoting good government', *Crossbow*, Autumn, pp. 4–5.

Hutchcroft, P. D. (1991) 'Oligarchs and cronies in the Philippines: the politics of patrimonial plunder', *World Politics* 43, pp. 414–50.

Hyden, G. (1985) *No Shortcuts to Progress: African Development Management in Historical Perspective* (London, Heinemann).

IBRD (International Bank for Reconstruction and Development) (1989) *Articles of Agreement* (Washington, DC, The World Bank). Also available at the World Bank website: http://www.worldbank.org/html/extdr/backgrd/ibrd/art1.htm

IDS (1977) *IDS Bulletin* 9(2) (Brighton, Institute of Development Studies).

IDS (1989) *IDS Bulletin* 20(3) (Brighton, Institute of Development Studies).

IDS (1998) *IDS Bulletin* 29(2) (Brighton, Institute of Development Studies).

Illich, I. (1969/1973) *Celebration of Awareness* (Harmondsworth, Penguin).

ILO (1976) *Employment, Growth and Basic Needs* (Geneva, International Labour Office).

IMF (1999) *Articles of Agreement* (Washington, DC, The International Monetary Fund).

Independent Commission on International Development Issues (chair Willy Brandt) (1980) *North-South: A Programme for Survival* (London, Pan Books).

Ingham, B. (1995) *Economics and Development* (Maidenhead, McGraw Hill).

International Social Development Review (1971) 'Social policy and planning in national development', *International Social Development Review* 3, pp. 4–5.

Jackson, K. D. (1978) 'Bureaucratic polity: a theoretical framework for the analysis of power and communications in Indonesia', in K. D. Jackson and L. W. Pye (eds) *Political Power and Communications in Indonesia* (Berkeley, CA, University of California Press), pp. 3–22.

Jackson, R. H. (1990) *Quasi-States: Sovereignty, International Relations and the*

Third World (Cambridge, Cambridge University Press).

Jackson, R. H and Rosberg, C. G. (1986) 'Why Africa's weak states persist', in A. Kohli (ed.) *The State and Development in The Third World* (Princeton, NJ, Princeton University Press), pp. 259–82.

Jessop, B. (1982) *The Capitalist State* (Oxford, Basil Blackwell).

Johnson, C. (1981) 'Introduction: the Taiwan model', in J. S. Hsiung (ed.) *Contemporary Republic of China: The Taiwan Experience, 1950–1980* (New York, Praeger), pp. 9–18.

Johnson, C. (1982) *MITI and the Japanese Miracle* (Stanford, CA, Stanford University Press).

Johnson, C. (1987) 'Political institutions and economic performance: the government-business relationship in Japan, South Korea and Taiwan', in F. C. Deyo (ed.) *The Political Economy of the New Asian Industrialism* (Ithaca, NY, Cornell University Press), pp. 136–64.

Johnson, C. (1995) *Japan: Who Governs?* (New York, W. W. Norton and Co.).

Johnson, C. (1998) 'Economic crisis in East Asia: the clash of capitalisms', *Cambridge Journal of Economics* 22, pp. 633-61.

Johnson, C. (1999) 'The developmental state: odyssey of a concept', in M. Woo-Cumings (ed.) *The Developmental State* (Ithaca, NY, Cornell University Press), pp. 32–60.

Jolly, R. (1975) 'Redistribution with growth: a reply', *IDS Bulletin* 7(2), pp. 9–17.

Joseph, R. A. (1983) 'Class, state and prebendal politics in Nigeria', *Journal of Comparative and Commonwealth Politics* XXI(3), pp. 21–38.

Joseph, R. A. (1987) *Democracy and Prebendal Politics in Nigeria* (Cambridge, Cambridge University Press).

Kabwit, G. C. (1979) 'Zaire: the roots of the continuing crisis', *Journal of Modern African Studies* 17(3), pp. 381–408.

Karl, T. L. (1986) 'Petroleum and political pacts: the transition to democracy in Venezuela', *Latin American Research Review* 22(1), pp. 63–94.

Kasfir, N. (1984) 'Relating class to state in Africa', in N. Kasfir (ed.) *State and Class in Africa* (London, Frank Cass), pp. 1–20.

Kaviraj, S. (1996) 'Dilemmas of democratic development in India', in A. Leftwich (ed.) *Democracy and Development* (Cambridge, Polity), pp. 114–38.

Kerkvliet, B. J. (1974) 'Land reform in the Philippines since the Marcos coup', *Pacific Affairs* 47, pp. 286–304.

Kerr, C., Dunlop, J. T., Harbison, F. and Myers, C. A. (1973) *Industrialism and Industrial Man*, 2nd edn with postscript (Harmondsworth, Pelican).

Kiely, R. (1995) *Sociology and Development: The Impasse and Beyond* (London, UCL Press).

Killick, T. (1989) *A Reaction Too Far: Economic Theory and the Role of the State in Developing Countries* (London, ODI).

Kitching, G. (1982) *Development and Underdevelopment in Historical Perspective* (London, Methuen).

Kitching, G. (1983) *Re-thinking Socialism* (London, Methuen).

Kohli, A. (1986) 'Democracy and development', in J. P. Lewis and V. Kallab (eds) *Development Strategies Reconsidered* (New Brunswick, NJ, Transaction Books), pp. 153–82.

Kohli, A. (1989) 'Politics of economic liberalization in India', *World Development* 17(3), pp. 305–28.

Kohli, A. (1991) *Democracy and Discontent: India's Growing Crisis of Governability* (Cambridge, Cambridge University Press).

Kohli, A. (1993) 'Where do high growth political economies come from? The Japanese lineage of Korea's "developmental state"', *World Development* 22(9), pp. 1269–93.

Kohli, A. (1994) 'Centralization and power: India's democracy in comparative perspective', in J. S. Migdal et al. (eds) *State Power and Social Forces* (Cambridge, Cambridge University Press), pp. 89–107.

Kornblith, M. (1991) 'The politics of constitution-making: constitutions and democracy in Venezuela', *Journal of Latin American Studies* 23, pp. 61–89.

Krasner, S. D. (1985) *Structural Conflict: The Third World Against Global Liberalism* (Berkeley, CA, University of California Press).

Kumar, K. (1978) *Prophecy and Progress: The Sociology of Industrial and Post-Industrial Society* (Harmondsworth, Penguin).

Kuper, L. and Smith, M. G. (eds) (1969) *Pluralism in Africa* (Los Angeles, CA, University of California Press).

Kuznets, S. (1955) 'Economic growth and income inequality', *American Economic Review* XLV(1), pp. 2–28.

Lal, D. (1983) *The Poverty of Development Economics* (London, Institute of Economic Affairs).

Lall, S. (1975) 'Is "dependence" a useful concept in analysing underdevelopment?', *World Development* 3(11/12), pp. 799–810.

Lamb, G. (1987) *Managing Economic Policy Change: Institutional Dimensions*, World Bank Discussion Paper 14 (Washington, DC, The World Bank).

Lancaster, C. (1993) 'Governance and development: the view from Washington', *IDS Bulletin* 24(1), pp. 9–15.

Lane, D. (1996) *The Rise and Fall of State Socialism* (Cambridge, Polity).

Lane, J.-E. and Ersson, S. (1994) *Comparative Politics* (Cambridge, Polity).

Larmour, P. (1995) 'Democracy without development in the South Pacific', in A. Leftwich (ed.) *Democracy and Development* (Cambridge, Polity).

Larrain, G. (1989) *Theories of Development: Colonialism and Dependency* (Cambridge, Polity).

Laver, M. (1997) *Private Desires and Political Action* (London, Sage).

Lee, E. (1979) 'Egalitarian farming and rural development: the case of South Korea', *World Development* 7, pp. 493–517.

Lee, J. M. (1967) *Colonial Development and Good Government* (Oxford, Clarendon Press).

Leftwich, A. (1983) *Redefining Politics: People, Resources and Power* (London, Methuen).

Leftwich, A. (1990) 'Politics and development studies', in A. Leftwich (ed.) *New Developments in Political Science* (Aldershot, Edward Elgar), pp. 82–106.

Leftwich, A. (1992) 'Is there a socialist path to socialism?', *Third World Quarterly* 13(1), pp. 27–42.

Leftwich, A. (1993a) 'Governance, democracy and development in the third world', *Third World Quarterly* 14(3), pp. 601–20.

Leftwich, A. (1993b) 'States of underdevelopment: the third world state in theoretical perspective', *Journal of Theoretical Politics* 6(1), pp. 55–74.

Leftwich, A. (1995) 'Bringing politics back in: towards a model of the developmental state', *Journal of Development Studies* 31(3), pp. 400–27.

Leftwich, A. (1996) 'On the primacy of politics in development', in A. Leftwich (ed.) *Democracy and Development* (Cambridge, Polity), pp. 3–24.

Leftwich, A. (1997) 'From democratization to democratic consolidation', in D. Potter et al. (eds) *Democratization* (Cambridge, Polity), pp. 517–36.

Leftwich, A. (1998) 'Forms of the democratic developmental state: democratic practices and developmental capacity', in M. Robinson and G. White (eds) *The Democratic Developmental State* (Oxford, Oxford University Press), pp. 52–83.

Lele, S. M. (1991) 'Sustainable development: a critical review', *World Development* 19(6), pp. 607–21.

Lemarchand, R. (1988) 'The state, parallel economy, and the changing structure of patronage systems', in D. Rothchild and N. Chazan (eds) *The Precarious Balance: State and Society in Africa* (Boulder, CO, Westview), pp. 149–70.

Lempert, D. (1987) 'A demographic-economic explanation of political stability: Mauritius in a microcosm', *Eastern Africa Economic Review* 3(1), pp. 77–90.

Lenin, V. I (1918/1970) *State and Revolution* (Peking, Foreign Languages Press).

Lerner, D. (1958) *The Passing of Traditional Society: Modernizing the Middle East* (New York, The Free Press).

Levi, M. (1981) 'The predatory theory of rule', *Politics and Society* 10(4), pp. 431–63.

Levi, M. (1989) *Of Rule and Revenue* (London, University of California Press).

Levine, D. H. (1989) 'Venezuela: the nature, sources and prospects of democracy', in L. Diamond et al. (eds) *Democracy in Developing Countries, vol. 4, Latin America* (Boulder, CO, Lynne Rienner), pp. 247–90.

Leys, C. (1975) *Underdevelopment in Kenya* (London, Heinemann).

Leys, C. (1976) 'The "overdeveloped" post colonial state: a re-evaluation', *Review of African Political Economy* 5, pp. 39–48.

Leys, C. (1995) *The Rise and Fall of Development Theory* (Oxford, James Curry).

Liddle, R. W. (1992) 'Indonesia's democratic past and future', *Comparative Politics* 24(4), pp. 443–62.

Lijphart, A. (1974) 'Consociational democracy', in K. McRae (ed.) *Consociational Democracy: Political Accommodation in Segmented Societies* (Toronto, McLelland and Stewart).

Lijphart, A. (1984) *Democracies* (New Haven, CT, Yale University Press).

Lim, Hyun-Chin (1985) *Dependent Development in Korea, 1963–1979* (Seoul, Seoul National University Press).

Lind, M. (1992) 'The catalytic state', *The National Interest,* Spring, pp. 3–12.

Linz, J. J. (1978) 'The breakdown of democratic regimes: crisis, breakdown and re-equilibration', in J. J. Linz and A. Stepan (eds) *The Breakdown of Democratic Regimes* (Baltimore, MD, Johns Hopkins Press), pp. 8–76.

Lipset, S. M. (1960) *Political Man* (London, Heinemann).

Lipset, S. M. (1994) 'The social requisites of democracy revisited', *American Sociological Review* 59, pp. 1–22.

Lipset, S. M., Kyoung-Ryung Seong and J. C. Torres (1993) 'A comparative analysis of the social requisites of democracy', *International Social Science Journal* 136, pp. 155–75.

Lipton, M. (1974) 'Towards a theory of land reform', in D. Lehmann (ed.) *Peasants, Landlords and Governments* (New York, Holmes and Meier), pp. 269–315.

List, F. (1885/1966) *The National System of Political Economy* (New York, A. M. Kelley) (first published in German in 1844, and in English in 1885).

Lodge, T. (1995) 'South Africa: democracy and development in a post-apartheid society', in A. Leftwich (ed.) *Democracy and Development* (Cambridge, Polity), pp. 188–209.

Lofchie, M. J. (1989) 'Reflections on structural adjustment', in *Beyond Autocracy in Africa*, Inaugural Seminar of the African Governance Program, The Carter Centre (Atlanta, GA, Emory University).

Longhurst, R., Kamara, S. and Mensurah, J. (1988) 'Structural adjustment and vulnerable groups in Sierra Leone', *IDS Bulletin* 19(1), pp. 25–30.

Lonsdale, J. (1981) 'States and social processes in Africa: a historiographical survey', *African Studies Review* XXIV(2/3), pp. 139–225.

Low, L. et al. (1993) *Challenge and Response: Thirty Years of the Economic Development Board* (Singapore, Times Academic Press).

Lubeck, P. M. (ed.) (1987) *The African Bourgeoisie: Capitalist Development in Nigeria, Kenya and the Ivory Coast* (Boulder, CO, Lynne Rienner).

Lugard, Lord (1923) *The Dual Mandate in Tropical Africa* (London, Wm Blackwood).

Lundahl, M. (1992) *Politics or Markets? Essays on Haitian Underdevelopment* (London, Routledge).

Maine, H. S. (1908) *Ancient Law* (London, John Murray).

Mainwaring, S. (1992) 'Transitions to democracy and democratic consolidation: theoretical and comparative issues', in S. Mainwaring et al. (eds) *Issues in Democratic Consolidation: The New South American Democracies in Comparative Perspective* (Notre Dame, IN, University of Indiana Press), pp. 294–341.

Mainwaring, S., O'Donnell, G. and Valenzuela, A. (1992) 'Introduction', in S. Mainwaring et al. (eds) *Issues in Democratic Consolidation: The New South American Democracies in Comparative Perspective* (Notre Dame, IN, University of Indiana Press), pp. 1–16.

Mann, M. (1986) 'The autonomous powers of the state: its origins, mechanisms and results', in J. A. Hall (ed.) *States and History* (Oxford, Basil Blackwell), pp. 109–36.

Manor, J. (ed.) (1991) *Rethinking Third World Politics* (Harlow, Longman).

Mardon, R. (1990) 'The state and the effective control of foreign capital: the case of Korea', *World Politics* 43(1), pp. 111–38.

Marshall, T. H. (1950) *Citizenship and Social Class* (Cambridge, Cambridge University Press).

Marx, K. (1852/1958a) 'The Eighteenth Brumaire of Louis Bonaparte', in K. Marx and F. Engels, *Selected Works,* vol. 1 (Moscow, Foreign Languages Publishing House), pp. 243–344.

Marx, K. (1853/1958b) 'British rule in India', in K. Marx and F. Engels, *Selected Works,* vol. 1 (Moscow, Foreign Languages Publishing House), pp. 345–51.

Marx, K. (1859/1958c) 'Preface to a Contribution to the Critique of Political Economy', in K. Marx and F. Engels, *Selected Works,* vol. 1 (Moscow, Foreign Languages Publishing House), pp. 360–5.

Marx, K. (1975) *The Poverty of Philosophy* (Moscow, Progress Publishers) (first published 1847).

Marx, K. (1976) *Capital I* (Harmondsworth, Penguin) (first published 1867).

Marx, K. and Engels, F. (1845/1965) *The German Ideology* (London, Lawrence and Wishart).

Marx, K. and Engels, F. (1888/1958) 'Manifesto of the Communist Party', in K. Marx and F. Engels, *Selected Works,* vol. 1 (Moscow, Foreign Languages Publishing House), pp. 33–65.

Mayegun, O. (1999) *The Conditions for Democracy in Africa*, unpublished MA thesis, Department of Politics, University of York, UK.

McCord, W. (1965) *The Springtime of Freedom* (New York, Oxford University Press).

McCoy, J. (1988) 'The state and the democratic compromise in Venezuela', *Journal of Developing Societies* 4, pp. 85–133.

McCoy, J. and Smith, W. C. (1995) 'Democratic disequilibrium in Venezuela', *Journal of Inter-American Studies and World Affairs* 37(2), pp. 113–79.

McGrew, T. (ed.) (1997) *The Transformation of Democracy? Globalization and the Post-Westphalian World Order* (Cambridge, Polity).

McNamara, R. S. (1970) 'The true dimensions of the task', *International Development Review* I, pp. 3–8.

Meadows, D. H., Meadows, D. L., Randers, J. and Behrens, W. H. (1972) *The Limits To Growth*, A Report of the Club of Rome (London, Pan).

Medard, J.-F. (1982) 'The underdeveloped state in tropical Africa: political clientelism or neo-patrimonialism', in C. Clapham (ed.) *Private Patronage and Public Power* (London, Pinter), pp. 162–92.

Meillassoux, C. (1970) 'An analysis of the bureaucratic process in Mali', *Journal of Development Studies* 6(2), pp. 97–110.

Meldrum, A. (1989) 'The corruption controversy', *Africa Report* 34(1), pp. 36–7.

Migdal, J. S. (1987) 'Strong states, weak states: power and accommodation', in M. Weiner and S. P. Huntington (eds) *Understanding Political Development* (Boston, MA, Little, Brown and Co., pp. 391–434.

Migdal, J. S. (1988) *Strong Societies and Weak States: State-Society Relations and State Capitalism in the Third World* (Princeton, NJ, Princeton University Press).

Migdal, J. S. (1994) 'The state in society: an approach to struggles for domination', in J. S. Migdal et al. (eds) *State Power and Social Forces* (Cambridge, Cambridge University Press), pp. 7–36.

Migdal, J. S., Kohli, A. and Shue, V. (eds) (1994) *State Power and Social Forces* (Cambridge, Cambridge University Press).

Miliband, R. (1969) *The State in Capitalist Society* (London, Weidenfeld and Nicolson).

Mill, J. S. (1848/1970) *Principles of Political Economy* (Harmondsworth, Penguin).

Minogue, M. (1987) 'Mauritius', in C. Clarke and T. Payne (eds) *Politics, Security and Development in Small States* (London, Allen and Unwin), pp. 125–40.

Mitra, S. K. (1996) 'Politics in India', in G. A. Almond and G. B. Powell, Jr (eds)

Comparative Politics Today 6th edn (New York, Harper Collins), pp. 669–729.

Molutsi, P. and Holm, J. D. (1990) 'Developing democracy when civil society is weak: the case of Botswana', *African Affairs* 89 (356), pp. 323–40.

Moon, C. I. and Kim, Y. C. (1996) 'A circle of paradox: development, politics and democracy in South Korea', in A. Leftwich (ed.) *Democracy and Development* (Cambridge, Polity), pp. 139–67.

Moore, B. (1966) *The Social Origins of Dictatorship and Democracy* (Boston, MA, Beacon Press).

Moore, D. (1991) 'The ideological formation of the Zimbabwean ruling class', *Journal of Southern African Studies* 17(3), pp. 472–95.

Moore, M. and Robinson, M. (1994) 'Can foreign aid be used to promote good government in developing countries?', *Ethics and Foreign Affairs* 8, pp. 141–58.

Moraes, F. (1957) *Jawaharlal Nehru* (New York, Macmillan).

Moran, J. (1999) 'Patterns of corruption and development in East Asia', *Third World Quarterly* 20(3), pp. 569–87.

Morawetz, D. (1977) *Twenty-five Years of Economic Development* (Washington, DC, The World Bank).

Mortimer, R. (1991) 'Islam and multiparty politics in Algeria', *Middle East Journal* 45(4), pp. 575–93.

Mosley, P. and Toye, J. (1988) 'The design of structural adjustment programmes', *Development Policy Review* 6(4), pp. 395–413.

Mosley, P., Harrigan, J. and Toye, J. (1991) *Aid and Power: The World Bank and Policy-based Lending,* 2 vols (London, Routledge).

Munroe, T. (1972) *The Politics of Constitutional Decolonization: Jamaica, 1944-1962* (Kingston, Jamaica, Institute of Social and Economic Research, University of the West Indies).

Muramatsu, M. and Krauss, F. S. (1984) 'Bureaucrats and politicians in policy-making: the case of Japan', *American Political Science Review* 78(1), pp. 126–46.

Murray, R. (1967) 'Second thoughts on Ghana', *New Left Review* 42, pp. 25–39.

Myrdal, G. (1957) *Economic Theory and Underdeveloped Regions* (London, Methuen).

Myrdal, G. (1968) *Asian Drama: An Inquiry into the Poverty of Nations,* 3 vols (New York, Pantheon).

Myrdal, G. (1970) 'The "soft state" in underdeveloped countries', in P. Streeten (ed.) *Unfashionable Economics: Essays in Honour of Lord Balogh* (London, Weidenfeld and Nicolson), pp. 227–43.

Nairn, T. (1977) *The Break-up of Britain* (London, Verso).

Nayar, B. R. (1976) 'Political mobilization in a market polity: goals, capabilities and performance in India', in R. I. Crane (ed.) *Aspects of Political Mobilization in South Asia*, Foreign and Comparative Studies, South Asia Series, 1 (Syracuse, NY, University of Syracuse), pp. 135–59.

Needler, M. (1968) 'Political development and socio-economic development: the case of Latin America', *American Political Science Review* 62, pp. 889–97.

Nelson, J. M. (ed.) (1989a) *Fragile Coalitions: The Politics of Economic Adjustment* (New Brunswick, NJ, Transaction Books).

Nelson, J. M. (1989b) 'The politics of adjustment in small democracies: Costa Rica, the Dominican Republic and Jamaica', in J. M. Nelson (ed.) *Fragile Coalitions: The Politics of Economic Adjustment* (New Brunswick, NJ, Transaction Books), pp. 169–214.

Nelson, J. M. (1989c) 'The politics of long-haul economic reform', in J. M. Nelson (ed.) *Fragile Coalitions: The Politics of Economic Adjustment* (New Brunswick, NJ, Transaction Books), pp. 3–26.

Nelson, J. M. (ed.) (1990) *Economic Crisis and Policy Choices: The Politics of Adjustment in the Third World* (Princeton, NJ, Princeton University Press).

Newman, B. A. and Thomson, R. J (1989) 'Economic growth and social development', *World Development* 17(4), pp. 461–71.

Nordic Ministers of Development (1990) 'Communiqué of the Nordic Ministers of Development Cooperation' (Molde, Norway, 10–11 September 1990).

Nordlinger, E. A. (1987) 'Taking the state seriously', in M. Weiner and S. P. Huntington (eds) *Understanding Political Development* (Boston, MA, Little, Brown and Co.), pp. 353–90.

Nowack, M. and Swinehart, T. (eds) (1989) *Human Rights in Developing Countries: 1989 Yearbook* (Kehl, Germany, N. P. Engel).

Nozick, R. (1974) *Anarchy, State and Utopia* (Oxford, Basil Blackwell).

Nyerere, J. K. (1968) *Freedom and Socialism* (Dar Es Salaam, Oxford University Press).

O'Brien, D. C. (1972) 'Modernization, order and the erosion of a democratic ideal', *Journal of Development Studies* 8(3), pp. 49–76.

O'Connor, F. (1956/1966) *Everything That Rises Must Converge* (London, Faber and Faber).

O'Donnell, G. (1973) *Modernization and Bureaucratic-Authoritarianism: Studies in South American Politics* (Berkeley, CA, University of California Press).

OECD (1984) *Development Cooperation: 1984 Review* (Paris, Organisation for Economic Cooperation and Development).

OECD (1989) *Development Cooperation in the 1990s* (Paris, Organisation for Economic Cooperation and Development).

OECD (1997) *Final Report of the DAC Ad Hoc Working Group on Participatory Development and Good Government,* parts I and II (Paris, Organisation for Economic Cooperation and Development).

Olson, M. (1982) *The Rise and Fall of Nations* (New Haven, CT, Yale University Press).

Önis, Z. (1991) 'The logic of the developmental state', *Comparative Politics* 24(1), pp. 109–26.

Oxfam (1998) 'East Asian "recovery" leaves the poor sinking', Oxfam International Briefing at: http://www.oxfam.org.uk/policy/papers/eabrief1.htm

Packenham, R. A. (1973) *Liberal America and the Third World: Political Development Ideas in Foreign Aid and Social Science* (Princeton, NJ, Princeton University Press).

Palma, G. (1981) 'Dependency and development: a critical overview', in D. Seers (ed.) *Dependency Theory: A Critical Re-assessment* (London, Pinter), pp. 20–78.

Pandit, K. (1995) 'Labour and employment under the "NIC" model of development: recent evidence from Mauritius', *Singapore Journal of Tropical Geogra-*

phy 16(2), pp. 158–80.

Pareto, V. (1966) *Sociological Writings*, selected and introduced by S. E. Finer (London, Pall Mall).

Payer, C. (1974) *The Debt Trap: The International Monetary Fund and the Third World* (New York, Monthly Review Press).

Payer, C. (1982) *The World Bank: A Critical Analysis* (New York, Monthly Review Press).

Pearce, D., Berbier, E. and Markandya, A. (1990) *Sustainable Development* (Aldershot, Edward Elgar).

Pempel, T. J. (1999) 'The developmental regime in a changing world environment', in M. Woo-Cumings (ed.) *The Developmental State* (Ithaca, NY, Cornell University Press), pp. 137–81.

Picard, L. (1987) *The Politics of Development in Botswana: A Model for Success* (Boulder, CO, Lynne Rienner).

Pittau, J. (1967) *Political Thought in Early Meiji Japan, 1868-1889* (Cambridge, MA, Harvard University Press).

Please, S. (1984) *The Hobbled Giant: Essays on the World Bank* (London, Westview).

Pollard, S. (1968) *The Idea of Progress* (London, Watts & Co.)

Pope, A. (1734) 'An Essay on Man', in John Butt (ed.) (1963) *The Poems of Alexander Pope* (London, Methuen).

Potter, D. (1997) 'Explaining democratization', in D. Potter et al. (eds) *Democratization* (Cambridge, Polity), pp. 1–40.

Potter, D., Goldblatt, D., Kiloh, M. and Lewis, P. (eds) (1997) *Democratization* (Cambridge, Polity).

Poulantzas, N. (1973) *Political Power and Social Classes* (London, New Left Books).

Prescott, W. H. (1843/1847) *History of the Conquest of Mexico and History of the Conquest of Peru* (New York, Modern Library).

Preston, P. W. (1982) *Theories of Development* (London, Routledge).

Przeworski, A. (1986) 'Some problems in the study of the transition to democracy', in G. O'Donnell et al. (eds) *Transitions from Authoritarian Rule: Comparative Perspectives* (Baltimore, MD, Johns Hopkins University Press), pp. 47–63.

Przeworski, A. (1988) 'Democracy as a contingent outcome of conflicts', in J. Elster and R. Slagstad (eds) *Constitutionalism and Democracy* (Cambridge, Cambridge University Press), pp. 59–80.

Przeworski, A. (1992) 'The games of transition', in S. Mainwaring, G. O'Donnell and A. Valenzuela (eds) *Issues in Democratic Consolidation: The New South American Democracies in Comparative Perspective* (Notre Dame, IN, University of Indiana Press), pp. 105–52.

Przeworski, A. and Limongi, F. (1993) 'Political regimes and economic growth', *Journal of Economic Perspectives* 7(3), pp. 51–69.

Przeworski, A. and Wallerstein, M. (1982) 'The structures of class conflict in democratic capitalist societies', *American Political Science Review* 76, pp. 215–38.

Przeworski, A. et al. (1995) *Sustainable Democracy* (Cambridge, Cambridge University Press).

Przeworski, A., Alvarez, M., Cheibub, J. A. and Limongi, F. (1996) 'What makes democracies endure?', *Journal of Democracy* 7(1), pp. 39–55.

Putzel, J. (1997) 'Why has democratization been a weaker impulse in Indonesia and Malaysia than the Philippines', in D. Potter et al. (eds) *Democratization* (Cambridge, Polity), pp. 240–68.

Rao, U. S. M. (1968) *The Message of Mahatma Gandhi* (New Delhi, Government of India).

Raphaeli, N., et al. (1984) *Public Sector Management in Botswana*, World Bank Staff Working Paper 709 (Washington, DC, The World Bank).

Redclift, M. (1987) *Sustainable Development* (London, Routledge).

Rhodes, R. (1995) *The New Governance: Governing Without Government* (Swindon, Economic and Social Research Council).

Riggs, F. W. (1966) *Thailand: The Modernization of a Bureaucratic Polity* (Honolulu, East-West Centre Press).

Riggs, F. W. (1991) 'Problems of presidentialism', unpublished paper, Department of Political Science, University of Hawaii, January 1991.

Riley, S. P. (1991) *The Democratic Transition in Africa* (London, Research Institute for the Study of Conflict and Terrorism).

Robertson, A. F. (1984) *People and the State: An Anthropology of Planned Development* (Cambridge, Cambridge University Press).

Robinson, M. (1993) 'Will political conditionality work?', *IDS Bulletin* 24(1), pp. 58–66.

Robinson, M. and White, G. (eds) (1998) *The Democratic Developmental State* (Oxford, Oxford University Press).

Rodney, W. (1972) *How Europe Underdeveloped Africa* (London, Bogle-L'Ouverture).

Romero, D. (1996) 'Venezuela: democracy hangs on', *Journal of Democracy* 7(4), pp. 30–42.

Rostow, W. W. (1960) *The Stages of Economic Growth: A Non-Communist Manifesto* (London, Cambridge University Press).

Roth, G. (1968) 'Personal rulership, patrimonialism and empire-building in the new states', *World Politics* 20(2), pp. 194–206.

Rothchild, D and Chazan, N. (eds) (1988) *The Precarious Balance: State and Society in Africa* (London, Westview).

Rueschemeyer, D. and Evans, P. B. (1985) 'The state and economic transformation: toward an analysis of the conditions underlying effective intervention', in P. B. Evans et al. (eds) *Bringing the State Back In* (Cambridge, Cambridge University Press), pp. 44–77.

Rueschemeyer, D., Huber Stephens, E. and Stephens, J. D. (1992) *Capitalist Development and Democracy* (Cambridge, Polity).

Rustow, D. (1970) 'Transitions to democracy', *Comparative Politics* 2, pp. 337–63.

Sachs, W. (1990) 'The archaeology of the development idea', *Interculture* XXIII(4), pp. 6–25.

Sachs, W. (1992a) 'Environment', in W. Sachs (ed.) *The Development Dictionary* (London, Zed Books), pp. 26–37.

Sachs, W. (1992b) 'Introduction', in W. Sachs (ed.) *The Development Dictionary* (London, Zed Books), pp. 1–5.

Said, E. (1978) *Orientalism* (New York, Pantheon).

Sandbrook, R. (1975) *Proletarians and African Capitalism* (Cambridge, Cambridge

University Press).

Sandbrook, R. (1985) *The Politics of Africa's Economic Stagnation* (Oxford, Oxford University Press).

Sandbrook, R. (1986) 'The state and economic stagnation in tropical Africa', *World Development* 14(3), pp. 319–32.

Sandbrook, R. (1990) 'Taming the African leviathan', *World Policy Journal* 7(4), pp. 672–701.

Sandbrook, R. (1992) *The Politics of Africa's Economic Recovery* (Cambridge, Cambridge University Press).

Saul, J. S. (1974) 'The state in post-colonial societies', in R. Miliband and J. Saville (eds) *Socialist Register, 1974* (London, Merlin), pp. 349–72.

Schneider, B. R. (1999) 'The *desarrollista* state in Brazil and Mexico', in M. Woo-Cumings (ed.) *The Developmental State* (Ithaca, NY, Cornell University Press), pp. 276–305.

Schumacher, E. F. (1973) *Small is Beautiful: Economics as if People Mattered* (New York, Harper & Row).

Schumpeter, J. A. (1943) *Capitalism, Socialism and Democracy* (London, Unwin).

Seers, D. (1969) 'The meaning of development', *International Development Review* 11(4), pp. 2–6.

Seers, D. (1972) 'What are we trying to measure?', in N. Baster (ed.) *Measuring Development: The Role and Adequacy of Development Indicators* (London, Frank Cass), pp. 21–36.

Seers, D. (1979a) 'The birth, life and death of development economics', *Development and Change* 10(4), pp. 707–19.

Seers, D. (1979b) 'The meaning of development', in D. Lehmann (ed.) *Development Theory: Four Critical Studies* (London, Cass), pp. 9–24.

Seers, D. (1979c) 'The new meaning of development', in D. Lehmann (ed.) *Development Theory: Four Critical Studies* (London, Cass), pp. 25–30.

Sen, A. (1999) *Development as Freedom* (Oxford, Oxford University Press).

Shapiro, I. (1993) 'Democratic innovation: South Africa in comparative context', *World Politics* 46, pp. 121–50.

Shihata, I. (1991) 'The World Bank and governance issues in its borrowing members', in I. Shihata, *The World Bank in a Changing World: Selected Essays* (Dordrecht, The Netherlands, M. Nijhoff), pp. 53–96.

Shivji, I. (1976) *Class Struggles in Tanzania* (London, Heinemann).

Short, C. (1997) *Democracy, Human Rights and Governance*, speech given at the University of Manchester, 30 June 1997 (London, Department for International Development).

Singh, I. (1983) 'The landless poor in South Asia', in International Conference of Agricultural Economists, *Growth in Agricultural Development* (London, Gower), pp. 379–400.

Sirowy, L. and Inkeles, A. (1990) 'The effects of democracy on economic growth and inequality: a review', *Studies in Comparative International Development* 25(1), pp. 126–57.

Sisk, T. D. (1994) 'Perspectives on South Africa's transition: implications for democratic consolidation', *Politikon* 21(1), pp. 66–75.

Skidmore, D. (1974) 'The Chilean experience of change', in A. Leftwich (ed.) *South*

Africa: Economic Growth and Political Change (London, Allison and Busby), pp. 213–48.

Sklar, R. (1979) 'The nature of class domination in Africa', *Journal of Modern African Studies* 17(4), pp. 531–52.

Sklar, R. (1991) 'Developmental democracy', in R. L. Sklar and C. S. Whitaker, *African Politics and Problems in Development* (Boulder, CO, Lynne Rienner), pp. 285–311.

Sklar, R. (1993) 'The African frontier for political science', in R. H. Bates, V. Y. Mudimbe and J. O'Barr (eds) *Africa and the Disciplines* (Chicago, IL, University of Chicago Press), pp. 83–112.

Sklar, R. (1995) 'The new modernization', *Issue* XXIII(1), pp. 19–21.

Sklar, R. (1996) 'Towards a theory of developmental democracy', in A. Leftwich (ed.) *Democracy and Development* (Cambridge, Polity), pp. 25–44.

Smelser, N. J. (1968) 'Toward a theory of modernization', in N. J. Smelser, *Essays in Sociological Explanation* (Englewood Cliffs, NJ, Prentice Hall), pp. 125–46.

Smith, A. (1776/1977) *The Wealth of Nations* (Harmondsworth, Penguin).

Smith, B. S. (1996) *Understanding Third World Politics* (London, Macmillan).

Soesastro, M. H. (1989) 'The political economy of deregulation in Indonesia', *Asian Survey* 29(9), pp. 853–69.

Sours, M. H. (1997) 'Comparative development strategies in Asian authoritarian national regimes', unpublished paper delivered to the International Studies Association Annual Convention, Panel C-3, Toronto, Canada, 20 March 1997.

Spencer, H. (1969) *The Principles of Sociology,* ed. Stanislav Andreski (London, Macmillan) (first published in three vols, 1876–96).

Staley, E. (1961) *The Future of Underdeveloped Countries* (New York, Frederick Praeger).

Stallings, B. (1990) 'Politics and economic crisis: a comparative study of Chile, Peru and Colombia', in J. Nelson (ed.) *Economic Crisis and Policy Choice* (Princeton, NJ, Princeton University Press), pp. 113–68.

Stanliand, M. (1985) *What is Political Economy?* (New Haven, CT, Yale University Press).

Stavrianos, L. S. (1981) *Global Rift* (New York, William Morrow and Co.).

Stein, S. J. and B. H. (1970) *The Colonial Heritage of Latin America* (New York, Oxford University Press).

Stepan, A. C. (1978) *State and Society: Peru in Comparative Perspective* (Princeton, NJ, Princeton University Press).

Stephens, E. H. and Stephens, J. D. (1986) *Democratic Socialism in Jamaica* (Basingstoke, Macmillan).

Stokke, O. (1995) 'Aid and political conditionality: core issues and state of the art', in O. Stokke (ed.) *Aid and Political Conditionality* (London, Frank Cass).

Stone, C. (1980) *Democracy and Clientelism in Jamaica* (New Brunswick, NJ, Transaction Books).

Streeten, P. (1979) 'Basic needs: premises and promises', *Journal of Policy Modelling* I, pp. 136–46.

Stretton, H. (1976) *Capitalism, Socialism and the Environment* (Cambridge, Cambridge University Press).

Sundhaussen, U. (1989) 'Indonesia: past and present encounters with democracy', in L. Diamond et al. (eds) *Democracy in Developing Countries, vol. 3, Asia* (Boulder, CO, Lynne Rienner), pp. 423–74.

Suret-Canale, J. (1964–72) *Afrique Noire* (Paris, Edition Sociales).

Swainson, N. (1989) *The Development of Corporate Capitalism in Kenya, 1918–1970* (London, Heinemann).

Tansey, S. D. (1995) *Politics: The Basics* (London, Routledge).

Tilly, C. (ed.) (1975a) *The Formation of National States in Western Europe* (Princeton, NJ, Princeton University Press).

Tilly, C. (1975b) 'Western state making and theories of political transformation', in C. Tilly (ed.) *The Formation of National States in Western Europe* (Princeton, NJ, Princeton University Press), pp. 601–38.

Tipps, D. C. (1973) 'Modernization theory and the comparative study of societies: a critical perspective', *Comparative Studies in Society and History* 15(2), pp. 199–226.

Todaro, M. P. (1997) *Economic Development* (Harlow, Addison-Wesley-Longman).

Tönnies, F. (1887/1955) *Community and Association* (London, Routledge and Kegan Paul).

Toye, J. (1987) *Dilemmas of Development* (Oxford, Basil Blackwell).

Transparency International (1998) *Corruption Perception Index* at http://www.transparency.de/documents/cpi/index.html

Trimberger, E. K. (1978) *Revolution from Above: Military Bureaucrats in Japan, Turkey, Egypt and Peru* (New Brunswick, NJ, Transaction Books).

Tucker, V. (1999) 'The myth of development: a critique of a Eurocentric discourse', in R. Munck and D. O'Hearn (eds) *Critical Development Theory* (London, Zed Books), pp. 1–26.

Turnbull, C. (1962) *The Forest People* (New York, Simon and Schuster).

Turner, M. and Hulme, D. (1997) *Governance, Administration and Development* (Basingstoke, Macmillan).

UNDP (United Nations Development Programme) (1990) *Human Development Report 1990* (New York, Oxford University Press).

UNDP (United Nations Development Programme) (1991) *Human Development Report 1991* (New York, Oxford University Press).

UNDP (United Nations Development Programme) (1992) *Human Development Report 1992* (New York, Oxford University Press).

UNDP (United Nations Development Programme) (1997) *Reconceptualising Governance*, Discussion Paper 2 (New York, UNDP).

UNDP (United Nations Development Programme) (1998) *Human Development Report 1998* (New York, Oxford University Press).

United Nations Environment Programme (UNEP) (1998) Website at http://www.unep.org

United Nations Environment Programme (UNEP) (1999) 'The Rio Declaration on Environment and Development' at http://www.unep.org/unep.rio

United Nations (1951) *Measures for the Economic Development of Underdeveloped Countries* (New York, United Nations).

United Nations (1962) *The United Nations Development Decade: Proposals for Action* (New York, United Nations).

United Nations (1964) *The Economic Development of Latin America in the Post-*

war Period (New York, United Nations).

UNRISD (1980) *The Quest for a Unified Approach to Development* (Geneva, United Nations Research Institute for Social Development).

Wade, R. (1990) *Governing The Market: Economic Theory and the Role of Government in East Asian Industrialization* (Princeton, NJ, Princeton University Press).

Wade, R. (1996) 'Japan, the World Bank and the art of paradigm maintenance: the East Asian miracle in political perspective', *New Left Review* 217, pp. 3–37.

Wade, R. (1998) 'The Asian crisis and the global economy: cause, consequences and cure', *Current History*, November, pp. 361–73.

Wallerstein, I. (1974) *The Modern World System* (New York, Academic Press).

Wallerstein, I. (1979) *The Capitalist World Economy* (Cambridge, Cambridge University Press).

Ward, P. M. (1989) *Corruption, Development and Inequality* (London, Routledge).

Warren, B. (1980) *Imperialism: Pioneer of Capitalism* (London, Verso).

Waterbury, J. (1989) 'The political management of economic adjustment and reform', in J. M. Nelson (ed.) *Fragile Coalitions: The Politics of Economic Adjustment* (New Brunswick, NJ, Transaction Books), pp. 39–56.

Weber, M. (1964) *The Theory of Social and Economic Organization*, ed. Talcott Parsons (New York, The Free Press).

Weber, M. (1965a) 'Bureaucracy', in H. H. Gerth and C. Wright Mills (eds) *From Max Weber: Essays in Sociology* (New York, Galaxy Books), pp. 196–244.

Weber, M. (1965b) 'Science as vocation', in H. H. Gerth and C. Wright Mills (eds) *From Max Weber: Essays in Sociology* (New York, Galaxy Books), pp. 129–56 (first published 1918).

Weber, M. (1968) *Economy and Society*, vol. 3 (New York, Bedminster Press).

Weiner, M. J. (1985) *English Culture and the Decline of the Industrial Spirit* (Harmondsworth, Penguin).

Weiss, H. (1995) 'Zaire: collapsed society, surviving state, future polity', in I. W. Zartman (ed.) *Collapsed States* (Boulder, CO, Lynne Rienner), pp. 157–70.

Weiss, L. (1998) *The Myth of the Powerless State* (Cambridge, Polity).

Weiss, L. and Hobson, J. M. (1995) *States and Economic Development* (Cambridge, Polity).

Weiss, R. (1994) *Zimbabwe under the New Elite* (London, British Academic Press).

Westminster Foundation for Democracy (1999) *Annual Report 1998/9* (London, Westminster Foundation for Democracy).

Whitaker, C. S. (1991) 'Doctrines of development and precepts of the state: the World Bank and the fifth iteration of the African case', in R. Sklar and C. S. Whitaker, *African Politics and Problems of Development* (Boulder, CO, Lynne Rienner).

White, G. (1984) 'Developmental states and socialist industrialization in the third world', *Journal of Development Studies* 21(1), pp. 97–120.

White, G. (1985) 'The role of the state in China's socialist industrialisation', in G. White and R. Wade (eds) *Developmental States in East Asia*, Institute of Development Studies Research Report 16 (Brighton, Institute of Development Studies), pp. 208–71.

White, G. (1991) *Democracy and Economic Reform in China*, Institute of Development Studies Discussion Paper 286 (Brighton, Institute of Development Studies).

White, G. (1996) 'Development and democracy in China', in A. Leftwich (ed.) *Democracy and Development* (Cambridge, Polity), pp. 209–29.

White, G. (1998) 'Constructing a democratic developmental state', in M. Robinson and G. White (eds) *The Democratic Developmental State* (Oxford, Oxford University Press), pp. 17–51.

White, G. and Wade, R. (eds) (1985) *Developmental States in East Asia*, Institute of Development Studies Research Report 16 (Brighton, Institute of Development Studies).

Whitehead, L. (1986) 'International aspects of democratization', in G. O'Donnell et al. (eds) *Transitions from Authoritarian Rule: Comparative Perspectives* (Baltimore, MD, Johns Hopkins University Press), pp. 3–46.

Wiarda, H. J. (1988) 'Toward a nonethnocentric theory of development: alternative conceptions from the third world', in C. K. Wilber (ed.) *The Political Economy of Development and Underdevelopment,* 4th edn (New York, Random House), pp. 59–82.

Wilber, C. K. and Jameson, K. P. (1988) 'Paradigms of economic development and beyond', in C. K. Wilber (ed.) *The Political Economy of Development and Underdevelopment,* 4th edn (New York, Random House), pp. 3–27.

Williams, D. (1987) *The Specialized Agencies and the United Nations: The System in Crisis* (London, Hurst).

Williams, R. (1963) *Culture and Society 1780-1850* (Harmondsworth, Penguin).

Wils, A. and Prinz, C. (1996) 'Living in a small crowded room: scenarios for the future of Mauritius', *Population and Environment* 17(3), pp. 217–42.

Wiseman. J. A. (1997) 'The rise and fall and rise (and fall?) of democracy in sub-Saharan Africa', in D. Potter et al. (eds) *Democratization* (Cambridge, Polity), pp. 272–93.

Woo-Cumings, M. (ed.) (1999a) *The Developmental State* (Ithaca, NY, Cornell University Press).

Woo-Cumings, M. (1999b) 'Introduction: Chalmers Johnson and the politics of nationalism and development', in M. Woo-Cumings (ed.) *The Developmental State* (Ithaca, NY, Cornell University Press), pp. 1–31.

World Bank (1984) *World Development Report 1984* (New York, Oxford University Press).

World Bank (1988) *World Development Report 1988* (New York, Oxford University Press).

World Bank (1988/9) *World Development Report 1988/9* (New York, Oxford University Press).

World Bank (1989) *Sub-Saharan Africa: From Crisis to Sustainable Growth* (Washington, DC, The World Bank).

World Bank (1990) *World Development Report 1990* (New York, Oxford University Press).

World Bank (1991a) *World Development Report 1991* (New York, Oxford University Press).

World Bank (1991b) *The African Capacity Building Initiative* (Washington, DC, The World Bank)

World Bank (1992a) *Governance and Development* (Washington, DC, The World Bank).

World Bank (1992b) *World Development Report 1992* (New York, Oxford University Press).

World Bank (1994) *Governance: The World Bank's Experience* (Washington, DC, The World Bank).

World Bank (1996) *World Development Report 1996* (New York, Oxford University Press).

World Bank (1997a) *World Development Indicators 1997* (Washington, DC, The World Bank).

World Bank (1997b) *World Development Report 1997* (New York, Oxford University Press).

World Bank (1998a) *World Bank Annual Report 1998* (Washington, DC, The World Bank).

World Bank (1998b) *World Development Report 1998/9* (New York, Oxford University Press).

World Bank (1999a) 'Development goals', at http://www.worldbank.org/data/dev/devgoals.html

World Bank (1999b) 'The World Bank's role' at http://www.worldbank.org/html/extdr/backgrd/ibrd/role.htm

World Bank (1999c) *World Development Indicators* (Washington, DC, The World Bank).

World Commission on Environment and Development (1987) *Our Common Future*, report of the Brundtland Commission (Oxford, Oxford University Press).

Yeager, R. (1993) 'Governance and environment in Botswana: the ecological price of stability', in S. J. Stedman (ed.) *Botswana: Political Economy of Democratic Development* (Boulder, CO, Lynne Rienner), pp. 123–37.

Yong-duck Jung (1999) 'Globalization, domestic political economy and the institutional persistence of the developmental state in Korea', paper delivered at the IPSA Structure and Organization of Government Conference, Madison, WI, 22–24 April 1999.

Young, C. (1978) 'Zaire: the unending crisis', *Foreign Affairs* 57(1), pp. 165–79.

Young, C. (1988) 'The African colonial state and its political legacy', in D. Rothchild and N. Chazan (eds) *The Precarious Balance: State and Society in Africa* (London, Westview), pp. 25–66.

Young, C. (1994) *The African Colonial State in Comparative Perspective* (New Haven, CT, Yale University Press).

Zakaria, F. (1994) 'Culture is destiny: a conversation with Lee Kuan Yew', *Foreign Affairs* 73(2), pp. 109–26.

Zartman, I. W. (ed.) (1995) *Collapsed States* (Boulder, CO, Lynne Rienner).

Zolberg, A. (1966) *Creating Political Order: The Party States of West Africa* (Chicago, IL, Rand McNally and Co.).

Index